LANCASTER VALOUR

The Valour and the Truth

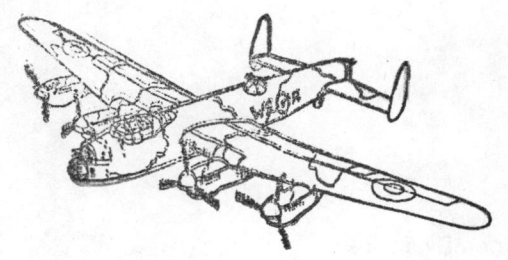

LANCASTER VALOUR

The Valour and the Truth

by

CLAYTON MOORE

COMPAID GRAPHICS
1995

Typeset using Ventura Publisher version 5
Fonts used NewTimes Roman, Courier, Swiss BT

Published in the United Kingdom by Compaid Graphics
Little Ash, Street Lane, Lower Whitley, Warrington, Cheshire. WA4 4EN

COPYRIGHT All rights reserved. No part of this publication may be reproduced, or transmitted in any form without the permission of Compaid Graphics (Publishers) and the Author.

Cover picture reproduced with kind permission of the Imperial War Museum ref CH12595.

British Library Cataloguing in Publication Data. A catalogue record for this book is available from the British Library.

First Edition January 1995

Published in co-operation with the Yorkshire Air Museum

ISBN 0 9517965 6 9

To Edith

Widow of Dick Jones, our first Mid Upper Gunner.

Table of Contents

FOREWORD 1

LANCASTER VALOUR 5
    ACKNOWLEDGEMENTS

CHAPTER 1 7
    IN THE BEGINNING

CHAPTER 2 11
    THE CALL OF ADVENTURE

CHAPTER 3 15
    INITIAL TRAINING

CHAPTER 4 19
    WINGS

CHAPTER 5 27
    OVERSEAS POSTINGS

CHAPTER 6 33
    OPERATIONAL TRAINING

CHAPTER 7 41
    THE LANCASTER

CHAPTER 8 47
    ARMAGEDDON

CHAPTER 9 55
    THE BIG TIME

CHAPTER 10 61
    CRASH LANDING

CHAPTER 11 67
    THE HOSPITAL

CHAPTER 12 73
    RECUPERATION

CHAPTER 13 77
    BACK IN THE SADDLE

CHAPTER 14 83
    THE SPIRIT OF RUSSIA

CHAPTER 15 89
    A GENTLEMAN'S AGREEMENT

CHAPTER 16 97
    ROSANNA

CHAPTER 17 103
    PATHFINDERS

CHAPTER 18 109
    JETSTREAM

CHAPTER 19 115
    THE CURTAIN GOES UP

CHAPTER 20 121
    ON WITH THE SHOW

CHAPTER 21	127
COMMISSIONED RANK	
CHAPTER 22	133
BACK TO THE BIG TIME	
CHAPTER 23	139
END OF SECOND TOUR	
CHAPTER 24	145
FRENCH LEAVE	
CHAPTER 25	151
HOMEWARD BOUND	
CHAPTER 26	157
WHERE ARE THEY NOW	
EPILOGUE	167
ON REFLECTION	

FOREWORD

by
Wing Commander A D White
Officer Commanding IX Squadron, RAF
BRUGGEN
BFPO 25

Lancaster Valour tells the story of one man and his crew - a crew that was but a small part of the most massive air campaign ever waged. Although only one of thousands of such crews, this one relates a most important account of the critical element of the campaign. It is the human story of the people who fought and died so valiantly over the battle fields of Europe.

Bomber Command and its crews faced many problems during the conflict, having to deal with aircraft operating at extreme range, the co-ordination of hundreds of aircraft, and suffering a loss rate that seemed barely sustainable. But throughout, the men and women of the Command continued with their vital task of taking the war to the enemy - a task that, for a significant part of the war, could only be achieved through air power. Without the efforts of those brave people, the war might have ended quite differently.

For a part of the war the crew was posted to IX Squadron, where they undertook the first of many operations. Today, the Squadron differs little from what it was all those years ago. True, the equipment has changed, but it is still the aircrews that take the war to the enemy. As before, they often have to fly to extremes of range as a part of large composite air operations, and there is ever present the prospect of losses. In the period to which Lancaster Valour relates (20th July, 1943 to 23rd January, 1944), IX Squadron took part in fifty-two raids on various West European targets. In that period seventeen of the Squadron's Lancasters failed to return; two ditched in the North Sea; three crashed on return, and one crashed on a test flight. In total, one hundred and thirty-nine members of aircrew were killed as a result. During the Gulf conflict (Operation Granby), IX Squadron Tornadoes shared in twenty raids without loss, although other Tornado equipped Squadrons involved were less fortunate. Air power today, as visibly demonstrated during the Gulf war, is now of age. It was born in the hands of Lancaster Valours, and has reached fully-fledged maturity through the expertise of their descendants over Iraqi airfields, both by day and by night.

Lancaster Valour gives an insight to the pressures faced by the Bomber Command crews. It tells of young men and their battles with the enemy and with officialdom. The latter serves to indicate the origin of the unofficial IX Squadron motto "There's always Bloody Something" - a turn of expression often uttered by the young aircrew of today in the Squadron crewroom.

FOREWORD

FOREWORD

LANCASTER

'Ungainly blackened brute' I read
What foolish tongues speak of beauty thus ?
So did unseeing eyes, long dead
To beauty's charm describe to us
Poetically the slender
Creature of the night that flies
So gracefully and does lend her
Wings to Youth in darkened skies

Such shapely wings, dihedral proud,
Silhouetted in a searchlight's beam.
Each star reflecting fin, supreme
In contour, flirts gaily with a cloud.
No lack of beauty here tonight
Where bombers rendezvous with 'flak'.
'Ungainly blackened brute' you write
Yet never flew a 'Lanc' to hell and back.

From "The Moon Shines Bright", a book of poems published by Jim Brookbank, a 9 Squadron Navigator of the period to which this book refers.

FOREWORD

LANCASTER VALOUR

ACKNOWLEDGEMENTS

In the task of recalling events which took place many years ago, my failing memory has been greatly revived by the kind co-operation of a number of establishments, sources of reference and people, without whose guidance Lancaster Valour could not have been written. As a consequence, I wish to express my sincere appreciation as follows:

In dealing first with people, special mention must go to Barry Nixon, the son of the late Paddy Blanch, our Mid Upper Gunner. Barry spent countless hours at the Public Records Office in Kew, pouring over the many operational records of the two squadrons on which we served. Equally deserving of special mention are those who contributed snippets of personal information and photographs of the various crew members. These came from surviving members, plus widows and decendants of those no longer with us, ie., Mary Wilson, widow of the late Jock Wilson, and her son Andrew; Steve Lodge, son of the late Dick Lodge, and Bunty MacDonald, sister of the late Bill Siddle. Traceable surviving crew members consist of Mike Machin of Coventry; Reg Moseley of Nuneaton, and Allan Macdonald of Marble Mountain, Nova Scotia, Canada. Others include Tom Mellors, former ground crew member, Nine Squadron; Fred Whitfield, also ex Nine Squadron, author of the book "We Sat Alone", and Neville Franklin of Brayford Press for supplying a photograph of our crashed aircraft, which had previously been published in "Action Stations".

I have also received valuable advice and encouragement from fellow authors, all of which are much more deserving of an accolade than I, and mention must be made of Chas Bowyer, Martin Middlebrook, Walter Thompson (author of "Lancaster To Berlin"), Gordon Wagner ("How Papa Won The War"), Fred Whitfield ("We Sat Alone"), Eric Stofer ("Unsafe For Aircrew"), and the late John Searby ("The Bomber Battle for Berlin"). The works of these authors, plus frequent reference to "Lancaster - Story Of A Famous Bomber" contributed much to the authenticity of "Lancaster Valour".

Finally, I wish to record my appreciation of the considerable information supplied to me by the RCAF Records Office in Ottawa, Canada; the Public Records Office in Kew, and the Russian Embassy in London.

LANCASTER VALOUR

CHAPTER 1

IN THE BEGINNING

My interest in a flying career was greatly influenced by events which took place during my early childhood spent in central Canada. I was the youngest of a family made up of three units, both of my parents having been married previously, and both having produced offspring prior to the demise of their respective spouses. My mother was a war widow, and had emigrated to Canada, together with her young son and the rest of her Scottish family in 1920. Father was Canadian by birth, but of Irish descent, and his prior contribution had amounted to one daughter and four sons. My eventual arrival on the scene brought the final total to seven.

Mother had made no attempt to dispense with her broad Scottish accent, and always referred to her collective brood as "His, o'ors and mine". Not that there ever existed any real segregation apart from age difference. Most of the others had grown up and gone their separate ways by the time I showed up. Indeed, we were a large but happy family intent on wresting a reasonable living from a ten-acre plot of land which had been allocated to Dad under a settlement scheme run by the Canadian Government.

The allocation of the land imposed certain conditions, the principal one being that my father must grub out all the trees and brush, and produce a crop within a specific period of time. Once this condition had been met, the ownership of the land was to be transferred to him completely free of any charge other than the regular payment of the land tax. Because of his enthusiasm and drive, all of the conditions had been met within the required period. In addition, my father had constructed the house, the barn, and other outbuildings, and had transformed the place into an efficient market garden, specialising in the growing of fruits and vegetables which he sold to grocers in the nearby Saskatchewan town of Prince Albert. Because of its isolation, our farm lacked such services as water, electricity, gas and sewage, but Dad had sunk a well which provided an ample supply of clear water for ourselves and the stock, and we made use of a collection of coaloil lamps and lanterns as a means of lighting. Our heating consisted of a centrally positioned tin wood-burning stove, and there was a large cast iron cooking range in the kitchen. We had a telephone, and the sewage problem had been solved by the existence of a well-constructed but unheated privy which Dad had cited some yards distant from the house. All things considered, the amenities were sparse and primitive, but these were typical of living conditions in the more remote farming communities in Canada at the time. To us, it was home.

Our humble small holding was situated on the southernmost edge of the district of Whitfield, hard against the seven-mile deep Nesbit pine forest which separated us from the town. Our community was made up entirely of farms, except for an Indian reservation to the north-west, and the area was served by a straight dirt road which ran due north to the only other feature of significance: our local school. This was three miles distance from our farm, and consisted of a one-roomed timber building. It not only served as a seat of learning for the children of the District, but as a dance hall on Saturday nights, and as a place of worship each sabbath. There was no public transport.

My arrival on the scene was closely followed by the great depression, a period during which many farmers were forced into bankruptcy because of the Wall Street crash and the steady decline in world markets. However, we were fortunate in that the very nature of our small holding ensured the provision of most of the essentials required of such a large family. There was always an abundance of fresh fruit and vegetables at our disposal, and we kept a cow, a couple of pigs, and a flock of free range chickens, ducks and turkeys. As a result, we were more fortunate than the cereal producing farmers in the area because we were self-supporting in the provision of foodstuffs for our own consumption. Mother was an excellent cook, so we were all well catered for. Although we never went in need of good, wholesome food, clothing was the one essential that required money, and money was something we were short of. Dad usually managed to sell enough of his produce to keep us reasonably well clothed, and Mother made up any shortfall by knitting and sewing for us. We children all got a new pair of shoes from Eaton's catalogue each winter, but we usually went bare footed during the summer months, a necessity which we looked upon as a pleasure rather than a misfortune.

Although luxuries were mostly non-existent, we did have a radio. This curious example of modern technology had been designed, constructed and given to us by an uncle who ran a radio store in Saskatoon. It consisted of a large, brightly varnished wooden cabinet, on top of which stood an enormous horn-like contraption from which a profusion of cacophonous sounds emanated when one twiddled the many knobs and dials on the front of the set. As a child, I was fascinated by the radio, and Dad had to make frequent trips into town so that the accumu-

IN THE BEGINNING

lators which powered it could be recharged. Depending on the ability of the knob-twiddler, it was not unknown for the atmospherics to be replaced by reasonably lucid sounds of music and voices, some of which came from far-flung parts of the North American continent.

Of the many stations and programmes I could tune in to, I soon became a firm fan of the Saturday night broadcast of the "Grand O' le Oprey" and the weekly hour-long shows put out by such radio stars as Bing Crosby, Bob Hope and Jack Benny. But my undoubted favourite was a fifteen minute soap opera known as "The Adventures of Howie Wing". This was broadcast nightly, and depicted the heroic airborne exploits of an American air ace and his blundering adversary, Pylon Potter. As was to be expected, the programme was subject to sponsorship, and I recall having badgered my mother to buy the products so that I could send away the tops for my shining 'pilot's wings' which I then wore with such boyish pride.

Our farm was situated directly beneath the flight path of the small single-engined float planes used to transport supplies and equipment from Prince Albert to the gold miners and trappers at Lake Athabask some three hundred miles to the north. These planes - mostly the C-64B Norseman high-winged cabin monoplane - often passed low over our house, at which time I would run outside and wave frantically. Sometimes the pilot would catch sight of me and wave back or dip a wing in salute, thus making one small boy supremely happy.

Once a week, my father loaded up our horse-drawn wagon with produce, which he then took to town for sale to either the Magnet or Safeway stores on Central Avenue. Weather permitting, I usually accompanied him on these trips, which were to me the highlight of the week. Once we had reached the town, Dad would leave me to wander around on my own while he disposed of his wares. I would then hurry along Central Avenue until I came to the Fire Hall at the northernmost end, where the broad North Saskatchewan river flowed. it wasn't that I (like most boys of my age) was all that interested in fire engines, but I knew that a few hundred yards down stream from the fire hall I would find at least one Norseman tied up at its moorings. Usually, I just stood on the river bank and watched the activity taking place around the planes as they were serviced and loaded in readiness for their next flight, knowing that Dad would collect me on his way back home. But sometimes the crews (who soon got to know me) would invite me down onto the mooring platform for a closer look, and I would then bombard my hosts with unending questions on the aircraft, and on what flying was really like. Although quite small in comparison to the types of aircraft I was later to become familiar with, The Norseman impressed me as being enormous, and I found myself wondering how such a large thing could fly. On one of my many visits, I was actually allowed to board one of the planes, and the experience became my one topic of conversation for weeks afterwards.

On one such Saturday afternoon, Dad took me into Woolworth's fifteen-cent store and bought for me a model aeroplane kit. On getting the kit home. I commandeered the kitchen table for two whole days while I laboured mightily with a razor blade and a tube of cement to place together the many bits of balsa wood and tissue paper until I had finally constructed something that vaguely resembled an aeroplane. Having done this, I took my masterpiece out into the yard and proceeded to wind up the elastic band that served as its means of propulsion. Unfortunately, this resulted in the placing of too great a strain on the flimsy and inexpertly constructed fuselage, causing it to telescope within itself. My ensuing distress knew no bounds, but Dad succeeded in stemming my tears by promising to buy me another kit the next time he was in town. This he did, and the new kit, together with the several others that he later presented to me, served to promote in me a degree of improved expertise in the art of building and flying model aircraft.

I soon launched into my new-found hobby with great enthusiasm, and was delighted to see my second creation soar several feet from the ground before it spun into a nearby gooseberry bush. My subsequent attempts were favoured with progressive improvement, and these served to fill in the long winter months that followed my first attempt at model aircraft construction.

The long winter months in central Canada could only be described as severe. During this time one could expect a covering of at least three feet of crisp, dry snow, and a temperature which, although frequently well below minus forty degrees Fahrenheit, scarcely rose above freezing for much of the time. The strong winds that swept virtually unchecked across the prairies created mountainous drifts of snow, and these made travel by any means other than skis, snowshoes, horse-drawn sleighs or snowmobiles extremely difficult, if not impossible. Whitfield's one dirt road remained hazardous for much of the winter because the overworked snow ploughs seldom reached our region. The lakes and rivers froze over, and each Norseman had its cumbersome pontoons replaced by skis.

The summers were most pleasant, with a weather pattern that seldom varied from the seasonal norm. Late April signalled the awakening of nature with the appearance of a profusion of wild flowers and shrub-

IN THE BEGINNING

bery, and the woodlands near our farm became rich with the colour and song of the many species of birds that visited the area each year. During the first or second week in June, we could expect what was known locally as 'the general rain', a period of about two weeks during which it rained almost continually, thus ensuring the success of the newly-planted crops.

The remainder of the summer was mainly hot and dry, with temperatures which could reach as high as one-hundred degrees Fahrenheit by about mid-day. This usually brought about the arrival of a violent electrical storm in the early evening, and this could be frightening in it's magnitude and ferocity. However, the storm seldom lasted for more than an hour, and left in it's wake an atmosphere that was clean, fresh and pleasantly cool, with a light breeze that traced a pattern across the tall-standing fields of wheat and barley that bordered on three sides of our small holding. This weather pattern could be expected to prevail until about mid-September, by which time the flat prairie landscape became a blaze of autumn tints, and the harvesting began. There then followed the calm, hazy days of Indian summer, when the skies were filled with vic formations of migrating wild geese intent on reaching their distant winter quarters before the end of October brought with it the first snow fall of the long, cold winter.

Because of the predominantly severe winter conditions, and Whitfield's total lack of public transport, only those of us children who lived in close proximity to the school could attend during the period. It followed that the standard of education attained by many of the children in the district was subject to the dictates of geography rather than their personal ability to make a full use of the limited education facilities to be had.

It was fortunate that the other children of the family had completed their education before I reached the age of five. My parents were thus free to concentrate on me whatever level of tuition they could provide for me during the time when I was unable to attend. With their inducement, I had learned to read and write before the time that I reached school age, and was at all times encouraged to slake my thirst for knowledge by reading anything that held my interest. Nevertheless, on reaching the age at which one's primary education was deemed to be at an end (seventeen years), I had only succeeded in amassing eight years of graded education (completion of Grade Eight). However, this had been finished within a cumulative total of just six years of actual attendance, instead of the requisite eight. This in itself was a considerable achievement.

The degree of success I had attained at school was due largely to the remarkable teaching skills of Whitfield's only teacher. To Eddy Brooman had fallen the formidable task of imparting knowledge to some forty children ranging in age from five to seventeen years. These were split up into ten "grades", each of which was grouped together within the school's only classroom. Because of the demand on the time available to our teacher, the children in each Grade usually received two fifteen-minute periods of actual instruction at their level during each day.

Mr Brooman's enthusiasm for the job was without bounds, and he possessed that rare quality which enabled him to recognise a pupil's thirst for knowledge. Having sensed an attraction to a particular subject, he would go all out to encourage whatever degree of interest was evident, regardless of whether or not the subject was in the school curriculum. He soon noticed that I had a number of such interests, one of which was English. Of course, this was the result of the many books I had read during the long winter months of enforced home study, but it rated a poor second to my affinity to things aeronautical. Later in my education, when I became sufficiently advanced in age and stamina to wage a six-mile battle with the winter elements each day -and was thus able to attend school regularly - I was appointed to the post of president of the school debating society and was also made editor of the school magazine, an unpretentious but sincere bi-monthly publication to which I made regular contributions of amateurish journalistic quality. As could be expected, most of my articles were concentrated on the subject of aviation.

At the end of each full term, a prize-giving ceremony was held, during which the exam results were announced, and prizes were presented to the top-scoring pupils of each Grade by the School Board. In addition to this, Mr Brooman personally supplied and presented special awards to the two members of his charge (one boy and one girl) who in his estimation had shown the most promise during the past year. I sometimes qualified for such an award, and this invariably consisted of (in my case) either a model aeroplane kit or a book on aviation. One of the books I thus received dealt in some detail with light aircraft construction, and repetitive reading of it soon made me familiar with such technicalities as formers, strings, dihedrals, wing roots, wing loading, et cetera, and this knowledge did much to assist me in the practicalities of building and flying model aircraft.

I was still two years short of school leaving age when war was declared, an event which created great excitement amongst we older boys at Whitfield. To our minds, it was an adventure which was not to be

IN THE BEGINNING

missed, and the chance to become heroes occupied our thought and formed our main topic of conversation for much of our free time. Our one concern was the possibility that the war might end before we became of age to enlist in whichever branch of the Canadian forces we had chosen to join.

My burning ambition was to become a fighter pilot, and my youthful mind was filled with fantasies based on the content of the many films and newsreels to be seen at the time, plus the newspaper reports on the progress of the war in Europe. Things were not going well for the Allies, and I was keen to get into the fray.

By the summer of 1941, the British Empire Air Training Scheme had been established in Canada, and the skies above Whitfield were filled with the sight and sound of the many Tiger Moths that were based at the newly-constructed airfield east of Prince Albert. The field had been set up as an initial training school for fledgling pilots, and Whitfield had become the favourite area over which to train, it being the nearest piece of cleared ground north of the town. During the hours of daylight, there was scarcely a moment during which there wasn't to be seen at least one of these delightful little two-seater biplanes above our small holding, with its brightly doped yellow canvas-covered wings flashing in the sunlight as it looped, rolled and spun to my boyish delight. As I watched, I allowed my imagination to picture me at the controls as I relentlessly pursued an equally imaginary Hun to his ultimate and unavoidable destruction, and the thought that I too would be up there amongst them within the year was uppermost in my mind.

At the end of term in July, 1941 I was finally compelled to leave school, having already exceeded the leaving age by two months. Because I had not completed grades nine and ten. I did not qualify for a place at High School, so my father arranged for me to begin work as a hired hand on one of the big farms in the district. The work was arduous and the hours were long, but the pay was good, and I enjoyed the healthy outdoor life that it provided. Unfortunately, like all agricultural work in Canada, it was seasonal, and the job ended with the completion of the harvest.

At this time, I heard from a relative in Saskatoon that there was a vacancy in a dry cleaning plant there, so I caught a ride on "The Skunk" (an early diesel train, so named because of its odorous exhaust gasses) for the one-hundred mile journey south. I got the job, which involved me in the operation of the machines used in the process of dry cleaning articles of clothing for the local populace.

Saskatoon also had its Empire Training Scheme field, situated at the end of Avenue A on the northern outskirts, and this (No 4 FSTS) was equipped with a flight of twin-engined Cessnas. We often got RAF and RCAF uniforms in for cleaning, and it was not unusual for me to be seen trying on one, particularly if it bore pilots wings and a high rank.

The dry cleaning job was poorly paid in comparison to my wage as a farm labourer, but it offered security, and a means of subsisting until I could enlist in the RCAF. Meanwhile, I found city life to my liking, and had soon gathered together quite a few friends of my own age. As a small boy I had learned to play guitar reasonably well, so I landed a part-time job as rhythm guitarist with a five-place outfit called "The Trail Rangers", one of the many Country bands around at the time. This usually accounted for a couple of evenings each week, and the remaining free time was invariably spent in attending parties or ice skating at the rink down on 19th Street - home of the Saskatoon Quakers' ice hockey team.

As the winter progressed, and the time neared at which I could at last apply for enlistment, I was compelled to restrain by some means my mounting impatience. This I did by curbing some of my social life and concentrating instead on the reading of any available literature on the subject of flight. I had been told that the RCAF medical examination would be a tough one, and that many aspirants were being rejected on detection of the slightest medical defect, so I launched myself into a programme of strict physical training.

When at last Tuesday May the 5th, 1942 (my eighteenth birthday) arrived, I managed to wrangle a day off from the dry cleaning plant, and caught a street car down to the RCAF recruiting office in the centre of town.

CHAPTER 2

THE CALL OF ADVENTURE

Number 4 RCAF Recruiting Centre in downtown Saskatoon sadly lacked the space required of its intended purpose. On entry, I found it packed to overflowing with an assortment of fresh-faced young hopefuls waiting to be processed. I threaded my way through the assembled throng to the reception desk at the rear, where a young WAAF added my name to her already lengthy list, after which I was instructed to wait until called. The few chairs provided were all occupied, so I took up a leaning position against a wall and prepared myself for what looked like being a long wait. The gathering of fellow aspirants was made up mainly of teenagers like myself, with just a few who looked more advanced in years. No doubt there were some unemployed men amongst them, but it was probable that most were exchanging safe and secure jobs for the glamour and adventure of a career in flying. My supposition was confirmed as I joined in the various conversations that were going on around me. In general, the atmosphere was one of excitement and anticipation, and I could detect nothing of the solemnity of the occasion on the faces of those around me.

After approximately one hour, my name was finally called out and I was shown into a small ante-room at the rear. There I was asked to present my education and birth certificates. The information shown on these, together with other personal particulars were carefully noted by a man wearing the rank of Sergeant, after which I was supplied with a printed questionnaire and instructed to complete it within a specified time. On glancing through the paper, it became apparent that the questions were not in any way related to flying, so I supposed it to be some form of intelligence test. In each instance, the candidate was required to select one of three answers to the question, and I was relieved to find that there was only one question requiring a mathematical calculation - not my strongest subject. On having completed the paper, I handed it to the Sergeant, and was again returned to the reception area to await an interview with the Recruiting Officer. Soft drinks were on sale, so I selected a bottle of Coke and rejoined my fellow hopefuls.

The Recruiting Officer, a Flight Lieutenant was busily studying my documents as I entered his office. Without looking up, he signalled me to take a seat, saying "I'll be with you in a minute". The minute became several as he silently leafed through the questionnaire, pausing occasionally to make a note on a pad.

At last he spoke: "So you want to join the Air Force, Lad", he remarked, smiling.

"Yes, Sir".

"Why?"

The question threw me because I wasn't sure of the answer he was looking for. During the brief time that I had been in the office, I had been trying to assess the man, and had concluded that he was nobody's fool. I reckoned him to be in his late thirties and, because he was not wearing wings, must be in the Administrative Branch. His job was to screen those wishing to enlist so that only suitable candidates were accepted. The question I had been asked was of a psychological nature, and I at once realised the importance to me of whatever reply I might give. Of the possible answers I could offer - patriotism, the search for adventure; job security; a career in aviation - I chose the last of these.

"I want to fly, Sir", I said quite simply, then added, "I want to be a pilot".

The smile on the F/Lt's face quickly disappeared, giving way to a look of surprise, and he studied me for some time before responding:

"Laddie", he said, almost apologetically, "I'm sorry, but there's no chance of you ever being accepted for flying duties in any of the present categories, least of all as a pilot".

For a time I was struck speechless, not being able to fully grasp the significance of what had been said. I thought about the years I had spent in day dreaming about a future career in aviation; of building up hope; of trying to keep in check an ambition that refused to be checked. And now this man was telling me that the Royal Canadian Air Force had no use for me! I felt almost overcome with disappointment and anger.

"Why not?", I demanded to know, making no attempt to conceal my emotions. He paused, studying me carefully before making his reply, and there was a look of genuine, almost fatherly compassion on his face as he spoke:

"The truth is, your education doesn't meet with our requirement, son. Grade eight just isn't high enough for aircrew category. However, if you're so keen to get into the RCAF, I can offer you a slot in ground crew. As a matter of fact, according to this" (he held up the questionnaire) "You are a natural airframe mechanic, and we need as many of those as we can get".

THE CALL OF ADVENTURE

I silently cursed the book on aircraft construction that I had studied so diligently back at Whitfield. There was no doubt that the knowledge I had gained through reading it had in some way influenced the answers I had given to the questionnaire, and there was nothing to be done about that. Equally disturbing was the realisation that my education fell two years short of the RCAF's minimum for acceptance to aircrew, and I was forced to accept for the first time in my young life that I was confronted by Bureaucracy - The System - The Powers That Be. I didn't like it, and, like most young men of my age group, I was prepared to fight it.

"But Sir..."

"Listen, Lad", he interrupted, and he held up my education certificate as he spoke. "This piece of paper tells me that ..."

Now it was my turn to obtrude. "You said it, Sir. We're dealing with a piece of paper. A clock card. It tells you that I attended school just long enough to pass grade eight. What it doesn't tell you is that I completed those eight years of graded education in just six, and therefore it gives no indication of the degree of intelligence and personal ability required of such an achievement.

Even as I ended my outburst, I realised the futility of the argument I was presenting. No doubt the F/Lt was bound by regulations made at a much higher level, and it was unlikely that he would attempt to supersede such rulings, but I felt that I had to try. There followed a long silence, during which he studied me thoughtfully, and I found myself hoping that perhaps my tenacity and determination of purpose had produced the desired effect. At last he spoke:

"I get a lot of young fellows like you in here, and believe me, I know something of the frustration and disappointment you must be sensing right now, because I've been through it. I wanted to fly, but I was rejected on medical grounds. You see", he continued, "I have to work to a set of rules - and don't ask me to bend them", he said, having seen me draw breath to interrupt again. "I can't do that, much as I'd like to in your case. I can see that you have a strength of character and purpose that is admirable, and it is for that reason that I strongly advise you to accept the airframe option. I think you'd do well at it".

"Sorry", I said, "but I want to fly, Sir".

"In that case, there's nothing more I can do for you", he said as he gathered up my papers and handed them over to me. I accepted the documents, turned, and walked out of the office.

The weeks that followed my rejection brought about a period of great indecision for me, and it seemed that there was no remedy for my despondency. At that time, young men of my age were to be seen in uniform on the streets of Saskatoon in ever-increasing numbers, and I felt that I should be with them. One of my half brothers was already serving overseas with the Canadian Army, and another was established as a commissioned officer in the RCAF, based in Winnipeg. Two members of our Country band were on the point of enlisting in the Canadian forces, as were a number of my friends. I could see by watching the newsreels and reading the papers that Hitler's plan of world conquest was in danger of succeeding, with most of western and central Europe and North Africa already under the jackboot, and the Japs had decided to get in on the act out in the Pacific. Although Canada was not yet under direct attack, it was certain to be a tempting prize for any enterprising would-be conqueror. Patriotism was beginning to influence my thoughts, but my youthful thirst for adventure was still my main driving force. The RCAF would not let me fly, but there were plenty of other opportunities for adventure still open to me. All that was required of me was to decide on which alternative to choose. Not that there was any need for me to become involved at all, since conscription for the Canadian forces was still non-existent.

The thought occurred to me that it might be a good idea to take up the F.Lt's advice and sign on as an airframe mechanic. True, it would be a groundcrew job, but I would probably get an overseas posting, and the promotion prospect was entirely up to my ability to do the job. I liked building model aircraft, and working on the real thing would be interesting. Furthermore, I had been told by a friend that groundcrew sometimes got a chance to go up on an air test after having carried out a repair. No doubt this concession was designed to test the mechanic's confidence in his own workmanship, but it provided a means whereby I could indulge in my primary ambition.

I was on the point of making application for the airframe job when the RCAF announced that the required minimum standard of education for certain categories of aircrew had been lowered to that of grade eight. There was no doubt that the decision had been taken in order that a greater number of recruits could be obtained, but it meant that I could at last pursue my ambition.

On hearing the news, I immediately requested and was granted a further day off work, and again joined the band of hopefuls down at the Recruiting Centre.

THE CALL OF ADVENTURE

In view of my previous experience of the procedure, I now felt reasonably confident of success. Although my earlier tilt at the system had proved disastrous, my inadequate education had been the only hurdle that had tripped me up, and this obstacle had been removed for the re-run. No doubt there wold be other tests to be taken, and the medical examination looked like being the most demanding of these. However, I knew my general physical condition to be good, and I considered my eyesight to be excellent, so I was harbouring few fears of failure this time.

In less than an hour after my arrival at the Centre, I found myself seated in front of the same F/Lt as before, and he recognised me at once. This time the interview, although brief, was a much happier event. Yes, I was to be accepted as a candidate for enlistment as air gunner, but I was warned that it was as yet too early for any form of celebration. I still had the medical examination ahead of me, and it would demand a high standard of physical fitness. On completion of the interview, I was instructed to report back at the reception desk, where appointments for the various segments of the medical would be made. Before dismissing me from his office, the F/Lt shook my hand warmly and wished me good luck.

The medical was indeed thorough, taking four full days to complete. The first day consisted of a detailed and at times rude appraisal of my general physical condition, as a result of which it was discovered that I was in need of some dental treatment, and that I was possessed of unusually high insteps. The dental work was to be carried out by a service dentist, and my foot irregularity presented no real problem, it being the policy of the RCAF to excuse such freaks from having to wear the standard issue lace-up boots. The second and third days were spent in undergoing a series of extensive eyesight tests, and on the fourth day, I was instructed to attend the local hospital for a chest x-ray. I took this to indicate that I had so far passed all the previous tests and examinations, otherwise I would have been ejected from the system forthwith. Having had the x-ray, I reported back at the centre, and was instructed to go home to await the result.

It was with a much easier frame of mind that I returned to my digs that Saturday afternoon. I felt confident that I had passed the medical, and that the RCAF would soon be launching me into the flying career that I had dreamed of for so long. My one regret was the knowledge that I would never become a pilot, but I was to be given the chance to fly, and my excitement at the prospect was almost limitless.

Back on Civvy Street, the band had been booked for a Country music slot a couple of nights later at the Roxy picture house on 20th Street. Our brief appearance called for just three numbers, and we were to appear during the interval, sandwiched somewhere between Clark Gable and Donald Duck. Of the lineup, one member had been rejected for military service on medical grounds; one was already serving in the Canadian Army as a bandsman (and was home on leave from his unit), and the other three - including me - were in the process of joining up. A hurried rehearsal was called, at which the three numbers were chosen and gone over several times, until we considered that we had them sounding right.

Audience appreciation proved to be moderate on the night. Country music bands were a dime a dozen at the time, and our performance was hardly professional despite the careful preparation. The large number of people in the auditorium included a good sprinkling of uniformed men and women, and our first two numbers earned only moderate applause. Before finally bringing our diminutive gig to a close, the lead vocalist announced that our next number would be the last that we would perform together because we were disbanding to join the Canadian forces. This effectively brought the house down, and the applause we got on completion of the final number was the kind to which such Country greats as Hank Williams were accustomed.

Of the friends I had made during my stay in Saskatoon, one was Margaret, the sister to one of the band members. I had been dating her for some time, and I found her great fun to be with. she enjoyed Country music and ice skating, and I suppose it was this sharing of common interests that attracted us to each other. We were frequently seen together down at the rink, and she always went with us whenever the band was booked to play at a gig. We liked each other's company, and it was generally accepted by our circle of friends that the relationship would grow. Not that there was as yet anything really serious between us. She was younger than I, and neither of us was as yet sufficiently matured to be ready for the solemnity of a romantic relationship.

After the gig I took Margaret into Eddy Malouf's soda bar for a coke. As we drank, we talked about my pending involvement with the Air Force. In answer to her many questions, I told her that I would be posted away for training soon, and that I would probably be sent overseas soon after that. To me, the future was filled with adventure of the kind I had been waiting for long to sample, but she seemed genuinely concerned about my welfare. Finally, she suggested that we should keep in touch with each other, and I promised that I would drop her a letter as soon as I had taken up my first posting.

THE CALL OF ADVENTURE

CHAPTER 3

INITIAL TRAINING

Two days later, I received orders to report to the Recruiting Centre. On presenting myself I was informed that I had been accepted into the Royal Canadian Air Force as aircrew 'for a term of voluntary service during an emergency'. I was then required to sign various papers, and was presented with a pay book and a printed list of instructions pertaining to my first posting. This was to a Manning Depot at Edmonton, Alberta. I also received a travel warrant, and was ordered to catch a train on the following afternoon. On enquiring about the issue of uniforms, I was told that this would be supplied at the manning Depot on my arrival.

The next twenty-four hours were hectic. First of all, my parents had to be informed, also my employer. Next came packing. Fortunately, this had been greatly simplified by a list of instructions I had been issued with. This imposed severe limitations on what I could or could not take with me, and, because no mention was made of musical instruments, I took this as an indication - wrongly as it happened - that these were not allowed. As a result, my guitar, together with various other items of personal accoutrement, were passed to a relation for safe keeping until my return.

In the evening, I made hurried calls on my friends and fellow musicians, after which I had a brief and impromptu date with Margaret. This consisted of a meal at a downtown restaurant, after which I walked her to her home through streets lit by the garish, flashing neon signs that were a feature of Canadian cities, even during wartime. As we walked, we discussed what the future might have in store for us, and she appeared to sense more than I did the circumstances that might ultimately affect our relationship. For the first time ever, she made no attempt to conceal her fondness for me, and I experienced a sense of shame at being sufficiently insensitive to consider us both too young to become involved in anything serious. It was true that we still had a lot of growing up to do, but we were getting there, she more quickly than I. At the time, I could think of little else than the great adventure that was about to begin for me. But to Margaret, the dangers with which I would soon be faced were clear and explicit, whereas I, being fired with the blind exuberance of youth, could only envisage the glamour and excitement of it all. In just over a year my views were destined to suffer a sharp reversal as the full horrors of warfare were revealed to me. But in the meantime, I looked upon her fears as a product of her unrealistic exaggeration of reality. After our walk, we had our very first kiss outside her door, after which I turned and walked off in the direction of the digs.

The overnight train journey from Saskatoon to Edmonton was a new experience for me, it being the first time that I had ventured so far from home. The RCAF had provided me with an upper berth on a sleeper near the rear of the train. Although the "The Canadian" (the trans-Canada passenger express) numbered at least twenty carriages in length, I could distinctly hear the whistle of the big steam engine up front as we passed through the wheat fields and forests of the prairies and steamed on into the sunset. The Canadian was in effect a self-contained hotel on wheels, and was adequately equipped to cater for the needs of the many passengers during the five day trans-continental journey. The sleepers were designed to serve as standard coaches during the day, but were speedily transformed as if by magic by the attendants as night approached, when the seats became lower berths; the upper berths were brought down from their stowage in the roof, and curtains were fitted in place. The change-over took place during the evening meal when all the passengers in the carriage were allocated a sitting in one of the dining cars.

As the evening progressed, I learned that there were a number of others on board bound for the Manning Depot, and I became friendly with a tall, gangling fellow 'stubble-jumper' from Saskatchewan. Known as 'Cowboy' McKinnon, he was to remain with me for most of my training, but lost his life while flying with a Canadian Squadron in England later.

The Canadian rumbled on into the night, and I was soon lulled to sleep by the swaying of the carriage and the frequent distant moaning of the whistle at each of the many level crossings in our path.

Sunrise found us steaming through the slightly undulating landscape Alberta, and, after a shave in the washroom at the end of the car, we were again ushered into one of the dining cars, this time for breakfast. By the time we had returned to our re-converted carriage, the train was nearing the outskirts of the city of Edmonton. Anyone who has travelled this route will know that, just prior to entering the city, the train is routed across a wide, deep gorge by means of a viaduct which has no sides. The crossing gives a quite realistic delusion of flight because nothing can be seen of the viaduct from the windows of the train. The view is exclusively of the grassy canyon floor far below.

An RCAF transport awaited our arrival, and several of us were loaded into this for the short trip to the

INITIAL TRAINING

Depot. I had expected to find an airfield there, but the entire establishment appeared to consist of nothing more than an enormous parade ground, surrounded by a conglomeration of timbered buildings of various shapes and sizes.

We were at this point handed over to a Sergeant who escorted us to what was to be our billet for the duration of our eight weeks' stay. This was a single dormitory, and each of us was assigned to a space occupied by a bed and a tall tin locker. Each bed space had a sash window, and the floor covering consisted of plain, light brown linoleum. This had been waxed and polished to a mirror-like sheen, and it was forcefully pointed out to us that responsibility for the upkeep and cleanliness of the interior would be ours.

After having deposited our belongings in our lockers, we were marched off to the camp barber shop for hair cuts. Despite my protests at having had one the week previously, I was obliged to occupy the chair, from which I stepped down three minutes later, looking like a recently released inmate of the local penitentiary. There then followed a visit to the medical centre, where I was subjected to the painful removal of three teeth and the filling of two others. The task was performed by an overworked F/Lt with hands like banana bunches and a chairside manner that left much to be desired. This ordeal being over, I was next confronted by a medical orderly whose task was to inject each of us with an assortment of serum's (seven in all) which were allegedly capable of protecting us from all known allergies.

At the end of it all, we were told that we had been excused duties for the remainder of the day, so our newly-formed squad of twenty-three raw, closely shorn, and somewhat groggy recruits stumbled back to the billet to await the call to lunch. We entered to find a Corporal awaiting us, and he immediately launched into a course of instruction on the making of beds. He began his carefully rehearsed dissertation with the words, "Beds shall be made up as laid down in Standing Orders". As was to be expected, this unfortunate turn of phrase brought forth gales of laughter from us, but our mirth was quickly ended when we saw the Corporal's unchanging facial expression. He had failed to see the humorous side of it, and he soon made known his displeasure by informing us that we were confined to barracks for the rest of the day on the grounds that our outburst had constituted insubordination.

Once the corporal had left, we busied ourselves by stowing our possessions and discussing our immediate prospects. We were to begin 'square-bashing' the next morning, and not one of us was looking forward to it, having witnessed the spectacle out on the square that morning. The eventual result of our discussion was a commitment to surrender to 'the system'. We couldn't beat it, so we might as well join it. After all, we reasoned, it would only be for two months, then we would be free to do what we had joined up to do in the first place - fly.

However, our resolve was severely tested next morning when, on presenting ourselves on the square, we were perturbed to learn that we had been allocated to 'Old Bulldog Face' for the duration of our training period. Unsmiling, he introduced himself as Corporal Kosick, and proceeded to deliver a stern lecture outlining his dislike of rookies and the total lack of tolerance he was prepared to give to such rabble. Like the others, I was greatly impressed by his tirade, and formed the opinion that he could not have looked more fearsome and officious had he been wearing the uniform of an Air Chief Marshal.

We had not yet been issued with uniform, so were hardly equipped to contend with the conditions. Our squad was confined to a part of the crowded square which was grassed, and a recent rainstorm had made the going distinctly soft. Like the others, I was dressed in the same outer garments that I had been wearing when I arrived. Mine consisted of two-tone patent leather shoes, yellow socks, off-white trousers (cuffed), and a pink shirt. The rigout was topped by an off-white doeskin zip-up jacket which was garishly trimmed with contrasting pigskin pipings. There was no doubt that my choice of attire mirrored my dedication to the prevailing fashion of my generation, but the result was totally unsuited to the rigours of square-bashing in the mud.

Our problem was resolved the next morning when we were sent to the stores section. There, we were each grudgingly supplied with a large armful of items of uniform and equipment by a stores attendant who seemed intent on ensuring that none of us got anything that fitted. This accounted for most of the morning, and we spent the afternoon in the billet, engaged in a lengthy session by means of which most of us, through a system of unofficial exchange and barter, managed to end up reasonably well dressed for the part we were to play.

Our wardrobe consisted of three uniforms (two 'Number One Blues' and one 'tropical'); one greatcoat; one forage cap; three shirts (each with two detached collars); two black ties; three pairs of socks, and two pairs of black boots (shoes in my case). Other items included a blue canvas kit bag; a safety razor and shaving brush; a set of aluminium mess tins; two sets of collar studs, and a 'housewife'. This was a small canvas pouch containing a selection of needles and thread, a threader, and a brass

INITIAL TRAINING

button stock. The three tunics and the greatcoat sported a profusion of standard RCAF brass buttons, and it was widely rumoured that these, together with the cap badge, were expected to be maintained in pristine condition by means of the frequent and laborious polishing thereof.

The pressing of the various items of uniform, plus the sewing on of shoulder flashes continued into the late evening, with the result that the matter of polishing the buttons came a poor second to our desire to bed down in readiness for the long and tiring day that lay ahead of us.

Corporal Kosick's reaction to the display of store-soiled buttons facing him on the morning parade was a masterful example of unbridled indignation and rage. As he proceeded to make known to the entire population of the parade square his extreme displeasure at our apparent indifference to the basic principles of spit and polish. I made what I later considered to be the most foolhardy decision I was ever likely to arrive at: I took it upon myself to act as spokesman for the Squad. Timing my intervention to coincide with a time when the Corporal was forced to interrupt his tongue-lashing in order to draw a much needed breath, I stepped smartly forward and, standing at attention, pointed out that, with respect, we had not yet been supplied with the required polishing materials.

There followed a brief period of silence which was almost ear-splitting in it's intensity, as the corporal fixed me with a stare that made me wish I was somewhere else. His expression told me that I had placed myself in line for a first-rate rebuke, and I feared what was to come. Not that there was really any need for him to speak, because his demeanour said it all. Words of profanity oozed from his every pore, and I watched the gradual build-up of pressure as the veins at his temples stood out, and his complexion took on a deep shade of purple. When the explosion finally came, I swear that the ground beneath me shook as he made it known to me and the Squad - and everyone within a half-mile radius for that matter - that ample stocks of the required liquid were available in the canteen, and could be purchased for a few cents a can!

I had given Margaret the address of my posting before I left Saskatoon, and her first letter to me came a few days after my arrival at Edmonton. Nothing of importance had transpired during the few days that I had been away, so the content of the letter was mainly an expression of her regret that we could no longer enjoy each other's company on a more regular basis. The remaining members of the band were in the process of joining up, and she would be giving further detail as soon as she could. The letter was signed "with Love", and she had added a row of kisses beneath her signature.

As the weeks progressed and our policy of surrender to the system began to pay dividends, so the quality of life became more acceptable. Gradually, as we adjusted ourselves to the pace, the training schedule became less difficult and demanding, and we even grew to accept the bullying and seemingly needless discipline to which we were frequently subjected. Like the other members of the Squad, I at first looked upon square-bashing as quite unnecessary to the mean efficiency of any fighting force other than the infantry, but I gradually began to envisage the need for discipline under combat conditions. As I saw it, our willingness to accept orders quickly and without question could one day prove vital to our survival, and I then came to realise that the purpose of the training was to instil that acceptance.

By the end of the sixth week of our training, we had become quite expert in the technique of squad drill, and had begun to take pride in our smart and efficient bearing. A spirit of competition had built up between us and the other squads occupying the square, and I also sensed the presence of a similar spirit between the various instructors. As our proficiency progressed, and a bond of near friendship began to build up between us, I personally regarded Corporal Kosick as a man of impressive bearing, integrity and character, and considered him to be deserving of a much higher rank than that which he carried.

As the penultimate week of our course neared it's end. Corporal Kosick fell victim to a sever case of laryngitis, and this rendered him incapable of giving voice to his various commands in the way to which he was accustomed. This was a blow to us, because our final week was to be taken up by a series of parade ground tests which would be observed and assessed by a senior officer. During these, each squad would be put through it's paces, and each member of each squad would be called upon to take command and execute a drill of the officer's choice. Finally, the squad considered to be the most proficient was to be selected for service as a display unit, and would be held back for an unspecified period so that it could take part in ceremonial parades. Although I was keen to avoid an extension to our stay at Edmonton, I was concerned that we were to lose the man who had moulded us into the smart and efficient Squad that we had become. However, despite our impassioned pleas that he should remain with us, the Corporal was ordered to rest, and we were handed over to the charge of another Corporal named Wright.

INITIAL TRAINING

Corporal Wright was no stranger to parade ground techniques, and our pride and self confidence was soon restored. When the big day finally arrived, we put up a good show despite our nervous state, and we derived comfort from the sight of Corporal Kosick standing at the edge of the square observing our performance.

When my turn came to take command, I was ordered to size the squad. This was a complicated manoeuvre which called for the giving of a number of successive commands, one of which I got in the wrong sequence. My blunder was quickly corrected by the examining officer however, and the remainder of the test was completed without further complication. On presenting the newly-sized squad to him, the officer returned my salute, and I detected a slight smile of understanding as he dismissed me.

The nail-biting wait for the results of our tests proved mercifully brief, and we were informed of these in the late afternoon. It was with a great sense of relief I learned that we had all passed, although our squad had not won the ultimate accolade of being chosen as the elite, a failure for which I felt no remorse, being keen to get on with my flying training.

After receiving our results, we were told that we were to be granted a week's leave (plus travelling time) commencing on the following day; that we were all promoted to the rank of LAC (Leading Air Craftsman) forthwith, and that the entire squad was to report to No 3 Bombing and gunnery School at Macdonald, Manitoba on September the 14th in order to begin air training.

Our jubilation at receiving the news of our leave and posting was too great to be contained, and there immediately sprang up in our billet one of those impromptu booze-ups that I was soon to accept as a feature of Air Force life. Cases of beer appeared as if by magic, and the room was soon ringing to the sounds of boisterous revelry as we gave vent to our exhilaration. Because Canadian law at that time prohibited the consumption of intoxicants by all those under the age of twenty-one years, most of us were in danger of doing a stretch, but none cared.

The party was just beginning to get interesting when the door suddenly burst open, and in strode Corporal Kosick. A mighty silence fell on the room as bottles were hurriedly concealed beneath beds and inside lockers, and we all had visions of exchanging our leave period for a spell in the camp lock-up. Hands on hips, the Corporal stood silently for a time, surveying the spectacle that we presented, and his face expressed everything that was evil. Anxiously, we waited for the expected trouncing, and we wondered if his laryngitis might to some extent serve to ease the impact. At last, it came:

"Well", he croaked, "isn't anybody gonna gimme a beer?"

The celebration was immediately restored to its former state of ebullience. Somebody struck up a popular barrack-room ballad, and we all joined in. A guitar appeared from somewhere, and this was at once taken in charge by the Corporal. Soon the billet was ringing to the strains of "Bless 'Em All", ably accompanied by some nifty guitar picking.

"Bless all the Corporals and W.O. Ones..." we chorused. "... For we're saying goodbye to them all, as back to their billets they crawl..." In just a couple of weeks we would be starting our flying careers, but corporal Kosick and his fellow drill instructors would tomorrow be presented with another batch of raw recruits, and it was likely that the new intake would prove just as reluctant to conform to the dictates of military training and discipline as we had in the beginning. I found myself wondering if our Corporal and his associates derived any job-satisfaction from their humdrum existence.

"You'll get no promotion this side of the ocean...". We were already just one notch below the rank of corporal, and our promotion to Sergeant would accompany our wings in a few week's time. But there was no guaranteed system of promotion for these men. "So cheer up, my lads, bless; 'em all".

Late the following evening, those of us who were heading homewards to the east were loaded into canvas covered transports, and, with numerous toilet rolls streaming from the open back of each vehicle, were transported through the brightly-lit streets of downtown Edmonton to the railway station.

CHAPTER 4

WINGS

My brief stay in Saskatchewan was taken up by visits to my various friends and kinsfolk in Saskatoon, plus train journey north to Prince Albert. Harvest time was just beginning, and Whitfield was resplendent with the tall, ripening fields of grain that were a feature of the district. Dad had planted the usual selection of fruits and vegetables, and the crop looked good. He always made use of a gang of squaws from the nearby indian reservation for the potato harvest, and Mrs TwoBear, who organized her own work force for the purpose, was waiting when Dad and I arrived at the farm. She was a jolly but quiet-spoken lady whose command of the English language was limited.

"How!", she greeted me as I walked into the kitchen, where she was sipping a cup of tea that Mother had given her. "Hello", I replied as I shook her hand. "You fly in big bird?", she asked with difficulty. I wanted to reply in her native language, but found that I had forgotten most of the Indian lingo she had taught me when I was a small boy. "Not yet, but soon", I replied.

"You want moccasins?", she asked, and I recalled that, over the years that I had known her, Mrs TwoBear had been in the habit of presenting me with a pair each harvest time. These were fashioned with loving care from cured and tanned deerskin, and were richly adorned with an intricate pattern of brightly coloured beads. They were also without doubt the most comfortable footwear I had ever owned, and had proved to be an ideal form of protection against the severity of a Canadian winter. Unfortunately, I was forced to decline her offer on trying to imagine the response I would get from someone like Corporal Kosick if I was to present myself on parade in a pair.

Mother had prepared a veritable feast for my return, and we were soon sitting down to a meal of roast pork with dumplings and lashings of vegetables fresh from the garden. Dessert was a choice between apple pie and wild strawberries with cream, and the meal ended with a generous glass of her home-made choke cherry wine. Mrs TwoBear shared the meal with us, during which a date was set for her to attend with her gang of squaws to begin harvesting the potato crop. Her work force was always made up from the women of her community, it being customary for the more menial tasks to be shunned by the male members of the tribe. Having dined, she then left with her pony and trap for the two-mile return trip to the reservation.

After lunch, our conversation dwelt mainly on matters concerning the immediate farming community, but eventually drifted to include the war in Europe and the effect that it was having on the family. Brother Tom had closed down his blacksmith business in Debolt, Alberta, so that he could join up, and was serving with a Royal Canadian Electrical and Mechanical Engineers regiment somewhere out in North Africa, after having escaped from Dunkirk. Brother Joyce had enlisted in the administrative branch of the RCAF; had landed a commission, and was tied down to a desk job in Winnipeg. Bill, who was living our in Alberta, was in the Strathcona Horse regiment, and Arthur Bliss and been rejected for service on medical grounds. In all, it could be said that the Moore's were very much involved in the struggle.

Dad and Mother both expressed their concern at the dangers I would be facing in my chosen military career, and I tried to allay their fears by assuring them that I was getting the best training available, and that the aircraft and equipment I would be using was superior to anything that the Germans had. I argued that the Axis powers had put up a good show so far, but fortunes were beginning to improve for the Allies around El Alamein, and we had all heard of the pasting that Bomber Command and the American Eight Air Force were dishing out to the cities and war production centres of Germany and Italy.

The Tiger Moths were still milling around the sky above our farm, and I spent some time watching them during the two days I was at home. One of them came down to do some low flying, and the pilot - obviously a recent convert to the solo status - recognised my uniform, whereupon he promptly put on a mini display in my honour. This consisted of a loop and a roll, followed by a low pass over the farmyard, during which he waved to me and waggled the wings before heading off in the direction of Prince Albert. As the little yellow biplane chugged out over the Nesbit forest, I silently wished it's pilot luck in his flying career.

Once back in Saskatoon, I dated Margaret on the night before I left for Macdonald. We went to see George Formby in "It's In The Air" at the Tivoli down on Second Avenue, followed by a meal and a street car ride up to her place in Avenue Q. I gave her my new address and promised her that I would write as soon as I was settled in. As I rode the street car back to Avenue C, I reflected on our association. There was no doubt that Margaret was serious about our relationship, and I was at last beginning to see her in a different light. She was no longer just someone

WINGS

who was fun to be with. She was fast developing into a very attractive young woman. She had made her affection for me quite plain as we had kissed good night a few minutes earlier, and I had seen the tears well up as she begged me to "take care".

The sun was just setting as I climbed down from the train at Portage la Prairie, together with a few other members of the Squad. The usual RCAF transport was waiting to collect us, and we were soon established in one of the warm and comfortable timber billets that were a monotonous feature of the Gunnery School at nearby Macdonald. I selected a corner bed and found that the one next to mine was occupied by someone I had not met previously. Shy and soft-spoken, he turned out to be a young Polish Canadian from nearby Winnipeg, and had done his square-bashing at No 1 Manning Depot in Toronto. His name was Andy Mynarski, and he and I were to become close friends during the next few months, until our ways divided and he was posted to a Canadian unit (No 419 "Moose" Squadron) at Middleton St George in northern England. Unfortunately, he was destined to lose his life in circumstances which warranted the posthumous award of the Victoria Cross in recognition of an act of selfless courage and bravery which belied his timid personality. Later (in 1978), I was to visit a school in Machrae Avenue, Winnipeg. The building had been dedicated to his memory, and I saw in the main corridor a portrait of Andy which had been expertly painted by Chris Sheehan, a close friend and Air Force enthusiast from northern England. On completion of the portrait, Chris and I had together arranged for the RCAF to collect it at Teesside Airport and fly it out to Winnipeg.

The following morning, we were given an outline of what the course would entail. The first six weeks were to be taken up with classroom tuition on such subjects as airborne armament, aircraft recognition, Morse code transmission and reading (key and Aldis lamp), map reading, elementary navigation, gun turret manipulation, and a study of ballistics and trajectories. In addition to all this, we would be given practical instruction in shooting at a stationary target with a .303 rifle, and shooting skeet with a twelve-bore shotgun. The highlight of the ground course was to take place on the firing range, during which we would each be given a brief two-minutes in which to let fly at a stationary target with four Brownings mounted in a powered turret. We were told that we would not begin flying training until the seventh week, and that, during the first week of the period, we would be using only camera guns. During the remaining three weeks, we would be firing a single Vickers gas-operated .303 machine gun at either a drogue target or at smoke floats dropped on the surface of Lake Winnipegosis. We would be training mainly in the Fairey Battle. That evening we walked out to the airfield to have a look at the various aircraft. From their appearance, it was obvious that the Battles had seen action, and had probably been shipped out from England after Dunkirk. Many bore the scars of combat, with small -

Fig 1

The author (centre) with Jack Kendall and Hank Benis. No 3 Bombing and Gunnery school, Macdonald, Canada.

Winter 1942

and in some cases large - patches of aluminium riveted into place where bullet holes had once been.

As the ground instruction course progressed, and information on the armament and destructive capacity of the various German fighter aircraft became available, I found myself sufficiently informed as to be able to assess the dangers I could expect to meet during serial combat. It was obvious that the fighter was superior to the bomber in speed, manoeuvrability, and in the fire power and effective range of it's armament. The best that the heavy bomber could bring to bear during a rearward attack by an enemy fighter would be a total of six .303 Brownings, while most of the German fighters carried an equal number of 7.9mm machine guns, plus two - or, in some cases four - 20mm cannons. The 7.9mm gun was approximately equal to the .303 in range and rate of fire, but the British heavy bomber had no effective answer to the destructive potential of the cannon. This weapon made it possible for the fighter to inflict severe damage on the bomber from a position beyond the range of the Browning .303.

In my estimation, the only advantage that the bomber had over the fighter was the power-operated mid-upper and tail gun turrets. These enabled the bomber's fire power to be directed against the attacker without regard to the line of flight being taken by the bomber, whereas the fighter pilot had to aim his aircraft before he could hope to score any hits on his quarry with his fixed, forward-firing guns.

I was later to learn that the ponderous speed of a large and heavily-laden bomber could be used to advantage during a 'swerving match' with a fighter, and that the effective use of the cannon's range superiority depended on the fighter pilot's ability to see his target from an extended distance, especially under conditions of darkness. Nevertheless, I was inclined to conclude that there was little future in becoming involved in a lead-slinging match with one of those babies, and that, if I eventually found myself in Bomber Command, my role would basically be one of defence, tempered with all the cunning that I and my pilot could together contrive.

As a result of my assessment of the probabilities facing me, I decided that I must at all costs avoid like the plague a posting to the 'heavies'. Instead, I would try to get a slot in one of the other Commands which used air gunners - Coastal Command, even Fighter Command, still had two-seaters. Of these, the Boulton Paul Defiant with its four-gun turret impressed me as being a useful aircraft. it had nice lines, and it, together with the now defunct Fairey Battle, had given a good account of itself during the evacuation of Dunkirk, and had since then been used to some effect, together with the spitfire and the Hurricane, in the defence of London against the German night bombing offensive.

Since it appeared likely that I would end up in Bomber Command, i decided to become proficient in the handling of the equipment I would be using. With this in mind, I spent as much time as possible in the turret manipulation room, learning to perfect a degree of fine and rapid control over the Frazer-Nash gun turret. Each member of the course was expected to log at least eight hours, so the competition for time slots was fierce. In all, I managed to clock ten-and-a-half hours, and considered myself expert in driving the thing by the time the course ended. Not as expert as some of the lads, however. A favourite trick was to fix a pencil to the end of one of the guns, and demonstrate your skill at manipulation by writing your name on a piece of card, using the controls. Some even went so far as to illustrate their artistic qualities through the production of line drawings, most of which were unfit for public display.

Aircraft recognition became a favourite subject, and I was soon able to recognise and name most enemy aircraft as they were briefly flashed onto a screen. Having learned how to handle the .303 rifle and the twelve-bore shotgun, I soon became an efficient marksman, and particularly enjoyed skeet shooting. Aiming at a moving target presented a challenge which was more in keeping with my intended function, and I usually succeeded in marking up an above-average score.

Most segments of the ground course were found to be easy, although I did have some difficulty with the subject of Morse signalling. Navigation, because it involved some mathematical calculations, also proved to be something of a problem because of my limited mastery of things numerical, but I somehow managed to obtain a reasonable pass mark in all subjects.

Most of the instructors were men who had already completed at least one tour of operations overseas, and their attitude towards us presented a refreshing contrast to that which we had been subjected to back at the Manning Depot. Many had been decorated, and some were commissioned officers. Without exception, they were keen to pass on to us the benefits of their knowledge and experience, and they did not seem interested in sustaining the degree of regimentation to which we had grown accustomed during our initial training. These men were squadron types. They had seen it all, and they knew what lay ahead of us. The lectures were frequently interrupted while the instructor answered one of the many questions asked on what life was like on an operational squadron, and on what difficulties we could expect to meet during an attack on

WINGS

an enemy target. Of the answers we got, I considered most to be accurate, while some were downright awe-inspiring, and my general conclusion was that the career I had chosen fell far short of being a safe one.

The ground instruction course ended with a night-time visit to a nearby gunnery range, where each one of us was briefly installed in a gun turret for some shooting practice. I got the Boulton Paul turret for my session, and the sensation of power that I experienced as I depressed the firing button and heard the four Brownings chatter was most reassuring. As I watched the tracers impinge on the distant target (a wooden cut-out of a Messerschmitt 109), and the splinters began to fly off, my confidence in the future underwent a considerable improvement.

Completion of the ground course was rewarded with a forty-eight hour pass. This would not allow a trip home, so I, together with Andy Mynarski and a couple of the others caught a train down into Winnipeg. There we planned on spending a surreptitious evening visiting a few watering holes, after which we would book into a hotel for the night before returning to the Gunnery School next day. Unfortunately, we spent rather more time and hard cash on our infringement of the Canadian drinking laws than was wise. As a result, we discovered that our pooled resources were not sufficient to meet the cost of our proposed accommodation. A hasty conference was held, during which it was decided that the other two members of our party would book a double room in the cheapest doss house we could find after which Andy and I would be smuggled in.

The plan worked to perfection. In fact, on having sneaked upstairs and into the room occupied by the others, Andy and I discovered a door connecting the room with another. The door was not locked, so we gently opened it and peered inside, and were delighted to find that it was not only unoccupied, but that it contained two single beds, all made up and ready for use. These we gleefully commandeered, and were just getting ready to settle down to a night of comfortable, booze-induced oblivion when we heard the sound of a key rattling in the door leading out into the corridor. Fortunately, whoever was attempting access to the room must have been in a worse state of inebriation than we were, and was thus experiencing great difficulty in locating the keyhole. This gave Andy and me sufficient time in which to gather our belongings together and retreat back to the other room.

Fig 2

A Fairey Battle drogue ship. Macdonald

On re-entering we again faced the earlier problem. It was obvious to the four of us that, although broad-minded, there just wasn't any way that we were all going to fit into the narrow single beds that were a feature of our chosen flophouse. Consequently, Andy and I had to spend an uncomfortable night on the floor of the room, each wrapped in a single blanket which had been donated to our cause by our fellow sufferers. The night was cold, and (because there didn't appear to be any heating in the place) we were glad when it finally ended.

Ten minutes past nine o'clock on the morning of October 29th, 1942 marked the beginning of my flying career proper, as Fairey Battle number 2107/49, with Flight Sergeant Palmer at the controls came unstuck from the grassed, snow sprinkled airfield, and lifted in the direction of the drab grey cloudbase that hung above us. Peering cautiously over the rim of the open cockpit at the terrain slipping fast beneath us, I experienced disappointment at the lack of flight sensation. Once the rumbling of the wheels on the grass had ceased, there was no sensation of movement other than that which could be seen. Even the perception of speed was denied me as we gained height, and the backward movement of the receding fields beneath us appeared to slow. Our progress seemed smooth and effortless, and we soared into the overcast yet windless sky. Then, quite suddenly, we were enveloped in a grey world of cloud, and only the extremities of the aircraft itself could be seen. Just as quickly, the murk that surrounded us began to brighten, and our aircraft broke through the cloud tops and soared out into the dazzling morning sunlight. The sun, looking larger than I could recall having seen it before, was the only contrasting feature of the brilliant blue canopy above us, and the sensation of speed was renewed as we sped out over a carpet of billowing, unbroken cloud that stretched to the horizon in all directions.

A profound sense of freedom and isolation from all things artificial surged through me as I beheld for the first time the vastness and the beauty of our natural surroundings, and it occurred to me that we and our man-made machine were trespassers in a domain to which we had no right of access. Yet man, through his ingenuity and determination had succeeded in breaking the stern bonds of earth. Surely such an achievement earned us the privilege. We were far removed in time, distance and scientific advancement from 1903 and Kittyhawk, and there would doubtless be other more sophisticated examples of man and machine to follow, and I considered this to validate our presence. Nevertheless, I found my elation and sense of pleasure tinged by the knowledge that our prime purpose was to transform this wondrous playground into an arena in which death and destruction would predominate, at least until the war was ended.

In the meantime, I had other things to think about. This was not a familiarisation flight. I was required to operate a camera gun during the exercise that was about to take place, and I wasn't absolutely certain on how to load the camera. The thought also struck me that, although I had a parachute with me, I had not during the many lectures I had attended been instructed in how to use the thing, so resolved to enquire of someone as soon as we returned to earth.

My preoccupation was interrupted as the Battle dropped its starboard wing to the vertical and began a tight right-hand turn. For the first time, I felt the pull of gravity as we changed direction, and my weight was pressed hard against the floor. Just as quickly, the aircraft righted itself and began to descend rapidly, causing me to chafe against the rim of the cockpit as weightlessness took control and my feet lost contact with the floor beneath me. Fortunately, I had remembered to fasten my safety belt to the floor-mounted cleat prior to take-off.

"Target aircraft below and to starboard, gunner, commence filming as soon as you are ready", came the voice of F/Sgt Palmer over the earphones. I managed to load the camera without too much difficulty, and began to film as the black and yellow striped target aircraft (another Fairey Battle) began to perform dummy attacks from the stern quarters, and I tried to remember all that I had been taught about closing speeds and deflection. The available film footage was soon exhausted, so we turned in the direction of the airfield. My first flight had lasted a total of just fifty-five minutes. I was to take part in a further twenty flights, and would log a grand total of a mere fifteen and a half hours in the air before becoming fully qualified as a gunner.

The camera gun was only used on the first six flights of the course. The remaining exercises permitted the use of a single Vickers gas-operated .303 machine gun mounted on a swivel at the edge of the cockpit. This was fired at either a canvas drogue or at a smoke float dropped on the surface of Lake Winnipegosis. During one of the drogue exercises, I was credited with my first combat victim, having earned the distinction of being the one member of the course to have shot down the drogue! As I watched the thing fold up and drift lazily down towards the surface of the lake, I was convinced that I must surely receive some sort of an award for such an achievement. As it transpired, my pilot (Pilot Officer Macdonald) was accused of having positioned us too near to the towing aircraft, and I was told that I had allowed too much deflection, otherwise I would have hit the drogue, not the tow rope. I had expected to land a DFM at least. Instead, I got a rocket, and was ordered to go up and rerun the exercise.

In all, the resulting hits we usually managed to score on the drogue were a big disappointment to all of those on the course. Having let fly at the drogue with a thousand rounds, one would expect the thing to end up looking like a hair net. In truth, you were lucky if you managed to make up a five percent score when the holes were counted.

My final flight of the course consisted of a map reading exercise in an Avro Anson. Seven bods (two pilots and five sprog air gunners) were crammed into every available nook and cranny of the ancient aircraft, and we staggered into the air with orders to navigate the province of Manitoba. Our first objective, the city of Winnipeg, presented no problems. Having located it, we jointly plotted and set a course which should have taken us on to Brandon, but didn't! The pilots, being sufficiently foolhardy to have complete confidence in our ability to navigate, had not been keeping a chick on our progress, with the result that we found ourselves to be hopelessly lost. After having spent a lot of time in searching for an identifiable landmark, we happened on an irregular-shaped body of water, which we recognised as Devil's Lake, which lies about fifty miles south of Canada's border with North Dakota, U.S.A. Having thus violated American airspace, we eventually arrived back at Macdonald, where we found the airfield in the grips of a heavy snowstorm. The pilots (neither of which had ever flown a twin-engined aircraft before) managed to get us down in what loosely resembled a safe landing. As we walked away from the aircraft, one member of the course was heard to remark that any landing that we could walk away from was a good one. I was later to learn the wisdom and truth of his observation.

Although we found that life on the gunnery course was markedly free of the discipline we had been subjected to at the manning Depot, there were still occasions when we were reminded of its continued presence. On one such day, we and the entire station complement were ordered to report in number one blues for a special parade. This turned out to be a ceremony in which an unfortunate Sergeant pilot was to be carpeted and expelled from the service for having caused his Battle to collide with a power cable whilst engaging in a spot of illicit low flying locally. We were formed up into a hollow square, into the centre of which the offender was marched between two Service Policemen. There then followed a series of events which I would have found incredible had I not witnessed them personally. First of all, the man's forage cap was snatched from his head and thrown violently to the ground. This was followed by his pilot's wings, which had been unstitched earlier and pinned in place. Finally, his stripes were similarly removed and disposed of, and he was marched off in the direction of the guard room, leaving behind the pathetic trappings of his henceforth defunct flying career. As I observed the spectacle, I found myself questioning the need for such a costly and time-wasting display of pompous ceremonial, and I experienced a sense of shame at being part of a service that could be so callous. No doubt the man deserved to be stripped, but I couldn't help thinking that things might have been different had the incident taken place in a theatre of war.

During my stay at Macdonald, letters from Margaret had been arriving at weekly intervals. Their content consisted mainly of news about our mutual friends, but there was also present an element of romantic innuendo which grew in significance with each letter that she wrote. She frequently gave expression to her concern for my safety, and the wording of her letters made it plain to me that, whether I liked it or not, I had romance on my hands. I was troubled by the realisation that her attitude to our relationship had only become apparent on my enlistment with the RCAF, and I was afraid that she was being motivated by infatuation rather than love, so I had decided to deliberately withhold any response until I could be certain of the true nature of her emotions.

Night life on the station was mostly taken up by extra-mural studies, but there was available (to those more confident of successfully completing the final exam paper) a camp picture house and a games room. The latter contained a couple of pool and ping-pong tables, a bar, and a juke box which belted out "Don't Fence Me In" by Bing Crosby and the Andrews Sisters non-stop. The pool tables were put to good and frequent use by myself in the company of either Don Hendries of Kipp, Alberta, or Tom Buchak of Edmonton. As we played our appetites were kept happy with numerous Sweet Marie bars, washed down with gallons of coke or Seven-up.

On Thursday, December the 3rd, 1942, the results of our final examination were announced. We had all managed to get through all right, and I was pleased to learn that I had obtained a pass mark of 71.7%, which was about average for the course. There then followed the wings parade, at which we all turned up wearing our brand new Sergeant's stripes. I took up my position (in alphabetic order) in the line-up, with Andy Mynarski standing on my left, as Squadron Leader Ross, the Chief instructor moved along the line, pinning the Air gunner's brevets to our otherwise unadorned tunics. On Friday, we entrained for the journey to our respective home towns, with orders to await instructions on our next move.

Fig 3. Gunnery course photograph, Macdonald, autumn 1942.
Standing L to R: Don Stanchfield, Jack Peet, A Fredrickson, the author, Jim Seaton, E Johnson, Raymond Day.
Seated L to R: Jack Buchak, Jack Kendall, R Hughes, W McBain, A Archibald, Wally Anderson, Harold Dawson, Donald Hendries, Hank Bennis

WINGS

CHAPTER 5

OVERSEAS POSTINGS

Embarkation leave lasted just twenty-one days, most of which I spent in visiting relatives and friends in Whitfield and Saskatoon, attending parties and dating Margaret. I got orders to catch a train from Saskatoon at eleven p.m. on Christmas Eve for Halifax, Nova Scotia. I was thus obliged to leave a lively Christmas party at its peak and catch a taxi down to the station. Margaret accompanied me, and a number of friends and relatives were already at the station when we arrived. During my leave, I had managed to dispel any doubts I had concerning her affections - and mine - and, as 'The Canadian' steamed out of the station and into the darkness, my gaze was fixed only on Margaret, as she waved to me from the front of the group standing in the pool of light that surrounded the boarding area. Later, as I settled into the warmth and comfort of my sleeper berth, and my train rumbled on into the night across the snow-clad, moonlit prairies, I recalled the sight of her receding into the night until the steam from the stack obscured her from my view, and I could see her no more. At last, the soporific moan of the train whistle took effect, and I drifted into sleep. wondering if I would ever see her again.

The two-and-a-half day journey to Halifax proved pleasant enough. Andy and a few of the others joined the train at Winnipeg during the early hours of Christmas morning, and we were all treated to full Christmas fare in the dining car that afternoon. Each coach of the train had a combined smokeroom and washroom at one end, and we spent much of the two days in this, talking about our future prospects, playing poker, or just watching the changing landscape roll by as we progressed steadily eastwards.

The Halifax embarkation centre was our home for just seven days, during which we were readied for our shipment to Britain. There wasn't a lot going on at the centre, so we frequently visited one or other of the many beer parlours in the town. Because Halifax was a port, the Canadian Navy was in prominence, and the presence of us 'Brylcream Boys' in such a maritime stronghold was not welcomed by our bell-bottomed buddies. Bar room battles between the two factions were a frequent occurrence, and - during one of these - an unfortunate member of our camp was stabbed to death by a grog-crazed fellow combatant. Come to think of it, most of us were mere teenagers, and we had a lot to learn about our capacity for the booze. Even I was beginning to acquire a taste for it, and had indulged too freely on more than one occasion. Maybe the Canadian age limit on drinking wasn't such a bad idea after all, I thought.

On the morning of January the 14th, 1943, we were loaded onto a special CNR train for the non-stop ride to new York. On arrival, we were transferred to a number of small craft for the short trip down the Hudson river, past the Impressive Manhattan skyline and the burnt-out, capsized hulk of the French liner Normandie, and on to where our ship was moored. This turned out to be the Queen Elizabeth, one of the two largest and most luxurious liners of the British mercantile fleet. We were going to war, but we were going in style, if not in the comfort for which the "Lizzy" had been designed. My berth was on E Deck, just above the water line. Originally meant to accommodate two passengers, the cabin had been fitted with three sets of two-tier bunks, in common with most of the cabins on board. The 15,000 passengers consisted mainly of American troops bound for the European theatre, with just a sprinkling of RCAF airmen and airwomen, plus a contingent of the Canadian Army.

The following morning (Tuesday the 15th), we awoke to the feeling of movement, and were told that we had set sail during the night. Out on deck, the only sight to be seen was a lone Sunderland flying boat circling overhead. Because of her speed, the QE seldom sailed in convoy, but relied on her twenty-eight knots and a change of course every eight minutes to make it difficult for any enterprising U-boat to launch a successful torpedo attack on us.

The four-day trans-Atlantic voyage represented just one more of the many 'first' I was to experience over the next couple of years. Prior to leaving Whitfield a few months previously, I had never ridden a train or flown in an aircraft. The farthest I had been away from home was the seven-mile trip to Prince Albert in Dad's horse-drawn wagon. Now I was sailing abroad on one of the world's largest luxury liners. A voyage that would take me several thousand miles away from all the places and people that were familiar to me. No doubt there lay ahead many more new and unfamiliar experiences, some pleasant, some not so pleasant. I would make new friends, walk strange lands, learn strange customs, and listen to strange dialects. I was going to war, and although I looked on it as an adventure, there was no way that I could foresee just what was in store. I was to witness death and destruction on a scale that defied the imagination of one so young. I was to learn much of the horrors of war, of man's capacity to kill and maim his fellow men, women and children. I would see at first hand the suffering of a land whose people were in the front line, and I would share with those people their sorrow, and I would marvel at their

OVERSEAS POSTINGS

courage and their determination to win at all cost. I was to join them in the struggle against the tyranny that threatened us all. Would I survive? Would I ever see Canada again? And, what about Margaret? There were so many questions, and only the passing of time could reveal the answers that I wanted so much to hear.

During the voyage, apart from a daily lifeboat drill, we had little to do but eat, sleep, or spend long hours pacing around the promenade deck in an anti-clockwise direction. Sometimes we just stood at the rail watching the big North Atlantic rollers slipping past. The skies were clear and sunny for much of the trip, and most of us spent the time on deck in our shirt sleeves as we enjoyed the winter warmth of the Gulf Stream. On our first day out, I noticed a large sea mammal, which I took to be a porpoise, as it tagged along behind the ship. I was surprised to find it still following us the next day. In fact, it remained with us throughout the four-day voyage, and I found myself intrigued by the seemingly limitless stamina of so large and graceful a creature, and its ability to maintain a non-stop rate of twenty-eight knots for such a lengthy period.

Although the sleeping quarters were cramped, the on-board dining facilities were excellent, although somewhat regimented. The food was well cooked and plentiful, and was delivered to each of the long tables in large metal pots, from which we helped ourselves to the contents. Because the tables were fitted athwartships (running from side to side), and because the QE could roll as much as thirty degrees during a heavy swell, a close watch had to be kept of the voluntary movement of the pots throughout the meal, otherwise the table could be cleared completely when the ship heeled over.

The American G.I. contingent on board was made up mostly of whites, but with a conspicuous number of blacks included in their ranks, and it grieved me to see how these men were deliberately segregated from the rest and quartered on the lowest decks of the ship. They were all sons of the great USA; they wore the same uniform, they would soon be fighting the same enemy, even dying, perhaps. Yet, although these men were prepared to die along with their fellow Americans, they could never share the same life. On the rare occasions when a few of them were to be seen on the promenade deck, they always walked alone or with another of their kind - never with a white G.I. One day I asked one of the latter why this was. His reply was terse and simple: "They stink!", he scowled. My mind took me back to the radio reports I had heard coming from America, in which lynchings were frequently reported. Usually the report would concern some unfortunate negro who had been seen associating with a white woman.

The American way of dealing with the offender was to tie him behind a car and drag him through the streets until he was dead. I recalled that we had a family of negro farmers living at Whitfield. They were hard working, honest, and they were friendly. They had been given the opportunity of joining the community on an equal footing, and had proved themselves worthy of the trust we had placed in them. Why couldn't the great USA do this? Why should a line drawn on a map make such a difference.

The Saturday afternoon of January the 9th, 1943 was dull and miserable as we sailed up the Clyde to Greenock, passing a number of shipwrecks lying out in the Firth. The bombed and upturned hulks were the first indication to us that we were in a theatre of war. We were met by a bustling flotilla of small craft, and the RCAF detachment was finally loaded onto a paddle steamer for the short trip from our moorings to the nearby dockside. As we headed for the shore, a member of the crew related a graphic description of the part his small pleasure craft had played in evacuating troops from the beaches of Dunkirk in 1940.

On landing ashore we were told that we were being sent to a place called Bournemouth, and that we would be travelling overnight by train. Like the other members of our party, I was feeling a bit frayed after all the kit-carrying I had done during the day, and was looking forward to a hearty meal and a good night's sleep. Imagine our surprise and disappointment when we learned that our train had no sleeping berths, and that the seats we were to occupy during the long journey to the southern end of the British isles were of the wooden, slatted variety. In addition to this, we found that the train had no dining car, but we were assured that subsistence would be brought around to us during the journey. I had heard tales of the Flying Scotsman, and wondered if this was it. If so, it was a poor substitute for the luxurious comfort of 'The Canadian'.

When the refreshments finally arrived, we found them to consist of a couple of sandwiches containing a product known as 'spam', a commodity with which we were to become familiar during our stay in Britain. This, the main course, was supplemented by a small packet of board-like biscuits which closely resembled and tasted like asbestos roof shingles. A solitary jam tart completed the content of the paper bag with which each of us had been presented, and this was followed by a mug of hot cocoa dispensed from a trolley-borne tin urn by a jovial British Army Corporal. Having satisfied himself that we were all fed and watered, the corporal sat down amongst us and proceeded to give, in answer to our many questions, a vivid account of what life was like in

OVERSEAS POSTINGS

wartime Britain. Austerity was the keynote of his revelation, and we who had originated from a land of plenty found difficulty in grasping the implication that such hardships as shortages, rationing, the blackout and the blitz were all conditions to which we would have to adjust. We were more than slightly perturbed to learn that such staple requirements as beer and cigarettes were in short supply, and we were advised to avoid visiting the larger cities when on leave - London in particular - because of the danger of enemy bombing raids, which were said to be frequent.

As darkness closed in and we could no longer see the rain-soaked Scottish countryside through which our train was passing, our thoughts turned to the discomforts we would have to endure throughout the coming night. It was obvious that the wartime British transport system had nothing to match the comfort to which we were accustomed, so we began to consider whatever improvisation we could come up with. The problem of where to sleep was solved for Andy and myself when we discovered that there were two large wooden luggage racks at one end of the carriage. We immediately took possession of these and, having offloaded the collection of kit bags into a corner, we settled down as best we could, using our greatcoats in an unavailing attempt to shelter ourselves from the cutting mid-winter draughts that invaded our coach from all directions.

Six o-clock the following morning found a band of miserable, complaining, and disgruntled Canadian airmen standing on a cold platform at Bournemouth, surrounded by kitbags and gloom. After a roll call, we and all our items of kit were loaded on transports for the short journey to our billets. Andy and I were off-loaded in front of an imposing pink edifice known as the Bath Hill Court Hotel, one of several such establishments which had been taken over by the RCAF as a receiving depot for airmen arriving from Canada.

I had been allocated a room on the fifth floor, and was dismayed to find that none of the lifts were working. I presumed this to be the result of a temporary electrical or mechanical fault, but learned later that it was a feature of a national power conservation plan, and that the inconvenience caused by the absence of this facility was just one more of the many hardships I would have to meet in the interests of the war effort. After much perspiring and complaining. I (together with two kitbags and a back pack) finally reached the fifth floor, where I found that I would be sharing a room with Andy Mynarski; Hank Bennis, who haled from Medicine Hat, Alberta, and a character called Eric Plunkett from somewhere in Ontario. Eric and I were to remain together for most of our flying careers, but as members of different crews.

The hotel, because it had taken on the role of a barracks, had no dining facility, the kitchens having been closed 'for the duration'. But we had each been issued with a dining card, and this entitled us to enjoy regular meals at the Pavilion down on the sea front. This was a modern and impressive building set amidst well laid gardens, trees and shrubbery, at the end of the central park, right next to the sea. We found the large dining hall a pleasant place to visit, and the food was excellent. The only snag was the one-mile hike between the Pavilion and our hotel perched high above the town.

Next day, Eric and I walked down the hill and along the tree lined park with its small stream running down the middle. The day was sunny but breezy, yet the park was well peopled by a selection of the local inhabitants. Most were elderly people sitting on the park benches, but there were also a few of the younger set, mostly female. We found the girls to be friendly and eagre to talk to us, and we spent a pleasant afternoon conversing with them on topics which centred mainly on the effect that the war was having on their lives. We learned that, although Bournemouth had not been entirely ignored by the Luftwaffe, damage and casualties had been light, with London appearing to be the main focal point. On enquiring about the night life in the area, we were told that there was plenty of action to be had, with the local dance halls providing the best facilities for any fraternisation we might like to indulge in, and we got the impression that most of the girls we met were hungry for male companionship.

After a time, we strolled into the town to have a look at the shops, and to purchase cigarettes. We found great difficulty in coming to grips with the complicated British money, and could not understand why the 'Pound' should be divided, first into twenty units and then by twelve. Our confusion was further compounded by frequent references to 'quid', 'bobs', and 'tanners' and 'half-crowns' by the shop assistants.

We had been told that the purpose of our stay at Bournemouth was to await a posting to a place of further flying training, but no one could say when such a posting was likely to take place. Meanwhile, there was little that we could do, although route marches through the town were lain on as a frequent but ineffective means of dispelling our boredom. Usually, a body of fifty or so men with an officer at the head of the column would set out, only to return an hour later with most of the marchers missing, they having sloped off into various public houses along the route. indeed, it was not unknown for an entire column (including the officer in charge) to disappear

OVERSEAS POSTINGS

completely from the face of the earth during such a sortie.

Fire watching duty was another laid-on diversion. Each of us was assigned a four-hour period during the night, and were given the responsibility of ensuring that Bath Hill Court was blacked out in keeping with the regulations. My first stint was scheduled between the hours of ten p.m. and two a.m. Unfortunately, this coincided with the closing of the pubs and dance halls, and proved to be the busiest period of the night. consequently, infringements were widespread and frequent, with brightly-lit windows appearing all over the building. When this happened, lack of communication made necessary a climbing of the stairs in order to apprehend the offender, who was almost invariably resident on one of the upper stories.

My first English pub crawl might have been a memorable occasion but for the fact that I can't remember much about it. Although Bournemouth featured a good selection of ale houses, the prime commodity of such establishments was always in short supply. Usually the shout, "Beers off!" would be called half an hour after opening time, leaving the disgruntled clientele to either leave in search of another possible source, or to be content with whatever alternative refreshment was on offer. I can recall that, on the night in question, I was in company of Harvey Renaude, a French-Canadian from Montreal, and we had not yet had time to consume our first pint of beer when the dreaded call rang out across the crowded bar. Because the weather was wet and cold outside, we decided to remain where we were for the rest of the evening, so enquired of the barkeep just what was on offer. Neither of us fancied hitting the hard stuff, so we plumped for a drink which was known locally as 'Scrumpy'. Because of its mild taste, we considered the liquid (of which we had no prior knowledge) to be some kind of soft drink, so proceeded to consume vast quantities of the stuff. It was at about this time in the evening that my powers of perception were abandoned, and I can only guess at how Harvey and I managed to struggle through the blacked-out, rain-soaked streets of the town, and up the steep hill that lay between us and our hotel.

One morning, Eric Plunkett and I were strolling along the seafront promenade when we heard for the first time a sound which was later to become familiar to us. It was the wail of the air raid sirens. Not knowing where an air raid shelter was to be found, and being anxious to view whatever was about to happen, we decided to remain where we were. Soon we saw the condensation trail of a lone aircraft high above us in the clear blue sky, with small black puffs of smoke bursting close to the small, unrecognisable shape. This we took to be a German reconnaissance plane which was probably engaged in photographing the area. Despite the fierce attention it was getting from the anti-aircraft batteries around the perimeter of the town, the aircraft still managed to survive the barrage, and was soon seen to be heading back in the direction of the continent.

Once the roar of the guns had ceased, Eric and I began to discuss what we had seen, but our conversation was again interrupted as an aircraft, which we instantly recognised as a Fairey Battle, came screaming in at low level across the beach and over the town with its wheels down and its landing lights glowing, as it urgently wagged its wings, and we were forced to take a dive as the shrapnel began to cascade down all around us. Fortunately, the trigger-happy gun crews seemed to be having a bad day of it, so the Battle also managed to dodge their fury.

As the tumult died away and the all-clear was sounded, we picked ourselves up and continued our leisurely stroll along the beach, discussing the implications of what we had seen. It was plain that the likelihood of a high-flying aircraft being brought down by the flak was very much a matter of luck, but we drew no comfort from the fact that we had just seen a friendly aircraft being fired on by our own defences. Even after supposing that the officer in charge of the gun crews had failed to recognize the outline of his target, its markings should have indicated its nationality. On considering it, we reckoned (rightly so) that the incident represented just one more of the many hazards we would have to contend with in the future.

We were gradually coming to terms with the knowledge that, although Canada was at war, Britain was in the front line. The golden sands that sloped down the beach and slid beneath the gently lapping waves were scarred by long coils of barbed wire and ugly concrete tank traps, while equally unattractive pill boxes and observation posts lined the cliffs overlooking the scene. The flock of seagulls that had flown off in alarm a few minutes earlier had returned to continue foraging the shoreline, and Eric and I were alone with them on a beach which would probably be thronged with holiday makers in peacetime. But this was war. There were no children playing, no swim-suited bathers frolicking in the surf. Only the trappings of war could be seen.

Since our arrival in Britain, we had seen many indications of the conflict that was taking place: the sunken ships in the approaches to the Clyde; the austerity and discomfort of our train journey south; the blackout; the shortages; rationing; the queues, and the lack of fashion (few women could be seen wearing stockings). Then, there were the gaps in the street where houses and shops had once stood,

OVERSEAS POSTINGS

only to be replaced by large metal emergency water supply tanks after the rubble created by an enemy bomb had been cleared away. Windows were criss-crossed with adhesive tape, and sandbags were everywhere. There was a marked absence of young men on the streets, and a lot of the women were wearing black arm bands. Yet, despite all this, the people that we met and got to know showed little of the stress and sorrow that they must have been feeling. There was always a smile and a friendly handshake for anyone wearing a uniform bearing Canada flashes, and we were frequently plied with questions about life back home. We soon found that we were warming to our new-found acquaintances, and were never short of the warm hospitality that was lavished on us wherever we went. But most of all, we had nothing but profound admiration for the spirit and courage of the British people, and it was with a sense of personal pride I realised that most of us were descendants of the people of these islands. Britain alone had halted the advance of Nazism at the Channel back in 1940. Surely, I felt, we must be on the winning team.

Letters from Canada had begun to filter through during my stay at Bournemouth. I got one from home and two from Margaret. Mother's letter contained the usual news about the family and the farm, and asked for details of anything I might need because she was preparing to send a parcel to me. Margaret's letters were mainly about how much she was missing the good times we used to have together, and - as always - expressed here concern for my well-being. All three letters had been opened by the censor, and mother's in particular had been severely decimated in the process of cutting away that which was not permitted. Because she had written on both sides of the paper, there wasn't a lot left that made sense to me. From what there was, I deduced that she was anxious to find out exactly where I was. I was unable to supply this information since the only address I could give was my name, rank and service number, followed by the phrase, "RCAF Overseas".

After replying to Margaret, I prepared a letter to mother in which I requested a supply of cigarettes and six pairs of nylon stockings, taking care to point out that the latter were not intended for my use, but that I propose to give them to any deserving female I happened to become acquainted with. I then mentioned that I was planning on visiting some of my mother's relatives, knowing that this would indicate Scotland, thus revealing to her my approximate whereabouts.

During our long stay at Bournemouth, we were each required to undergo a number of tests, including an examination to determine our ability to see in the dark. We were also asked to fill in a questionnaire which appeared to be designed to afford us a choice, but didn't. We were asked to indicate our preference of (1) the Command we wished to serve in, and (2) the make of aircraft we wished to fly in. I listed, in order of preference (a) Fighter command, (b) Coastal Command, and (c) Bomber command as my choice of group, and (a) Defiant, (b) Sunderland, and (c) Lancaster as the make of aircraft I wished to fly in. The ultimate decision that I should spend my service career dicing in Lancasters for Bomber Harris was a fair indication of the choice which was available to me.

My posting to an operational training unit took effect on Wednesday, March 3rd, 1943. At this stage, the 'old gang' to which I had become attached during my training at the Gunnery School underwent a drastic decimation at the hands of those in charge of our respective fates. In all, I found that I was to be accompanied on my new posting by only two close acquaintances of the original draft from Macdonald. Most of the others were heading for recently formed Canadian units for their final preparation, but I was being fed into the English part of the system.

OVERSEAS POSTINGS

CHAPTER 6

OPERATIONAL TRAINING

So it was that I, together with Eric Plunkett, Harvey Renaude, and a couple of other fellow Canadians, found ourselves in attendance at a course of operational flying training at No 16 OTU, Upper Heyford, in the English county of Oxfordshire.

We found the unit to be a hive of activity, with plenty of flying going on at all hours of the day and night. A pre-war drome with concrete runways, brick hangars and administrative buildings, Heyford was equipped with a fleet of war-weary twin-engined Wellington bombers, but could boast excellent messing facilities and comfortable living accommodation. The latter included 'married quarters' to which we had been assigned. These were made up of several rows of small, two-storey, terraced houses, each one complete with the usual domestic amenities - kitchen, lounge, bedroom, nursery and bathroom. But, because there was a war on, domesticity had been dispensed with, and all of the rooms (including the kitchen) had been transformed into dormitories, with single metal beds occupying most of the available floor space. Each room sported an open grate for the burning of coal as a means of heating the room and the provision of hot water.

Although the skies above Heyford were filled with the sight and sound of the lumbering old Wellingtons for much of the time, there existed for us the unavoidable period of ground instruction through which we must progress before being allowed to get the personal posterior airborne. Our stay at Heyford was to take up more than three months, the first half of which consisted of lectures and other chairborne pursuits, followed by the flying segment. Two courses were always in attendance at the same time, and we had been assigned to Course 52. During our period of classroom confinement, Course 51 was engaged in flying, and a new batch (Course 53) would be waiting to take our places before the seats had time to cool.

Social activities were plentiful, with frequent evening visit to either Banbury or Oxford rated high on the list of popular boozing haunts to be found within a short bus ride of the camp. At either of these venues, female companionship, although sparse on the camp itself, was plentiful amongst the civilian population, particularly at Banbury. This was because Oxford had a goodly supply of male University students. While a large section of the eligible young men of Banbury had been conscripted into the armed forces. This accounted for the marked shortage of suitable escorts available to the bored young girls to be seen sipping drinks together or taking to the dance floor with each other.

It soon become obvious to the Canadians amongst us that Britain was a philanderers paradise in which opportunities for pleasurable pursuits were not too difficult to find. Unlike our native Canada, Britain was in the front line, and this called for a total effort, including the conscription of all those of service age who were not in a reserved occupation. As a result of this, we found ourselves to be in popular demand. We were foreign; we were well paid, and there was an element of glamour about us that most young girls found difficult to resist. True, there were those of us who took full advantage of the situation, and there are those within the generation following upon ours who are not fully aware of their true nationality. For my part, my growing relationship with Margaret precluded any thoughts of promiscuity, and it is probable that many of my compatriots were similarly committed.

Genuine and close relationships between ourselves and members of the civilian population were not unknown, but most were destined to be of a short duration. This also applied to friendships formed within our own group. A posting to another location was only one of the limiting factors which could obstruct the establishment of a long-term association, as I had already learned in the preceding months.

One other snag was the element of personal uncertainty of which we were all aware, but never put into words - 'the chop'. Even at that early stage in our flying careers, death was no stranger to us. During one disastrous night at Heyford, two Wellingtons crashed, killing all ten trainee aircrew and a couple of instructors. In the same night, an unfortunate member of the ground staff was beheaded by a whirling prop at one of the dispersals. I was one of those detailed to perform pollbearing duties at a nearby cemetery a few days later. As we gently lowered the flag-draped coffin into the grave, I became aware of how impersonal my involvement in the whole exercise seemed. It occurred to me that I did not even know the name of the man I was helping to lay to rest - probably had not even met him, because he had been on the other course to mine. But he was one of us. A young man, no doubt. Probably about my age. Keen to experience the thrill and glamour of flying, and fired with the same thirst for adventure that I knew so well. Like me, and most others of our generation, he had chosen to ignore the dangers that war could bring; to think that 'it' could never happen to him; that he would succeed in dodging the chop.

OPERATIONAL TRAINING

The pallbearing detail had been instructed that, after having lowered the coffin into the grave, each man was to come to attention and salute the grave, after which he would turn and march alone from the cemetery. It transpired that I was last in line, so that all the other service representatives had gone, leaving only myself, the clergyman and the small group of mourners at the graveside. As I delivered my salute, I sensed that all eyes were on me, and, as I turned to leave, my gaze swept across the tear-stained faces of the little knot of grieving relatives. The group was made up of people ranging in age from children to the elderly, but my attention was caught by the misery so evident on the face of a young woman standing at the front. I reckoned her to be about twenty - possibly a sister of the deceased, or his fiance, perhaps. Maybe she was his young widow - I did not know, and I was ashamed of my ignorance. I felt that her loss and that of the others was a personal thing, and that we had no right to be there. Surely the term 'full military honours'; gave little comfort to those people. In truth, we represented that section of the establishment that had caused their sorrow, and I felt that our presence was an incursion on their personal grief and privacy. Then, partly on an impulse, and partly as a means of conveying to them the sympathy that I felt, I paused and saluted the small, wretched gathering before turning to walk away and join the others.

The relative freedom from discipline that I had enjoyed at Bournemouth and at the Gunnery School in Canada had in no way prepared me for the rigours of life on an English Operational Training Unit. Inspections of kit and living quarters were frequent, and the danger of confinement to barracks of those found to be lacking in the required standard of cleanliness and proficiency was a threat that had to be expected. On one such occasion, when we had failed to satisfy the requirements of an inconsonant Warrant Officer as to the general condition and upkeep of our particular section of the married quarters, we were compelled to forego a planned evening visit to Banbury in order to subdue his rage. Our task included not only the polishing of the floors throughout the building, plus the cleaning of all the windows, but the application of whitewash to the upper layer of coal in the outhouse. The execution of this ridiculous chore meant that the fires had to remain unlit once the required decoration had been applied to the coal. Because we were still in the month of March, it was decided that, in the interest of creature comfort, the coal would remain unadorned until the early morning, just before the threatened return inspection. By so doing, we avoided having to spend a night of abject discomfort in the interests of authority gone bonkers.

Inspections of premises and kit were not the only form of surveillance to which we were subjected. There was one other indignity which had to be endured whenever we arrived at a new posting: Popularly known as 'short-arm Inspection', this entailed us being lined up in some draughty hangar in what was picturesquely referred to as the 'down trousers and up shirt' configuration, by which certain items of personal equipment were exposed to the experienced eye of a medical officer whose task was the detection of any incipient flaws thereon. There existed in our midst one unfortunate individual who shall be nameless, but who had acquired a sinister scar through having been pecked by a chicken at some time during his early boyhood. Because of its exact location, the resulting decoration closely resembled the trace which would have been left by a previous infection, and this always resulted in the man being pulled out of the lineup and sent off to the medical centre for a more detailed examination, much to the amusement of all those present. Those of us who knew the man and his circumstances were merely amused by this, and expected it to happen. But those who were not aware of the details of his misfortune would knowingly nudge each other and remark with a smile, "he's got it!".

Although our rate of pay was inferior to that of our American counterparts, we members of the Canadian forces serving in Europe enjoyed a pay structure which was in excess of that to which British aircrew were accustomed. We sensed that this was largely responsible for our popularity, not just with the girls, but equally so with our British associates, and we suspected that the welcomed presence of a Canadian in an otherwise all-British crew was not entirely accidental. He was looked upon as a rich uncle, and provided a most convenient source of financial supplementation for the less affluent crew members.

Despite our undoubted prosperity, we, together with the Australians, New Zealanders and other sons of the Commonwealth, were always last to be called out on pay parade, when the call "Fall in the Colonials" would ring out across the hangar. This always brought forth loud protests, particularly from us Canadians, with the unfortunate Paymaster being forcefully reminded that Canada was not a colony. The inexact reference to our status within the commonwealth persisted until we eventually conspired to stand firm unless addressed correctly. The strategy worked, with the result that we were from that time referred to as "The Dominions".

On Monday, April the 19th, we began the flying segment of our operational training. The first part of the programme was made up of sixteen flights in the trusty old canvas-covered Wellington, an aircraft

OPERATIONAL TRAINING

Fig 4. Harvey Renaud and the author at No 16 O.T.U. Upper Heyford spring 1943.

which I found to be a delight to fly in despite the many draughts that invaded the fuselage during flight. The main problem was the dreaded narrow catwalk which ran the length of the aircraft. One had to be very careful when negotiating it, because more than one tail gunner had put a foot through the fabric whilst making his way down the darkened fuselage from the entry hatch in the nose of the aircraft. Each flight, which averaged about ninety minutes and comprised mostly bombing practice and 'circuits and bumps' with some camera gun and air-firing thrown in for the gunner, was made with a scratch crew drawn from the course membership. The formation of permanent crews had not yet taken place, and I was flying with a different collection of bods on each and every occasion. A few of the pilots were of commissioned rank, but most were Sergeants, and every bit as inexperienced as the rest of us. Because I was aware of the dangers involved in flying with 'sprog' pilots, I was looking forward to the time when I would become part of a regular crew.

After nine days of dicing with death, we were all herded into a large room at the side of one of the hangars, and were ordered to sort ourselves out into crews. Some of us had already formed unofficial partnerships but, because Harvey and I had decided to leave our selection purely to chance, we had no preconceived idea of what the final composition of our crews would be. Eric had earlier teamed up with a Canadian Flight Lieutenant named Mitchell, but Harvey and I were still unpicked after more than half an hour of wheeling and dealing, and the room was gradually emptying as groups of five left for a celebratory drink in the Mess. We had carried out a head count a few days earlier, only to find that there was a surplus of gunners in relation to the number of pilots, and this meant that those of us who failed to team up would be held back for the next course.

I had just decided that it was time to take some positive action when two pilots left the dwindling group on the other side of the room and approached Harvey and me. The Pilot Officer engaged Harvey in conversation, leaving me confronted by the Sergeant, a tall, slim, and distinctly untidy individual, with a face that looked as if it had been slept in. I estimated his age to be somewhere in the mid to late twenties, a calculation which categorized him as something of a father figure, if not an antique.

"I'm Bill Siddle", the sergeant announced softly with a broad toothy grin. "I'm looking for a gunner. Would you be interested in joining us?", he asked, indicating three other men who had followed him across the room.

I had seen Sergeant Siddle at various times during the course, but had only flown with him once. We had been detailed to do some bombing practice off the west coast on that occasion, after which I had let go a few hundred rounds of .303 at a smoke float. He had hedge hopped the elderly Wellington most of the way back from the exercise, and I had been impressed, not only by his sense of fun, but by his ability to handle the aircraft, and it was the latter

OPERATIONAL TRAINING

Fig 5. The original crew at Winthorpe H.C.U. spring 1943.

**Standing L to R: Sgt Dick Lodge (navigator), Sgt Bill Siddle(pilot), Sgt Clem Culley(wireless operator)
Front row L to R: Sgt Reg Moseley(flight engineer), Pilot Officer Ken Hills (bomb aimer), Sgt Dick Jones (mid upper gunner), Sgt Clayton Moore (tail gunner)**

quality which prompted me to accept the invitation.

On having agreed to throw in my lot with them, there followed a brief introduction to the other three. The navigator was named Dick Lodge, and he came from the east London suburb of Barking. Ken Hills, also a Londoner, was the bomb aimer, and - being a Pilot Officer - was thus the senior rank in the crew, all the others being Sergeants, including the wireless operator, Clem Culley from Leicestershire. Siddle was from a place called Penrith in Cumberland, where his parents owned the Crown, a residential hotel. As we chatted I could foresee that we were destined to have a few problems with dialects, particularly in the air, during use of the in-flight intercom.

The formation of the crew was the only aspect of Air force life in which the individual was allowed to exercise any real choice. Even so, the somewhat limited time factor imposed on the making of such an important selection precluded the degree of care I would have wished for. It was for this reason that I had decided to leave purely to chance whatever fate might lay in store for me. It was not as if I had known any of the men for more than a few weeks. Their character, background, temperament and personal ability were unknown yet important factors. How could I possibly gauge the merit of these men in so short a period? Only time could supply the answer. Although no formal contract had been drawn up, and there was nothing to be signed, the commitment had been made. And yet, despite the apparent lack of formality, I looked upon our newly-formed alliance as being akin to a marriage. Although unspoken, vows of honour and obedience had been implied, and these must of necessity be sanctified, at least until (as might well be the case in extreme circumstances) death did us part.

Lunchtime was almost upon us by the time we had finalised the formation of the crew. In order that those forming crews could get acquainted with each other, all training had been cancelled for the remainder of the day and evening, so we left the hangar and made our way over to the Mess.

After lunch, the five of us assembled in a quiet corner of the mess for what was to be the first of many crew meetings. These were to be a feature of our alliance, and would be held whenever a matter concerning operational strategy or discipline arose. From the

OPERATIONAL TRAINING

outset it was clear that Bill was a born leader, and that the show was going to be well organised. He had already formulated a basic crew strategy, and this was put forward for discussion.

Not only was it expected that we should each be efficient in our own particular function within the crew, but an interchange of responsibilities was to be encouraged. At least one other member would become capable of flying and landing the aircraft in the event of our pilot being indisposed, and all other crew positions were to be similarly duplicated. Because he had received instruction in gunnery, the wireless operator would be expected to stand in for an injured gunner, and the navigator was to make himself familiar with the duties of the bomb aimer. Furthermore the navigator, together with the bomb aimer and (eventually) the flight engineer, would be trained as substitute pilots. I would be expected to take over the radio if required, and, because I had some tuition in navigation, I was also to receive further instruction in that capacity. A stand-in for the flight engineer would be appointed once we progressed to the larger aircraft, at which time one would be joining the crew.

The next item concerned the operational tactics we should employ as a crew. Again, Bill Siddle had strong views on the subject. In his opinion, our prime function was the dropping of bombs on the enemy. The defence of the aircraft and its crew was of paramount importance, and the displaying of any unnecessary heroics was to be discouraged. We would not go out looking for a fight because our firepower would be very much inferior to that which a Jerry fighter pilot would have on offer, and Bill could see no future in us getting involved in a swerving match with a cannon-toting Messerschmitt. Ever since having joined up as air gunner, I had formed the opinion that I would be the poor relation of the crew, and would thus occupy a position of distinct disadvantage when it came to establishing the pecking order. But Bill had other ideas. Rank would be disregarded in the air at all times. If the aircraft was to come under attack by an enemy fighter, I would be in complete charge of the aircraft during the attack, and the issuing of instructions to Bill on how to evade the enemy would be my responsibility throughout the encounter. But he was of the opinion that the early detection of the enemy's presence was most important, and that this was my main function within the crew. My guns should only be brought into action as a last resort, and this would be looked upon as an indication of my having failed to spot the enemy much earlier. Because I did not agree fully with his last point, I suggested that other crew members be detailed as lookouts, and this was adopted.

The airfield at Upper Heyford boasted an unusual feature. Known locally as 'The Heyford Hump', this consisted of a small hill in the centre of the field, beyond which an aircraft, whether landing or taking off, disappeared from view during its run. Once the pilots had mastered the technique of landing up-hill and taking off in a downward direction, we were assigned to the night flying segment of the course. This was made up of only six of the twenty exercises to be flown, but supplied us with a number of anxious moments. On one occasion, our port engine's constant speed unit failed on takeoff, and this caused the engine to go out of control at maximum revs. Because we were too far down the runway when the fault showed up - over the dreaded hump in fact - we were unable to abort, so Siddle had to take us screaming around the circuit to make a hurried but safe emergency landing.

A second hair-raising incident befell us during our participation in a mock exercise or 'bullseye'. The trip was designed to give us sprogs an insight into what it would be like to take part in a real raid on an enemy target, and much preparation had gone into making it look like the real thing. Our 'target' was defined as a place called Hull on the Humber estuary, and we were told that this would be heavily defended by scores of searchlight batteries, and that Fighter Command would have a number of aircraft up looking for us.

We had been navigating a complicated route for about two hours, and had until then managed to keep out of trouble. Dick was keeping us on track, and I had successfully lost a fighter by calling on Bill to throw the old Wellington around in a way that Barnes Wallis would never have approved of. In truth, I was in the process of congratulating myself on my undoubted vigilance when, to my amazement, I was suddenly confronted by the spectacle of a Beaufighter sitting fifty yards astern with all its navigation lights on. My shame was further compounded when the Beaufighter's cockpit was lit up like the Palais de Danse on a Saturday night, and I saw the two occupants grinning at me and giving me the thumbs-down sign, thus indicating that we had in theory been blasted out of the sky.

But it wasn't over yet. We still had to attack our target. We had been told to expect a first-rate show of realism, and as we approached our objective, it became clear that we were not to be disappointed. Searchlights were everywhere, and there was even one poor sod coned over the middle of the city. It wasn't until we observed anti-aircraft fire rising into the sky ahead of us that we formed the opinion that too much was being done in the interests of simulation. Nevertheless, we pressed on towards Hull, feeling confident that the gunners down on the

OPERATIONAL TRAINING

ground must know what they were doing.

As we neared the target, Ken reported from his position down in the nose of the aircraft that he could see what looked like bomb burst on the ground. In almost the same instant, the shadowy but unmistakable shape of a Heinkel 111 went hareing past us in the opposite direction, causing us to realise just what was happening. The Jerries had decided to get in on the act! The fair city of Hull was indeed under attack, but by the professionals, not a collection of students. We were already high-tailing it for Heyford when the message instructing us to return to base was received.

One dark night an 'evasion and escape' exercise was laid on for all those crews taking part in the course. At about ten p.m. we were loaded into a fleet of canvas-covered lorries for transportation out into the countryside, where we were dropped off in pairs. It was supposed that we had been shot down over enemy territory, and our brief was to evade capture and return to base before six a.m., by which time the exercise would be deemed to have ended. The carrying of maps or compasses was forbidden, and we had been told that units of the British Army, together with our own Service Police and the local constabulary would all be doing their level best to apprehend us before we could make it back to Heyford.

I had been paired off with no less resourceful a person than Clem, the wireless op. and he had brought with him from the wireless section a 'flimsey' (a printed sheet listing the code letters being flashed by the various airfield beacons that night). In addition to this, I had purloined a map of the area and pocket compass, by the use of which I had hoped to learn in what direction the lorry was taking us as we were driven out through Oxfordshire.

In all, Clem and I were well equipped to deal with the situation, or so we thought. However, I soon found it impossible to work out our course because of the tortuous route our transport was taking, and anyway, conditions were too dark inside the curtained-off interior of the lorry for me to read either the compass or the map.

On us being off-loaded from the transport, Clem at once climbed a tree, with the intention of locating a beacon, but without success. My failure to ascertain the direction in which we had travelled meant that we had not the slightest idea of our location in relation to the airfield, and it would have been foolish to travel any distance before this information was known. Because it was wartime, there were no road signs anywhere, so we decided to find a village in the hope of being able to pinpoint our location by that means.

We soon found a small village complete with a corner shop, a public house and a post office, but all clues to the identity of the place had been carefully removed. The frequent levitation of my intrepid accomplice into the uppermost branches of numerous oak trees had resulted in nothing more remarkable than a large tear in the seat of his battle dress trousers. There just wasn't a flashing beacon to be seen anywhere, and we were still lost. The time was now nearing two a.m. and so far, we had only seen one Army patrol, but had managed to avoid being spotted. We had visited a number of rural localities, but had been unable to find any indication of their true identity, all such clues having long since been removed in the interests of national security.

We were once more reconnoitring a small hamlet in search of a clue when a voice behind us shouted "STOP!". Turning, we beheld a lone British Bobby pedalling furiously down the road on his bicycle, obviously intent on apprehending us. Both sides of the narrow road were lined with typical stone houses and farm buildings, so that there didn't appear to be an escape route other than down the road. I shouted to Clem to split up, whereupon he went galloping down the road, while I decided to vault over a nearby five-foot stone wall, thinking that the constable would not be able to follow me on his bicycle, but would probably continue to chase Clem.

My chosen plan of action produced the desired effect. On seeing my intention, the constable decided to continue his pursuit of Clem, and raced past me just as I vaulted over the wall. The one flaw in my plan was the fact that I was ignorant of what lay on the other side. This turned out to be an old sow, complete with a large litter of piglets, all slumbering peacefully. At least, they were until I landed heavily in their midst, causing all hell to break loose. As I struggled furiously to extract myself from the reeking mire into which I had tumbled, my progress was hampered by the profusion of panic-stricken pigs and piglets which were hurtling around the pigsty in all directions, and I feared that their strident squeals would awaken the local populace for miles around. On finally escaping the rough and tumble of the pigsty, I was struck by the thought that the farmer would at that moment be loading his trusty twelve-bore, intent on teaching me a lesson in the observance of rural protocol.

The pastureland at the rear of the enclosure sloped steeply down for about fifty yards to what looked like a line of small trees and undergrowth. I at once set off in the direction of this cover, zig-zagging as I went, trying desperately to avoid collecting a backside full of buckshot. On reaching my objective, I took a hasty

OPERATIONAL TRAINING

header into the welcomed seclusion of the bushes, only to find myself totally submerged in a small stream.

Feeling bedraggled and full of self pity, I went on alone in my quest for some sign of my exact geographic location. Some two hours later, I saw a shadowy figure in an adjoining field. It was Clem. The sky was beginning to lighten as we joined up and began to discuss our plight, the conclusion of which was that we still had no idea where we were, and there was little hope of us making it back to camp before the deadline in any case. We decided to give it up as a bad show, and soon found a main road. There we flagged down a passing motorist, who just happened to be an Air Force Flight Lieutenant. He was reporting for duty at Upper Heyford, so we got a lift, during which, as a result of my unwholesome state, I was made to occupy the rear seat, and all the windows had to be kept open throughout the journey.

Once back at the camp, I became interested in learning exactly how Clem had managed to dodge being nicked by the constable, but he proved elusive when I questioned him about it. Later in the day however, the increased activity of the Service Police (plus the presence on the camp of a couple of members of the local Constabulary) led me to suspect that Clem's method of avoiding capture had not been entirely statutory. Or perhaps, one of the many others involved in the exercise had perpetrated some dastardly act. Whatever the reason for the investigation, it soon ended, and nothing more was heard of it.

The third occasion on which a flight from Heyford went wrong for us was during yet another night cross country. We had been up for about seven hours; we had been lost for a time, and we were getting short of fuel. We were aware that the Wellington had a reserve fuel tank for such an emergency, but none of us knew the exact location of the vital fuel cock, except that it was situated somewhere down the fuselage on the port side, so Ken was hurriedly armed with a torch and dispatched down the catwalk in search of it. Both engines were beginning to splutter by the time he located the tap and opened it up, whereupon they resumed their quiet purr and we continued on to base, thankful at having survived the exercise that had spelled disaster for two crews from the previous course.

Bill called a crew meeting next day, at which our showing as a crew was subjected to close examination and criticism. He pointed out that the incident with the reserve fuel tank was a classic example of what could result from apathy on the part of any one of us. He accepted that he personally should have known the location of the cock, but that the incident was an indication of the need for all of us to be familiar with the more important components of the aircraft. Had Ken failed to locate the valve, the result would have been catastrophic. This caused me to realise that, although we had only been together for a few weeks, we already owed our survival to one of our number.

Dick was next in the line of fire. Although navigation was at this stage basic and difficult, getting lost in darkness was not to be tolerated, as Bill forcefully indicated. Then it was my turn to get a rocket for my mishandling of the Beaufighter incident. I considered the criticism to be justified; had already given the matter some thought, and had formulated a new plan. There was no doubt that I had failed to spot the fighter until it was too late., and there was no doubting the outcome had it been an enemy. Of course, I was not to know that the Beaufighter probably carried the latest top-secret aerial interception hardware, and that this placed me at a distinct disadvantage. I had learned from the experience that I was sweeping the sky too slowly, thus increasing the chance of a fighter sneaking up on me when my back was literally turned. I had also noticed that the quality of my night vision was best, no directly in my line of sight, but in the periferal region, so was already training myself to concentrate on what I could glimpse 'out of the corner of my eye', rather than what was directly in front of me. I had even succumbed to the mistakenly popular belief held by some senior medics that the consumption of copious quantities of carrots would improve one's night vision capability. As a consequence, aircrew were served carrots with everything except the prunes and custard. Unfortunately, the diet did nothing for me except to create a strong dislike of the vegetable, an aversion which was to remain with me throughout my life.

We completed the OTU course at a the end of May, 1943, and were immediately granted two weeks of well-earned leave. As a member of the Canadian forces serving overseas, leave always presented me with a problem. Apart from the members of my newly-formed crew and a few of those left over from my earlier period of training, I knew no one, and was at a loss to find something to do with so much free time. The rest of the crew were all heading for home, leaving myself, Eric, Harvey and the few remaining Canucks to fend for ourselves. At this early stage, most of us Canadians usually trooped off to "The smoke" (London) during these periods of imposed inactivity, but it was not unusual for a few of us to be seen just sitting around the Mess, or frequenting the local boozers on such occasions. Fortunately for me, Mother had supplied me with the addresses of some of her friends in Scotland, with the wish that I should visit them if I ever got the chance, so I boarded a train bound for Glasgow.

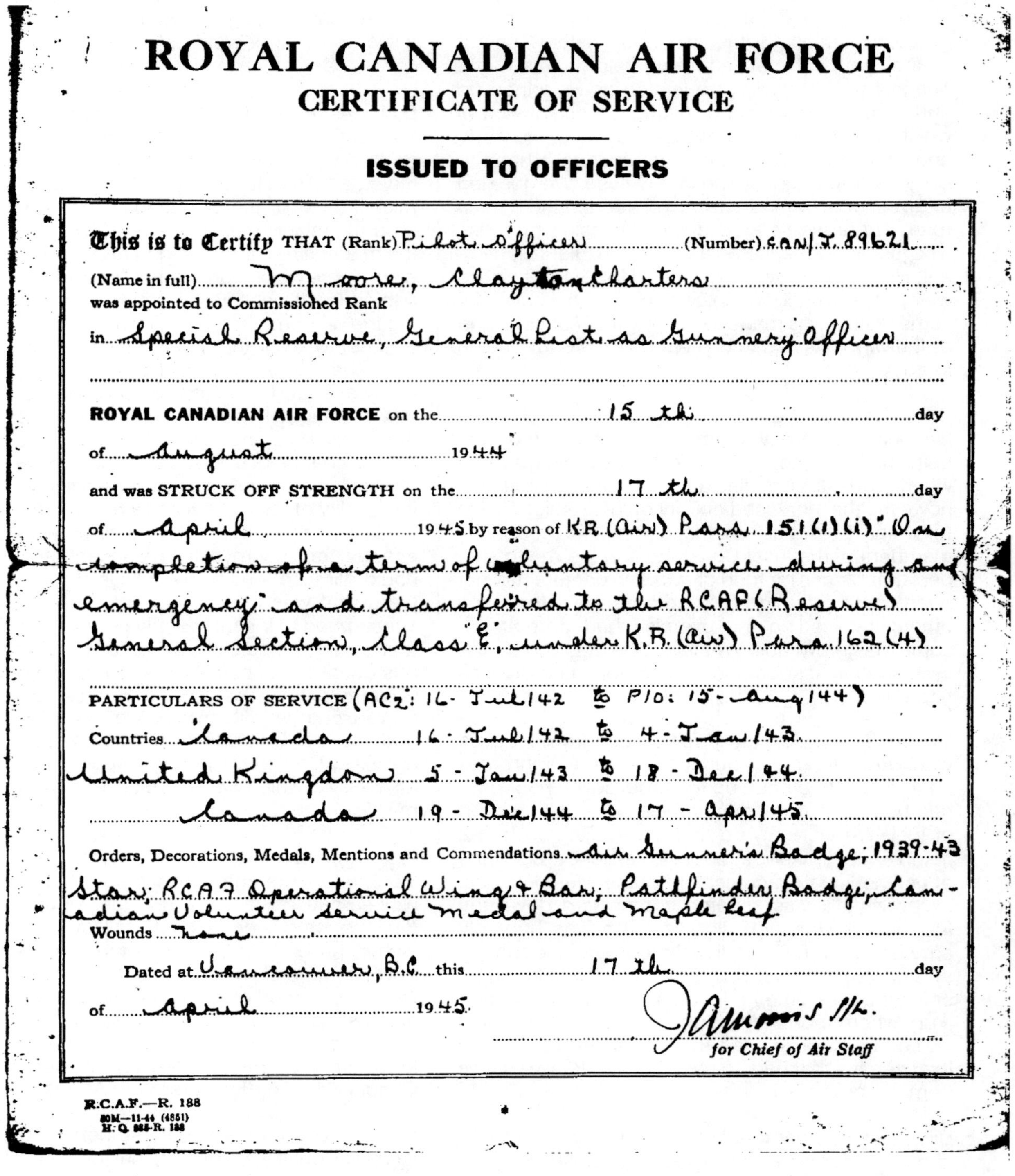

ROYAL CANADIAN AIR FORCE
CERTIFICATE OF SERVICE

ISSUED TO OFFICERS

This is to Certify THAT (Rank) Pilot Officer (Number) CAN/J. 89621

(Name in full) Moore, Clayton Charters

was appointed to Commissioned Rank

in Special Reserve, General List as Gunnery Officer

ROYAL CANADIAN AIR FORCE on the 15 th day

of August 1944

and was STRUCK OFF STRENGTH on the 17 th day

of April 1945 by reason of K.R. (Air) Para 151(1)(i) "On completion of a term of voluntary service during an emergency" and transferred to the RCAF (Reserve) General Section, Class "E", under K.R. (Air) Para 162(4)

PARTICULARS OF SERVICE (AC2: 16-Jul/42 to P/O: 15-Aug/44)

Countries Canada 16-Jul/42 to 4-Jan/43

United Kingdom 5-Jan/43 to 18-Dec/44

Canada 19-Dec/44 to 17-Apr/45

Orders, Decorations, Medals, Mentions and Commendations Air Gunner's Badge; 1939-43 Star; RCAF Operational Wing & Bar; Pathfinder Badge; Canadian Volunteer Service Medal and Maple Leaf

Wounds None

Dated at Vancouver, B.C. this 17 th day

of April 1945

J.A. Morris S/L
for Chief of Air Staff

R.C.A.F.—R. 188
80M—11-44 (4851)
H.Q. 885-R. 188

Fig 6. Certificate of Service. Issued by Squadron Leader J.A. Morris at Vancouver, Canada

CHAPTER 7

THE LANCASTER

I spent a couple of very pleasant days visiting a few of Mother's friends in a place called Kirkintilloch, a few miles out of Glasgow, during which time I was treated to the well-known brand of hospitality for which the Scots are famed. Amongst those I met were a few who had sung with Mother in the Kirkintilloch Girls Choir, and I was pleased to learn later that my visit had resulted in the renewal of some extensive trans-Atlantic correspondence.

After two days, I decided on a trip to London in order to take in some of the sights I had heard so much about. I had the address of an RCAF Club in Cromwell Road SW7, and was delighted to find on my arrival that Harvey Renaud had also booked a room there. Like me, he was at a loss for something to do, so we teamed up to do a round of the tourist attractions on offer, and spent the remainder of our leave looking at such places as Buckingham Palace, the Tower of London, Hyde Park, and (of course) Piccadilly Circus.

Harvey and I spent a particularly interesting afternoon visiting the world-famous wax works of Madame Tussaud. We found the entrance hall to be populated by a number of uniformed 'attendants', each one of which was identical to all the others in dress and facial features, and we were much impressed by the realistic detail that had been so painstakingly worked into each of the models. Only the glassy-eyed stare betrayed them as forgeries, and it was difficult to accept that the 'flesh' we could see was in fact coloured wax. In addition to those standing in the entrance hall, a number of stereotyped clones were positioned on each of the staircase landings which led up to the main exhibition, so we were not surprised to find yet another one standing at the top. Again we paused to admire the intricate workmanship - the hair; the facial detail; the realistic texture and colouring of the flesh; the smart and immaculate uniform. As we carried out our close-up inspection as before, I was struck by a minute detail which I had not noticed on any of the others, and remarked to Harvey, "Hey, this one could do with a shave!". Harvey at once came in closer for a look, and was about to feel for the tell-tale stubble when the 'dummy' smiled softly and turned to walk away, leaving us both doubled up with mirth. Considering that such a performance was deserving of some token of our appreciation, we tipped the man before entering the equally-notorious chamber of Horrors.

There was ample evidence throughout much of London of the effect that the German bombing was having on that city, and it was impossible to walk far without coming upon gangs of workmen busily engaged in clearing away the rubble left by a recent intruder. Again, we saw on the streets a lot of people wearing black arm bands, a tradition which we learned to be a mark of respect and remembrance for a family member who had been either killed through enemy action, or had by some other means been lost. Then there were the shortages, not just of beer and cigarettes (our staple requirements), but of many other consumer items as well. One of these was the common match. As smokers, we had all brought cigarette lighters with us from Canada, but it was impossible to purchase the fuel for these. We had tried gasoline (the British called it 'petrol') as a substitute, but found this impractical - particularly the hundred-octane stuff used to fuel aircraft engines. This was in plentiful supply, but one of the lads had witnessed the total destruction of his precious Ronson through his use of it, so we were obliged to rely instead on matches. Although it was quite impossible to locate a tobacconist with these in stock, we had learned that they could be obtained from the gambling machines in the many amusement arcades to be found around Piccadilly, and we soon became quite expert at manipulating the small model cranes until a box of the precious commodity had been won.

There was one other wartime shortage that caused us some concern, and that was the marked absence of sink plugs at each and every military establishment we had so far been posted to. The performing of the requisite ablutions in lukewarm water was bad enough, but your difficulties were compounded when you had to adapt a wad of screwed up toilet paper as a substitute stopper. We got the impression that, sometime during the early part of 1939, a rotter named Kilroy had pinched a sink plug, thereby setting up a chain reaction which had spread like wildfire throughout the British forces and beyond. In order to get a shave in reasonable comfort, you had to own a sink stopper, so these small rubber discs soon soared in value as a personal possession. Private hotels, public houses, railway rest rooms - any establishment in which cleansing facilities were on offer - all were subject to the scourge. The more skilful of those among us had taken the trouble to fashion a plug, using rubber obtained from a discarded tyre. Once this had been perfected, it was always carried on the person.

At last my leave came to an end, and I reported as instructed to the Five Group Training Flight at Fulbeck in Lincolnshire, together with Eric Plumkett. Harvey had been sent to a similar unit, but one somewhere else in the Midlands, and I was never to

THE LANCASTER

see him again, only his name listed in DRO's, reporting that he had failed to return from his first operational sortie. He was aged just twenty-one. No time was wasted in getting the training started, and I was airborne within a few hours of my arrival at Fulbeck. I was again flying in the Wellington, but not with my own crew this time. They were at 1661 Heavy conversion Unit at nearby Winthrope, where they would be getting instruction, first on the twin-engined Manchester, followed by their introduction to the aircraft we were destined to do our operational flying in - the Lancaster. The Fulbeck establishment was a sort of finishing school for air gunners, and the six-day course was made up of a series of camera gun exercises, using either a Martinet, a Spitfire or a Hurricane as the target aircraft. This time, the exercises were more realistic than previous ones I had taken part in, with the attacking fighter initiating his attack from different angles, and the bomber taking evasive action under the direction of the gunner. Because we were not bothered by bombing and navigation exercises, circuits and bumps, etcetera, nearly all of the air time was devoted to gunnery training, and I found this highly beneficial. Each film was developed and ready for assessment soon after it was shot, and my results indicated a progressive improvement as the course went on. I was beginning to formulate my own ideas on my duties as the chief defender of the aircraft, and each successive roll of film was an indication of the degree of success my ideas were producing.

I soon became adept at judging the optimum moment in which to give the order to 'corkscrew' in the appropriate direction, and I was pleased with the degree of difficulty the fighter pilot seemed to be having in carrying out a successful attack. Subsequent viewing of the film footage shot by both combatants did much to bolster my self confidence. I had plenty of shots of the attacking aircraft, and its position within the frame indicated that, in the main, my deflection angles were reasonably accurate. On viewing the shots taken by the fighter however, I noticed that the success attained by its pilot in getting my aircraft in his sights varied from one session to another. This I attributed to the individual aircraft handling ability of the various pilots I had been flying with on the course. Most of these had been capable of throwing the Wellington around the sky in a violent fashion during the corkscrew manoeuvre, and this had brought about the desired result as far as I was concerned. In the case of shots I had taken when flying with a more timid pilot, the fighter's results on camera were not to my liking, there being too many instances during which the attacking fighter had displayed a distinct advantage over me. From this it became obvious that dealing with an attack from a fighter was a situation which demanded the close co-operation and skill of both the gunner and the pilot.

Completion of the advanced gunnery training was immediately followed by a two-day commando course, the purpose of which was to provide us with the know-how to enable us to defend ourselves in the event of being shot down over enemy territory. In the main, it consisted of instruction in the art of unarmed combat, and we were shown a variety of holds, most of which were intended to render an opponent powerless, but some of which were capable of inflicting death. We were also given some useful tips on how to avoid capture if shot down, and were briefed on the use of a map and compass - tuition which Clem and I would no doubt have found of value a few weeks earlier! We were told that our first task would be the disposal of the parachute, preferably by its burial, and were advised to lay up in the bush during daylight, travelling only at night, avoiding roads whenever possible. Then we were told how we could subsist on pilfered farm produce and the emergency rations contained in the small pack which would be supplied prior to take-off for a raid.

All this information was dispensed by an ex-operational F/Sgt Wop/AG who appeared to be every bit as bored and disinterested in the subject as we were, and the entire course was, in the interests of realism, conducted out in the woods. Fortunately, the weather was kind to us, and we welcomed the fresh air and freedom that a smoke filled lecture room would have denied us.

On Wednesday the 23rd of June, 1943, I rejoined the crew at Winthorpe to discover that our number had increased to six. The new recruit was our flight engineer, a native of Bristol, and his name was Reg Moseley. I found him to be of a pleasant disposition, but with a boyish appearance which disaffirmed the importance of his intended purpose within the crew. I nevertheless warmed to his jocular demeanour.

There remained just one more position still be filled - that of a second gunner. Because the person chosen would be expected to work closely with me, Bill suggested that the choice should be mine, so I walked over to the gunnery section to have a look at what was on offer, and was directed to a side room where a dozen or so hopefuls were assembled. As I looked them over, I couldn't help thinking that the situation was akin to that of a Persian slave market, and that I was being cast in the role of an omnipotent sheikh in search of a concubine. After much searching of facial features, I finally plumped for the services of a handsome, wavy-haired lad of about my age who looked like he might fit the bill, so I walked over to clinch the deal.

"I'm looking for a fellow gunner for the crew. Would you like to joins us?", I asked.
He at once stepped forward and shook my hand.

He told me that his name was Richard (Dick) Jones, and that he was a Welshman from Wallasey. He was a qualified joiner, and had worked in the furniture manufacturing business before enlisting. Having mutually agreed to serve together in the same crew, we made our way over to the crew room for introductions to the others. Later that evening, we spent a few hours together in the mess, downing a few glasses of beer and getting acquainted.

Next morning, I had my first close-up look at the Lancaster. Although I had not been keen to get involved with heavy bombers during my intended flight career, I found the visual impact of the Lancaster most impressive. Despite its size, the aircraft was pleasing to the eye, and there was a look of solidity and power about it. My first impressions were to be confirmed later that day when we took one up, accompanied by a pilot instructor. This was the first time that the complete crew had flown a Lanc, the other members having been training on the twin-engined Manchester during my absence. During the previous evening's informal get-together, it had been jointly decided that I was to be the crew's Rear Gunner, and that Dick would permanently occupy the Mid Upper position.

The exercise was listed as 'stalling and recovery', so we climbed to eight or nine thousand feet so that we would have room to manoeuvre should we 'lose it'. Our instructor then throttled back and prompted Bill to raise the nose while Reg read out the diminishing air speed. The Lanc began to wallow unsteadily as our speed dropped back into double figures, and the aircraft began to shake and vibrate alarmingly at eighty MPH. It then dropped one wing and began to initiate a spin. On instruction, Bill quickly recovered control, and the process was repeated a few more times. The instructor then proceeded to illustrate the Lanc's ability to fly with one or more of its engines 'out' and began by feathering the starboard outer. This caused the aircraft to yaw to starboard, but Bill soon overcame this by carrying out the required adjustments. The starboard inner engine was then cut. More yaw. More need for adjustment, but we were still able to maintain height.

This was meant to be the completion of the exercise, but our instructor decided to demonstrate still further the Lancaster's remarkable performance, whereupon he promptly switched off the port inner engine, leaving just the port outer engine still running. Bill later remarked that, although we had been losing height steadily through loss of power, and full trim had been necessary, the Lancaster had remained stable, and had not been too difficult to control.

We experienced something of a panic during a training flight later in the course. We were being instructed in diving turns by a Canadian pilot who was being rested as an instructor after having completed a tour on ops. The Lancaster we were flying on that day was fitted with dual controls, and it turned out to be fortunate for us all that it was. Bill had executed a few fairly severe corkscrews at a signal from me, and I was impressed by his handling of the new aircraft type. Not so our instructor, however, "Look, Buddy", he shouted at Bill with impatience, "When one of yer gunners tells ya to dive port, get the Goddam nose down and GO!". At this, he thrust his own control column hard against the instrument panel, thus setting in motion a number of hitherto unexpected high jinks. Reg, who had been standing behind the two pilots, soared into the top of the cockpit canopy before coming down across the throttle bank, pushing all four levers through the gate. I banged my head against the top of my turret, and the Lanc went into a screaming vertical power dive. Meanwhile, back in the cockpit, it was taking the combined strength of four men to pull us out. As we began to level, I sensed the beginnings of a blackout. Although the day was bright and sunny, the sky began to turn grey, and I saw a large chunk of something go hurtling past on my left. I was already reporting this to the flight deck when we finally resumed level flight and went screaming out across the Nottinghamshire landscape at a height of about two hundred feet.

Bill was to tell me later that, during the power dive from which we had been fortunate to escape, the rate of climb and descent meter had registered the maximum descent, after which it had passed over into the 'climb' segment of the dial, and the air speed indicator had also 'gone off the clock', causing him to calculate that we had been travelling directly earthwards at something nearing four hundred miles per hour, if not more.

We had no sooner levelled out than the Mid Upper Gunner reported that the cover had been ripped off the dinghy stowage hatch, and it was this that I had seen going out over the starboard tailplane as we pulled out of the dive. By some miracle, the dinghy itself had remained uninflated inside its wing stowage compartment between the starboard inner engine and the fuselage, but was in real danger of being sucked out by the negative air flow over the upper surface of the wing, and we all knew what to expect in such an event: the large rubber dinghy would probably get entangled with the starboard tailplane, thus making control of the aircraft difficult. There was even the danger that the impact of the dinghy at the speed we were flying would be suffi-

THE LANCASTER

cient to damage the tailplane, and could even dislodge it completely. It followed that, although we had survived having treated a Lancaster in a way for which it had never been designed, we were still in serious trouble.

We knew that, should the worst happen, and the dingy caused us to lose control, we were too near to the ground to bale out safely, and any attempt at climbing would make it more likely that the dinghy would be sucked from its stowage compartment by the increased vacuum over the top surface of the wing. It followed that our only course of action was to just sit tight and try to land on a nearby airfield, which we did. As Bill gingerly throttled back and touched down, the dinghy finally tumbled out onto the runway and began to inflate as it was dragged harmlessly along by its lanyard.

The first half of the four-weeks course was taken up by a number of daylight flights which were designed to familiarise us with the new type. Apart from the two exercises previously described, these consisted mainly of 'circuits and bumps' (practice landings and take-offs) high altitude flying; some gunnery practice, and a four-hour cross country stooge. Dick Jones and I also had a couple of sessions with a Spitfire. The seven exercises we carried out on the night segment were of longer duration, being made up of a couple of four-hour cross country flights; some bombing practice, and yet another round of "Circuits and Thumps". We had adopted the modified term in describing the exercise because of a couple of occasions on which Old Bill had executed landings which were not strictly in accordance with the text book. He had requested further instruction on the correct technique, and insisted that we accompany him.

Early in our stay at Winthorpe, I received my regular six-monthly promotion from the RCAF - this time to Flight Sergeant. This made me the second highest rank in the crew at that time, and I considered it odd that I should out-rank my pilot.

The mail from Canada was at last beginning to filter through fairly regularly, although letters were taking on average three to four weeks to reach me. These usually arrived in a bundle, having been held back at Halifax awaiting the sailing of a convoy. One such bundle had contained three letters from home, a few from some friends, and several from Margaret, who had formed the habit of writing three times a week. The news from home was mostly routine. Everything was going well at the farm, and Mother had posted a parcel with one of her letters, but it was not with the consignment. The news from my friends was mostly about our fast-diminishing social group, and I was told that one of them, who had joined RCAF aircrew shortly after my enlistment, had been killed in a flying accident during training in Canada. Although he had not been a member of our country band, he had been a devoted fan, and was to be seen at most of our venues, and invariably took an active part in our many social activities. He was just the first of a number of close friends that I was to lose in the coming months.

The letters from Margaret were mostly repetitive in their content, and left me in no doubt that she was busily making plans for our future together, having presupposed that I was of similar intent. She also mentioned the death of our mutual friend, and her letters showed much of the concern she felt for my safety. I had no doubts concerning the seriousness of the relationship and the direction in which it was developing, and my one regret was the lack of time that we had had in which to get to know each other better. It had been only in the past few months that the ties of friendship that existed between us had taken on a more intimate identity, and the opportunity to develop the relationship along these lines had from that time been limited by the demands of my service career. Now that I was stationed overseas, and would within weeks be in action, it was probable that it would be months - even years - before we would see each other again, if ever. There was too much uncertainty standing in the way of a well-reasoned and far-reaching decision to be taken before my part in the war was at an end. Although it was comforting to know that I had someone who cared so strongly, I considered it callous of me to allow Margaret to build her hopes so high. Although (like all the others in my circumstances) I had no intention of 'getting the chop', I had to accept the possibility.

A part of the course at Winthorpe concerned the procedure to be followed on abandoning the aircraft in an emergency, and we placed a lot of importance on this in view of the couple of close calls we had experienced in the previous weeks of training. Together, we spent more than the prescribed time in practising the taking up of crash positions; the drill for abandoning the aircraft in the air, and the correct procedure for 'ditching' in the sea. All of these could be carried out on the ground, but Bill was not beyond springing one on us while we were airborne. As far as bailing out was concerned, the Tail gunner had the best exit of all, it only being necessary for him to rotate his turret to one of the beams; slide open the doors behind him, and roll out backwards. Of the other six men, the bomb aimer was the next most favourably placed, his crew position being situated directly over the escape hatch in the nose. This exit would also be used by the flight engineer and the pilot, although the latter could sometimes escape through a hatch in the top of the cockpit canopy, a route that was not to be recommended because of the danger of being struck by one of the many obstacles on the upper surface of the fuselage. The navigator, wireless operator and mid upper gunner would normally exit via the large boarding door, which was situated on the starboard side of the fuselage, about six feet in front of the tailplane.

The ditching drill called for the taking up of crash positions by all crew members (except the pilot) at the rear of the main spar, in readiness for the impact of landing in the sea. As soon as the aircraft was presumed to be down, there followed a mad but orderly scramble for the three escape hatches in the roof of the fuselage, having first made sure that the dinghy release toggle had been activated. This effectively cracked open a CO^2 cylinder which then commenced to inflate the dinghy within its stowage compartment in the starboard wing. This served to force off the plywood hatch cover which, being taped in position, formed a small part of the upper wing surface during normal flight. In theory, the dinghy would then take shape on the surface of the water, being tethered to the wing by a lanyard. However, it was at this stage that Sod's Law usually came into play, thus making sure that the dinghy would be found floating upside-down. However, it was possible for one man to right the thing, as had been shown to us during a training session at the Newark Municipal Baths. A Lancaster could remain afloat for some time, or it could sink in a matter of minutes depending on whether or not it had suffered structural damage, either through enemy action, or when landing in the sea. It followed that there was no time to be wasted in getting the crew into the dinghy and away from the aircraft as soon as was possible.

At last, just one year and five days after the date of my enlistment in the RCAF, my training came to an end. At nineteen years of age, I was the youngest member of our recently formed crew. I had logged a total of 137 hours in the air, only 41 of which had been flown in darkness, and I was thus considered to be a fully qualified air gunner. I had my coveted wings; I was wearing the rank of Flight Sergeant, and I had certainly done a lot of growing up in the past fourteen months. The one thing that I lacked was operational combat experience. There was plenty of that to follow.

On Wednesday, July 21st., 1943 the crew received its first posting to an operational squadron. We were to join Number 9 Squadron, Five Group, Bomber command, stationed at Bardney in Lincolnshire.

THE LANCASTER

CHAPTER 8

ARMAGEDDON

Our first impression of the Lincolnshire village of Bardney, as the train drew out, leaving us standing alone on the otherwise deserted platform, was one of rural peace and tranquillity. The stillness of our placid surroundings was interrupted only briefly by the raucous roar of a Lancaster from the nearby airfield as it clawed its way skywards over the rooftops, its passing ignored by a collection of silent sparrows watching us from a wayside hedgerow. The day was dull but dry, with thick clouds hiding the sun and creating in me a deep feeling of concern for our future. The events of my year of training had served to dispel much of the excitement of flying that I had enjoyed prior to this posting. In that time, flying had become an almost monotonous routine, and one which had instilled in me an awareness of the degree of danger and uncertainty that attended my chosen profession.

In the absence of service transport, we stacked our luggage at the end of the platform while the skipper went in search of a telephone. Meanwhile, someone had spotted a nearby public house, so Clem was sent over to find out whether or not it was open for business.

On Clem's return, we learned that the pub was closed, but that he had spoken to the licensee, who had invited us over for a drink while we waited for our transport. Meanwhile Bill had contacted the field, and was just in time to join us as we trooped into the bar.

Bardney's Station Hotel was a typical village inn with a friendly, cosy atmosphere and an equally affable tenanty. As we consumed our drinks, we chatted about the fact that we were a sprog crew just joining the squadron. On learning that Bill's father owned the Crown Hotel in Penrith, our host, who had stayed in the hotel several times prior to the war, invited us to take part in some after-hours drinking in his private quarters whenever we wished. Needless to say, we took frequent advantage of this concession during our stay with the squadron, particularly on the frequent occasions when our host announced to all others present that the pumps were dry.

On the eventual arrival of our transport outside the deserted railway station, we loaded our kitbags in the back and climbed in for the short journey to our first posting as an operational bomber crew.

We found that the home of Nine Squadron had been hewn out of the farm lands lying to the north-east of the village, and was in effect a satellite of the large peacetime aerodrome at Waddington, up the hill from the city of Lincoln. Nine Squadron, the first unit to occupy the new field, had only been in residence since April.

Because it was a wartime establishment, austerity was the keynote. Although the actual field had concrete runways and perimeter tracks to Class A Air Ministry specification all of the necessary buildings, including the hangars and administrative offices were of half brick construction, with steel frames supporting the corrugated sheet upper section and roof. There existed a Sergeant's and Officer's Mess, each with bedding accommodation, but these were of insufficient size to take the entire complement, so the overflow (mainly 'sprog' crews such as ours) was billeted in a collection of small Nissan Huts. These were dispersed throughout a wooded area on one side of the field, and each was designed to accommodate one complete crew, having seven beds and lockers, plus a centrally positioned cast-iron stove with a tin pipe leading out through the roof. As was only to be expected, we were assigned to one of these highly undesirable residences, and were fully aware of the fact that our only hope of gaining tenancy of the Mess was dependant on our ability to survive the conflict until such times as someone in the Mess didn't.

After having settled into our humble abode, we set out to explore our surroundings with a view to determining what creature comforts were available. We found that the ablutions block was situated about a hundred yards from our hut, and that it contained the usual offices, including a couple of shower cubicles and a long row of wash basins, all of which were devoid of plugs, of course. Nevertheless, this most utilitarian edifice was equipped with heating, and appeared to be in the sole charge of a mop-wielding, disinterested ACH/GD on whose unpretentious shoulders rested the responsibility of keeping the floor clean and the boiler stoked. From there, a path meandered out through the undergrowth in the direction of the main buildings. This had been liberally strewn with gravel in a vain attempt at neutralizing the mud beneath. The interior of the Sgt's Mess consisted of a large day room which bore some evidence of an attempt having been made to improve the decor. The walls and ceiling had been freshly painted, and the floor was covered in brightly bumped dark brown linoleum. There was a well appointed and substantially stocked bar at the far end of the room, and some enterprising individual had fitted colourful print curtains at the windows. The furnishings consisted of a collection of folding wooden chairs and card tables, plus several well-

ARMAGEDDON

worn upholstered arm chairs, none of which matched, and all seemed to be of uncertain age and origin. A carefully constructed brick fireplace and a battered old upright piano completed the inventory.

Within a few hours of our arrival on the squadron, we were detailed for a 'local jaunt', the purpose of which was to familiarize us with the local landmarks and the general layout of the countryside in the vicinity of the airfield. For this flight, we were entrusted with W-4132 (WS/S), a veteran Lancaster which had already completed a good number of raids, and was soon to be retired to Training Command. We found Lincolnshire to be mostly flat, with the triple towers of Lincoln Cathedral dominating the skyline some ten miles to the west. During the months that were to follow, we were to become familiar with the sight of those magnificent examples of British stone architecture as they welcomed our return from the many conflicts that lay ahead.

After a brief aerial look at the village of Bardney, the predominant feature of which was the sugarbeet processing plant at one end of the railway station, we flew out to The Wash to see the bombing practice range at Wainfleet. Two nights later, we again took off with S, this time for a night cross country flight lasting three and a half hours. Because such trips, carried out in darkness, were mostly monotonous from a gunner's aspect, Dick and I arranged with Bill for a couple of corkscrew sessions during the trip, much to the displeasure of Dick Lodge the navigator, who invariably lost all his pencils, rulers and protractors during such violent goings-on.

The following evening (Saturday, July 24th, 1943) Bill Siddle was detailed for a 'second dickie' trip with another crew. This was standard practise in Bomber Command, the aim being to give a new pilot first hand experience of an actual attack on a target before asking him to take his own crew to war. Rumour had it that Hamburg was the target, and there were whispers around the squadron of a secret device being used for the first time. Although a sprog pilot was usually teamed up with an experienced crew for his initiation, it was not unknown for a new crew to lose its skipper on one of these trips, so we were greatly relieved when old Bill presented himself in the Mess the following day and gave us a vivid account of the ride.

In the opinion of the more experienced participants, enemy opposition had been moderate, with a lot of flak and searchlight activity in the area of the target (which had been Hamburg), but this had been mainly ineffective, it was claimed that this was due to the use for the first time a device called 'window' which had served to swamp the German radar defence network, thus making it impossible to track and intercept our bombers by any means other than sight, and there was no doubt that the unusually low loss rate for the action was ample proof of the success that use of the device had achieved.

Our skipper described the trip as having been mainly uneventful. There had been a marked absence of fighters, and the ground based defences had appeared to be in serious disarray, with the searchlights waving aimlessly around the sky, and with the flak bursting in confused patterns at a height well below that of the main concentration of bombers. He had seen two aircraft being shot down in the target area, but both of these had been from the lower echelon, which consisted mainly of Stirlings and Halifaxes, and it had been obvious that the searchlight and flak battery crews were being forced to rely entirely on visual sighting because of the effect that 'window' was having on their equipment. Because the German night fighters were normally directed to within visual range of their prey by similar means, it was probable that they had been faced with an identical problem.

Bill had brought a sample bundle of window back with him. It consisted of about a hundred strips of tinfoil, each measuring about eight inches by one inch, with a black paper backing. The size of the strips was critical because it matched exactly the wavelength being used by the German tracking system. It had been decided that the job of dispensing the bundles from the aircraft at regular intervals during the flight would be that of either the flight engineer or of the wireless operator.

On the subject of conditions in the target area, Bill was keen to point out that there was a lot of light around, and he stressed the need for every available crew member to keep a sharp lookout for enemy fighters. Because he and the bomb aimer would be busy at that stage, it was decided that everyone else should do all that they could to assist the gunners in their task, a ruling with which I thoroughly agreed.

On the following night, we were again detailed for a cross country training flip. During the flight, we once more put our various crew tactics to the test under the critical control of our skipper, who was growing increasingly insistent on the efficiency and discipline of each and every one of us. As the flight progressed, I sensed the development of an element of unity and confidence within the crew which had not been so evident when we first came together.

At twenty-two hundred hours (10 p.m.) on the night of Tuesday, July the 27th, we took off in Lancaster DV-198 (WS/U) for what was to be our first operational flight as a complete crew. It was Hamburg again, and it was with a mixture of excitement, fear

ARMAGEDDON

Fig 7. July 27th 1943, Bardney, Lincolnshire. IX Squadron crews awaiting transport to dispersals. Target: Hamberg. Sgt Moseley, Sgt Culley and Sgt Siddle standing in line to the left of the photograph. This was to be our first operational sortie.

Taken from a Planet News photograph.

ARMAGEDDON

and foreboding that I prepared myself for whatever the next five hours in the air might bring.

Darkness was beginning to creep steadily westward, and the sky above Lincolnshire was filled with the sight and the sound of the big bombers as they wheeled and struggled to lift themselves and their heavy loads to their operational height. My location in the aircraft left me with the impression that we were almost on the point of stalling as, with tail down and engines roaring steadily, WS/U continued to claw for height. As we reached ten thousand feet, the order was given to don oxygen masks, and I adjusted the level of illumination on my reflector sight and set my four Brownings to 'fire'. At last we turned eastwards on a course that would take us out over the coast in the direction of Germany.

As we made our way out over the North Sea, still climbing, the other Lancasters around us gradually faded from my view as the darkness closed in. Now the only evidence of their presence was the turbulence of a slipstream, or the occasional glimpse of streaking tracer bullets as some over-zealous gunner tested his weapons. A routine which was generally accepted as standard, this was one of which I did not approve. Apart from the obvious danger of scoring a hit on an unseen friendly aircraft in the vicinity, I was of the belief that a correctly serviced and adjusted Browning could always be relied on to function when required.

The butterflies had been giving me trouble ever since I had learned that we were 'on' that night, but their effect was beginning to lessen now that we were on our way to the target. This was it. A year of intensive training was behind me, and I knew that, if I was to see a fighter out there in the darkness tonight, it wouldn't be a friendly Beaufighter or Hurricane, armed with nothing more lethal than a camera gun. There wouldn't be the comforting presence of an instructor to tell me that I wasn't getting it quite right. This time it was for real, and my reward for dropping a clanger would be a lot more severe that a low assessment or a telling off. The defence of this big bomber and its crew and cargo was the responsibility of Dick Jones and me, and we couldn't afford to give or expect any mercy if attacked. In accordance with the established crew policy, it was our job to spot the fighter first and dodge a confrontation. But would we see him in time? After all, I hadn't seen that Beaufighter back at the OTU until it was too late.

As we droned out over the water, I began the now familiar search pattern, and congratulated myself on having sighted a couple of Lancasters forging through the murky darkness that surrounded us. I was later to learn that this was unusual, it being possible to complete a trip along with several hundred other aircraft without seeing a single one, except in the vicinity of the target.

As we forged steadily onward, with only the pinpoints of light from the stars to relieve the darkness, I drew comfort from the business-like way in which we were functioning as a crew. Conversation was being kept to the minimum, with only regular crew checks by Bill, and the occasional course correction from Dick Lodge breaking into the familiar background noise of the engines. At one point, the aircraft began to buck mildly as it ran into the turbulence being kicked up by another one somewhere ahead of us, and our navigator remarked smugly that somebody else must be right on track. Such mild humour, although unnecessary, was nonetheless appreciated because it served to relieve the tension that affected all of us.

At last, after more than two hours in the air, we turned to starboard on the heading that would take us across Hamburg. Bill announced over the intercom that the target was dead ahead, and that he could see a lot of fires still burning from the previous raid. The sky around us was beginning to grow much lighter now, and I sensed a feeling of nakedness as the protective curtain of darkness was gradually drawn aside. Glancing over my left shoulder, I could see the big black starboard rudder and one distant wing tip held in stark profile against the bowl of flickering red and yellow light that lay ahead of and beneath us.

As we drew nearer to the city, I could see frequent flashes of blinding white light as the photoflashes exploded near the ground, interspersed with the dull red flashes of the four thousand pounders and other high explosive bombs as they slammed into the streets and buildings far below, each load accompanied by a long, narrow swath of twinkling light thrown up by the incendiary bombs igniting on impact.

As we neared the action that lay ahead of us, things began to happen with increasing frequency. We were into the bombing run. Ken, lying flat in his compartment in the nose, had ordered the bomb doors to be opened, and I could feel the aircraft making gentle course corrections as he calmly issued commands to the skipper. Beneath us, long strings of light ack-ack shells climbed lazily upwards, looking like strips of multi-coloured fairy lights, only to burn out before reaching us. The heavy batteries appeared to be aimed at about our height, each shell burst giving off a dull read flash which was quickly consumed by a cloud of thick black smoke left hanging in the air, and looking remarkably like a barrage balloon as it drifted past. The heavy ack-ack shells gave no visual indication of their approach, so that the first warning that you got of their coming was the "whump" of the explosion, a frightening sound that was frequently audible above the noise of the engines, depending on the nearness of the blast.

Early in my career of operational flying, I was to learn that the run up to the target could be the most traumatic part of a raid. This was because, at a time when you were openly exposed to the full destructive potential of a well defended target, and when the survival instinct was screaming at you to get the job finished and get to hell out of danger, the taking of evasive action was forbidden, except in cases of extreme necessity. There were two reasons for this: first, the bomb aimer required a steady run up in order that he could take accurate aim on the target, and I found this acceptable. It was the wisdom of the remaining directive which I considered to be iniquitous. This was concerned with the action to be taken after the bombload had been released. Each aircraft carried a fixed on-board camera which was automatically set to take a picture of the area beneath the aircraft at the exact time that the bombs would be detonated. Also involved was the photoflash, the function of which was to provide illumination of the target, thereby enabling the camera to record the result of the drop. In order for this to happen, it was imperative that the aircraft should be flying straight and level, so that the camera lens would be aimed correctly at the time when the exposure was to be made. Depending on the height at which the bombs were released from the aircraft, it could take in excess of one full minute (in addition to the run-up) for them to reach the target, and this was one hell of a long time to spend in morbid contemplation of a possible outcome.

As I saw it, there were two distinct reasons for taking a photograph, the first being that it would be of value in determining the degree of accuracy obtained by the bomb aimer, and would thus provide a good indication of the damage inflicted on the target. Again, I concurred with the need for this, except in circumstances when the target was either covered by cloud or obscured by smoke, in which case the recording of ground detail would be impossible, and only parachute flares (if in use) would appear on the film. The second reason for exposing a valuable aircraft and its crew to possible destruction and death (although ancillary to the first and therefore involuntary) was the attempt to monitor the integrity of the crews by requiring them to prove that they had actually carried out the attack. It was known that a small number of crews were not keen to attack their objective, and some ingenuity had gone into the perfection of ploys which were designed to cheat the system. However, these crews were very much a minority, and their existence did not warrant the exposure of honest men to unnecessary danger.

Nonetheless, there were those in authority who placed much importance on the use of the pictures for this purpose, and it is probable that a lot of time was spent in trying to detect the existence of the few who cheated.

Now that we were almost directly above the target, the excitement (and the fear) was intense. The light from the fires, photoflashes, and searchlights; the smoke drifting up, the thundering flak bursts, and the flash of the bombs as they exploded far beneath, had turned the darkness into near daylight. Other Lancasters could be seen all around us, each with its bomb doors gaping open, and with the bombs spinning and tumbling as they began their unstoppable descent. Amidst the turmoil and confusion of the battle that was taking place all around, I got the feeling that all eyes must be on us, and I noticed for the first time the perspiration that fear could generate as I frantically searched the sky above us for the fighter attack that I felt must surely come.

"Left...", came Ken's voice over the intercom. "Steady . . . steady . . . bombs going". While this was going on, I was searching the starboard quarter, high.

"Tally Ho!", warned Dick from the mid upper turret. "Fighter astern, diving port to starboard".

I quickly swung my turret around, saw and recognised our enemy at once.

"It's a Focke Wulf 190, skipper, but he's after somebody else. Watch him, Dick. I'll cover the tail".

There then followed the long, nail-biting ordeal as we waited for the camera to function. Meanwhile, all hell was breaking loose around us. The gunners down below were sending up a box barrage, and I reckoned that they had the range just about right. Flak shells were bursting all over the place, causing the Lancaster to wallow drunkenly each time one got a bit near. Down on the starboard quarter, somebody copped one, and I watched for the first time the spinning, flaming hulk of what had been a Lanc as it fell into the inferno below, comet-like, with orange and white flames streaming to a point behind it.

A wandering searchlight beam flicked across us, paused, then returned. Some eagle-eyed operator had spotted us, and he soon had us held captive in his all-revealing beam of light. A couple of others locked onto us, followed by several more, and Bill began to throw us around the sky in a vain attempt to shake them off, while I cursed our luck at having been coned by searchlights on our first trip.

ARMAGEDDON

As we careered around the sky in a corkscrew that threatened to tear the wings off, I felt totally disorientated by the violence of the manoeuvre and the effect that the blinding light was having on my sense of direction and surroundings.

"For God's sake everybody, keep your eyes open for fighters", Bill shouted down the intercom at us as, with the Merlins screaming in torment, the Lanc continued to dive, bank and climb, subjecting me to stresses that I had never before experienced in an aircraft. Now our predicament was being compounded by the action of the ack-ack gunners who had started to fire visually up the beams at us. Despite the confusion and noise that was all around us, I could distinctly hear the shrapnel rattling against the fuselage each time a shell burst got near.

During our participation in subsequent raids, I was to become sufficiently callous as to rejoice at the sight of someone else being coned as we were at this moment, because we could be assured that most eyes (both friendly and unfriendly) were indeed on the unfortunate sods in the cone. This meant that, for the time being at least, the heat of battle was a little less intense for the rest of us. I was also to learn that the chances of surviving such and experience were about even.

"Some bastard down there doesn't like us!", Ken remarked in broad cockney.

"Shut up, bomb aimer, Bill admonished, then added, "There's no future in this. I'm going to do a power dive. See if we can shake them off that way".

Almost at once, there was a falling off in the accuracy of the flak, and the searchlights began to thin out until only a couple still held us. Bill pulled out of the dive and went into another corkscrew, and we were soon surrounded once more by the comforting darkness. We had been held in the cone for a total of six minutes.

The emergency over, Bill began calling up each member of the crew for damage reports. It was then that we were told that Dick Jones had suffered an injury. A piece of shrapnel had penetrated the perspex dome of his mid upper turret, striking him in the left shoulder. The wireless operator was immediately detailed to take over the position while the flight engineer attended to the wound. Fortunately, this was only superficial, and Reg soon had Dick patched up and back in position. As for damage, the aircraft had collected a few small flak holes in the central fuselage, but nothing of vital importance was involved, and all engines and instruments were functioning normally.

A course for base having been set, I continued to search the sky behind us, this being made easier by the light from the inferno that was Hamburg. The city was well alight, with flames and smoke rising several hundred feet. A large ball of flame, probably from an exploding gasometer. rose steadily upwards amid the waving searchlight beams and pinpoints of flak.

As we drew further away from the target area, I observed high above the holocaust a lone bomber with its black surfaces looking surprisingly silver as it tumbled frantically this way and that, seemingly supported by a giant tripod of white light that stood among the burning streets below. Watching the drama, I came to realise that we had ourselves been in a similar situation only a few minutes previously, and I fervently hoped that our fellow combatants would escape as we had. But soon, the moth-like silver speck suddenly glowed orange and began to tumble slowly downwards, breaking up as it fell.

"Aircraft going down in flames over the target", I reported to the skipper.

Although I was not to know it then, we were taking part in "Operation Gomorrah", and this was the night of the firestorm, a man-made horror that was to be extensively chronicled and questioned by historians of both sides in later years. I was as yet very much inexperienced in such matters, and cared little about the political reasoning behind the conflict in which I was involved. Nevertheless, I was capable of imagining something of the terrible degree of death and destruction that was being inflicted on the City of Hamburg and its unfortunate inhabitants even as I watched. No doubt a lot of people, some too young to hold political beliefs, were dying at that minute.

Soon we were out over the North Sea, and Hamburg was nothing more than a deep red glow in the dark sky behind us. As was to happen frequently during the months that were to follow, I allowed my thoughts to dwell on memories of Whitfield and home, as I continued to search the darkness behind us. On this night, I was reminded of something that had happened during my early childhood: Our farming community was often visited by the members of some obscure religious sect, and my mother always invited them in for a meal and a chat. They would have with them a wind-up portable gramophone which would be set up to play a selection of speeches while the provisions on offer were disposed of. Before leaving for the next farm, these 'Bible students' as they were known, always left a selection of booklets for us to read. Crudely printed, and with badly drawn black and red illustrations, the publications concerned 'The coming of Armageddon', during which, it was prophesied, fire and brimstone would rain down from the skies, and all mankind would perish. From my high altitude as we drew near to The Wash, I could still see the fires that we had left raging through the streets of Hamburg, more than three hundred miles distant, and this caused me to reflect on the remarkably accurate forecasting of future events that I had read all those years before.

We touched down at Bardney at 3:20 am., to be met at WS/U's dispersal by 'Chiefy', the Flight Sergeant in charge of our ground crew. During all of my term of service with Bomber command, I never ceased to marvel at the keeness and devotion to duty displayed by these much underpaid and undervalued servants, whose expert skills were so essential to us. No matter what the hour of the night might be, and regardless of weather conditions, there was always at least one of them waiting to welcome us back, sometimes several. In the main, these men spent much of their tour of duty on the remote and isolated despersal, with nothing more than a makeshift hut of their own construction in which to shelter when the weather turned nasty.

We had hardly enough time to give Chiefy a run down on the extent of the damage before the transport arrived to take us over to the flight offices for debriefing. Dick Jones had been picked up soon after the landing, and was already on his way to the station hospital for treatment. The debriefing room was already thronged with weary yet spirited young men like ourselves, and we were pleased to be told that all of the squadron aircraft had returned safely. There were four long tables in the room, at each of which was seated a WAAF and a bomber crew. While waiting for a table to become vacant, we each helped ourselves to steaming hot cups of tea which we eagerly drew from a tall, chromed urn in a corner of the room.

After the debriefing, we all trooped over to the Mess for breakfast. During the meal, we discussed the trip, and agreed on the need for some modification to our existing crew tactics, these to be based on our experiences during the flight. In general, Bill was satisfied with our performance, but ruled that in future, only crew positions would be used when calling someone over the intercom, there being a danger of confusion arising because of the duplication of Christian names within the crew. It was also ruled that, in similar circumstances, we would adopt the shallow dive tactic on being coned by searchlights over the target. Using the corkscrew manoeuvre would only prolong the duration of our presence in the danger area, thereby increasing the chance of us copping a packet from the ack-ack gunners, as had happened that hight. The diving technique of evasion would not only shorten our stay within the area covered by the guns, but would also make more difficult the chance of the defenses to hang onto us, because of our increased speed and rapid change of altitude.

On arising from a well-earned sleep in the early afternoon, I was pleased to learn that Dick had been passed as fit for flying. I was also told that the squadron was 'dicing' that night, and that we were again on the battle order. It certainly looked as if we were going to complete our tour in record time at the rate we were going.

ARMAGEDDON

CHAPTER 9

THE BIG TIME

After a late, lunch, Dick and I caught a transport over to the dispersals to check out our turrets and guns for the coming operation. Because we had been flying the previous night, another crew had done the NFT on our aircraft during the morning, and the armourers were already busy winching the bombs on board when we arrived. On asking, we were told that the bombload was almost identical to that carried by the squadron aircraft on the previous night's trip, but that the flight duration could not be calculated until orders concerning the fuel gallonage were announced. We were soon to realise that, once these details were known, the ground crews were quite capable of predicting the approximate location of the target with remarkable accuracy.

For the pending trip we had been allocated a Mk III Lancaster, registration ED-666 (WS/G), which had arrived new on the squadron in May. Quite by chance, WS/J, another A Flight Lanc was parked in the next dispersal to ours. "Johnnie Walker" (as she had been named) was the pride and joy of fellow Canadian "Mitch" Mitchell and his crew, one of which was none other than Eric Plunkett, the one acquaintance left over from my months spent in training.

As I climbed into my rear turret, I was somewhat perturbed to find it piled high with packets of window on either side of my seat. I at once lodged a complaint with a nearby armourer, who informed me that this incursion into my already cramped domain had been decided on by 'the powers that be', and that the rear gunner would in future be expected to eject a bundle by means of his clear vision panel at regular intervals during the time that the aircraft was over enemy territory. I could see that the idea was fraught with problems, and decided to challenge the order at the first opportunity.

At the briefing, it was revealed that the target was again to be Hamburg, making a total of three attacks on the city by Bomber Command in just four nights. Like some of the others present, I was concerned by this display of repetition in target selection, and I wondered at the wisdom of sending a large force to the same target at such close intervals. I feared that, having been subjected to a pounding on two out of the three previous nights, the German defences would by now have realised that we were intent on the total destruction of Hamburg, and would be ready and waiting for us to put in an appearance. My belief was further strengthened by a warning from the squadron Gunnery Leader that we could expect to find an increase in fighter activity in the vicinity of the target.

The Met. Officer, standing beside his blackboard and easel with pointer in hand, explained the meaning of the multi-coloured chalk sketches he had prepared for us. Cloud over the target was expected to be sparse, and it had been planned that our return would beat the arrival at our bases of a mass of low cloud that was moving in from the north west. We would be flying at twenty thousand feet, and the winds were expected to be moderate.

A somewhat elderly intelligence Officer then rose to give an outline of the known defences we could expect to encounter in the area of the target, and warned that there was photographic evidence of mobile flak and searchlight batteries being moved into position. However, window was again in use, and this could be expected to limit the effectiveness of the German defences. He then went on to report on the detail contained in the reconnaissance photographs taken of the target earlier in the day. "There are a lot of fires burning out of control in many parts of the city, but there are still a few buildings with their roofs still intact", he said. Then, with obvious distress, he announced that he had just attended the funeral of some close relatives who had been killed in a raid on the East End of London. In the respectful and awkward silence that followed, he tearfully implored us to "go over there and give them hell", then added, "I won't be happy while there's still a roof left in Hamburg".

After the briefing, we next visited the aircrew Mess for the traditional pre-flight meal of bacon and two eggs, followed by the equally traditional bowl of prunes and custard, it was widely suspected that the desert course was the brain child of some high-up Air ministry Medic who, being aware of its propensity for keeping one 'functional' had prescribed the treatment. On discussing the value of the prunes as a laxative, Ken put forward his own evaluation which, roughly translated, was to the effect that they fell far short of the effect that could be produced by a German flak barrage.

Take off was scheduled for 22:50 hours, so we had about ninety minutes in which to prepare ourselves for the coming trip. Our next call was at the crew locker rooms, where we all got dressed for the part. The locker rooms resounded to the boisterous babble of anxious young men intent on dispelling the apprehension that they undoubtedly felt. Only a few of the jokes to be heard were new, and the laughter was too loud and spontaneous. After a time, I learned the art of separating the new crews from those which had completed more than the first half-

THE BIG TIME

dozen flights. While the new boys were noticeably noisy at this stage of their preparation, the 'veterans' went about the chore of donning their flying kit in a spirit which bordered on quiet resignation.

One of the more senior crews on the squadron at that time was that of Pilot Officer Jim Lyon, an Australian. His crew was nearing the end of its tour, having spent a number of months in service with the squadron, during which time some of the most heavily defended targets had been visited by them. Jim and his crew were to complete their tour, after which they would be dispersed throughout Training command for a rest period. Unfortunately, he was killed in a flying accident a few weeks after his posting.

The air gunners had to wear more clothing than the other crew members because of the lack of heating in the turrets. In fact, the rear turret was open to the slipstream because of the cut-out clear vision panel in front of the unfortunate occupant. This admitted a fierce gale, particularly when the turret was trained to one beam or the other. As a consequence, the 'clobber' consisted of: battledress trousers and tunic; one-piece electrically-heated suit; zip-up canvas flying suit (with huge imitation fur collar and spacious knee pockets); two pairs of thick woollen socks, and leather flying boots. On top of this livery went the May West and the parachute harness, and the ensemble was completed by a fleece-lined leather helmet, complete with goggles, oxygen mask and intercom (microphone and earpieces). Finally, leather flying gauntlets with electric inner gloves were worn, and most gunners included a thick roll-neck sweater worn beneath the battle dress tunic.

On leaving the crew room, fully clad, the next task was the collection of the various items issued for use during the flight. These amounted to a small sealed emergency escape pack containing a map of the territory over which we would be flying; a supply of the local currency; forged identity documents; a small compass; a selection of concentrated food capsules (including Horlic tablets), chewing gum, and a few pieces of chocolate. This pack was only to be opened in the event of us being shot down, and was otherwise surrendered on our return. The pack, together with one bar each of Fry's sandwich and Fry's Chocolate Cream was presented to us by an equally apprehensive-looking young WAAF who stood just inside the exit. She also had for disposal a supply of boiled sweets, plus a limitless supply of 'wakey-wakey' pills. These were always in great demand, not because of their faculty for preventing one from dozing off during the trip, but because it was popularly believed that they were an effective aphrodisiac. Resulting from this, the pills were jealously hoarded in readiness for the next leave period, during which they would be hastily consumed.

There now remained only a visit to the parachute section in order to collect and sign for a pack before boarding the trucks or busses that would take us around the airfield perimeter tracks to our waiting aircraft.

Having been dropped off at WS/G's dispersal, we at once busied ourselves in stowing our gear and running a final check on our equipment. This done, we then sat on the grass at the edge of the pan, discussing the coming flight, and making last-minute decisions on tactics. Although darkness had fallen, the weather looked promising. Soon it was time to take up our positions prior to the engine run-up, after which the wheel chocks were dragged away by the ground crew, and we taxied out to join the long line of Lancasters making their way to the end of the runway for takeoff. As we rumbled slowly along, I carried out one last check on my turret, tested the intercom, and fastened my seat belt. Came our turn for takeoff, and Bill lined us up with the runway. The intercom was buzzing with the voices of Bill and Reg as they made ready for receipt of the green light from the nearby control caravan, at one end of which stood the familiar group of well-wishers (the 'Press-on Gang', as it was known). As the Lancaster ahead of us lifted its heavy load from the runway and clawed for height, leaving four heavy black trails of exhaust streaming in its wake, we got the green light, and Bill opened the throttles wide. My turret began to bounce as the wheel brakes were held firmly against the wayward pull of the Merlins. Then, satisfied that the engines were set at the correct condition for takeoff, the brakes were released, and we began to roll down the runway, steadily gathering speed as we went.

Our Lancaster began to pound down the runway as the navigator began calling out the ever increasing airspeed. The tail wheel lifted, and I could see the big port rudder working as Bill countered the tendency of all Lancasters to pull over to the left on takeoff. As Dick Lodge called "One-twenty", the tail dipped low and the ride suddenly became smooth as we left the runway and soared out over the boundary fence.

Once airborne, we joined in the with rest of the heavily-laden bombers as they circled for height above the darkened Lincolnshire landscape. At ten thousand feet, we got the order to don oxygen masks, then turned onto the course that would take us out over The Wash on the first leg of the flight. We were still striving for altitude, and most of our comrades had faded from sight by the time we finally reached our operational height of twenty thousand feet, somewhere out over the North Sea.

THE BIG TIME

Two hours into the flight, Bill announced from the cockpit that the fires of Hamburg could be seen in the distance. "Seems a waste of time sending the Pathfinder boys out to mark this one", remarked Ken from the nose. One hour later, we were lining up for the dreaded bomb run. During much of the approach, I had been busy throwing out bundles of window. Soon the heavy flak began to burst near us, so I dispensed a few more, just for good measure.

"Bomb doors open. Markers in sight". The big stuff was bursting all over the place, and at about our height. "Two going down in flames to starboard" (this from the mid upper). "Another one astern", I put in. "Steady . . . right a little . . ., steady . . . , bombs going . . . , Bombs gone!", Now came the long wait for the photoflash to explode. "Flash gone!", came the welcome retort from Ken. Bill at once threw us into a tight diving turn to port. "Let's get to hell out of here", he yelled, just as a searchlight beam flashed across us, followed by two others.

The diving turn had the effect of shaking off the searchlights before they could catch us in a concentrated cone. It also did strange things to me and my turret: My stomach did a loop, and the sudden application of zero gravity sent the remaining bundles of window cascading in all directions around the turret, where they became lodged in various nooks and crannies - ammunition belts, gun mounts, on the floor, even down the back of my neck. As I retrieved them and hurled them out, I vowed that I would raise a strong objection to their presence in my turret on our return to base.

The remainder of the flight proved uneventful, and we touched down at Bardney just before 4:30 a.m., tired, but pleased at having got one more trip 'in the book'.

Compared to our first op, this one had been a piece of cake. Not so for Hamburg. That unfortunate city had been well alight by the time we dropped the bombs, and - even from a height of almost four miles, we could see whole streets plainly outlined by the burning houses on both sides. It was clear that vast areas of Hamburg were totally destroyed and, try as I might, I found difficulty in imagining the hell that the people down there must be experiencing. The treatment of the injured and the disposal of bodies would be a severe strain on the public utilities, and it was likely that loss of power, fractured water mains, and streets littered with the debris of fallen and burning buildings must be making the task of the unfortunate fire fighters and ambulance crews quite impossible.

After the debriefing, at which I complained about the stowing of window in the rear turret, we enquired about the fortunes of the other squadron crews involved, and were told that they had all returned to base safely. Not so on the following night however (July 30th). We were not down to fly that night, when Nine Squadron had been sent to bomb Remschied. During this attack, Lancaster JA-692 (WS/D) went down, taking with it the highly experienced crew of F/Lt Fox, plus an unfortunate Second Dickie. The aircraft had only been with the squadron for a month, and had completed less than one hundred flying hours since its arrival from the factory.

We were not called upon to fly again until the morning of Monday, August 2nd. When we were detailed to take ED-975 (WS/Y) for an hour of local flying, just to keep us on the ball. At a later date, this aircraft was to figure prominently in our fortunes (and otherwise). On return to base, we were told to get ready for ops that night. For this one, we were allocated ED-654 (WS/W). At briefing, we were surprised to learn that the target was again to be Hamburg, and one comedian was heard to remark on the danger of pilots becoming redundant because the squadron aircraft knew their own way to Hamburg and back. Our route was to be longer this time, with the main force jinking around northern Germany in an attempt to keep the Jerry defences guessing about the identity of our intended objective until almost the last minute.

Takeoff was later than usual - ten minutes before midnight -so it was to be yet another sleepless night for us and the survivors of Hamburg. Nevertheless, I reckoned that the rear turret of a Lancaster would provide greater comfort and safety than a Hamburg air raid shelter under the circumstances, and I much preferred my role in the proceedings to that of the unfortunate people down there beneath us. Window was again in use, but I was pleased to find that, as a result of my complaint (and that of others), the responsibility for its disposal had been passed to another member of the crew.

For us at least, the trip was again fairly straight forward and uneventful, although bad weather proved troublesome, and was probably the cause of the high loss rate (30 aircraft in all, representing almost 7% of those sent). The defences in the target area were less effective than before, and the smoke rising from the many fires which seemed to be raging totally out of control made bombing tricky. Nevertheless, I saw a number of aircraft going down, including one Lancaster which was under attack by a Focke-Wulf 190.

On arrival back at base after almost six hours in the air, we learned that one of the squadron aircraft had failed to return. This was ED-493 (WS/A). It had been on its thirty-seventh operation, and had been piloted by Sergeant D Mackenzie.

THE BIG TIME

Another batch of mail had filtered though from Canada, and this included the parcel I had been expecting from home, it contained the nylon stockings I had asked for, plus a large fruitcake which mother had lovingly prepared for me. Unfortunately, the time and handling involved in the eventual delivery of the parcel had proved to be more than the cake could withstand, so I ended up feeding it to the grateful sparrows and starlings that inhabited the trees and bushes around our Nissen Hut.

Included in the consignment were several letters from Margaret, the content of which was again centred mainly on the now familiar theme of her undoubted devotion to me and her concern for my safety. She had been following the progress of the European war as reported in the newspapers and on the cinema newsreels, and these had served to relieve her anxiety to some degree because, although she was not aware of it, they tended to report only the good news about the conflict. Since my posting to an operational squadron, there had been too much happening to distract my attention from the chore of letter writing, and, on reading hers, I felt shame at not having written to her more than once every week or so.

Since becoming operational, each member of the crew had been issued with a Smith and Wesson .38 revolver, but the carrying of this on a raid was optional. I had given much thought to the option, and had decided against taking the weapon with me on flights, as had most of the other crew members. I had reasoned that, in the event of me being shot down and captured, the Geneva Convention would provide me with some protection because I would thus have lost my aircraft, thereby becoming a non-combatant.If however, I was found to be carrying a hand gun, my impunity would be rendered invalid, thus exposing me to far greater risks at the hands of my captors.

Although, as previously mentioned, the carrying of revolvers was shunned by most crew members, I noticed that Clem, our wireless op, always had his with him on the raids, so I asked him for his reason. Although quite unexpected, his reply brought home to me just how personal the war had become, and the effect that our frequent exposure to danger was having on us. "If we ever get shot down", he said, "you won't find me screaming and panicking to escape a burning aircraft".

Eric Plunkett, my old friend from the earlier days of training in Canada - and the only one of those to be posted to the same squadron as I - soon found a secondary use for our new toys. We took to visiting a nearby farm on which was a wooded area rife with crows which the farmer was keen to get rid of. On first obtaining the farmer's permission, we spent many hours blazing away at the creatures in an attempt to rid him of the scourge. After a couple of afternoons at the sport, during which our total score amounted to just one crow, we armed ourselves with a couple of sten guns and a supply of ammunition drawn from the squadron armoury, and returned to the fray. However, we soon found that, despite our increased fire power, the number of hits we scored fell far short of that to be expected of two supposedly experienced and highly efficient Royal Air Force gunners, so we abandoned the project.

A regular feature of life on the squadron was the posting up in the Mess each morning of DRO's (Daily Routine Orders), and it was the responsibility of everyone to read these thoroughly each day because of the likely content. Apart from squadron business, the orders contained such items as postings, promotions, and the latest list of the names of those Air Force personnel who had been reported as missing or killed. On reading these on the day following my third visit to Hamburg. I read that Harvey Renaude had failed to return from his first operational sortie, a raid on the Renault works in France. This caused me to recall that I had been one of those who had joined him in celebrating his twenty-first birthday at Upper Heyford a few short weeks previously. It had been quite an occasion, and all those present had gone flat out to set up a new world record for the consumption in Harvey's honour of the local wallop. The night had seen a number of casualties, and the first to be carried back to the billet was no less a personage than Harvey himself. I, being sure of my ability to remain upright despite whatever quantity I might have consumed, set off alone one hour later in the direction of the billet, but got lost on a tennis court which separated it from the Mess, and was eventually roused and unceremoniously transported the rest of the way by the remaining revellers. Now the young, fun-loving Harvey was missing, and I found myself hoping that perhaps he had survived the ordeal, to be taken prisoner.

A week was to pass before we did any more operational flying. Apart from one bombing and air to sea firing exercise, most of our time was taken up by routine training and lounging around the airfield. One hour before midnight on Monday, August the 9th, 1943, we lifted off in DV-198 (WS/U) for a raid on Mannheim. 'U' was a recent arrival on the squadron, and was in spanking condition. We had a reasonably easy trip in her, but the short sea crossing and the much extended duration of flight over enemy territory called for a prolonged period of alertness on the part of us all. The target defences were on form,and we were treated to the now familiar assortment of punishment we had come to expect. I saw a few aircraft being shot down, and, in the light of the target, I saw an unfortunate Lancaster suddenly blow up for no apparent reason. It was on the bombing run (as we were at the time), and there were no flak bursts in the immediate vicinity. I could only presume that the Lanc had copped a load bombs from above.

One of our duties was to report and log all sightings of aircraft going down, and it fell to the navigator to note details of the time and approximate bearing in relation to our aircraft so that the point of impact could be plotted. No doubt such information was of use to the intelligence bods, but it could be time consuming, and I tended to dislike any duty which detracted from my main responsibility of searching the sky around us for enemy fighters.

On the night following our Mannheim trip, the squadron attacked Nurnburg, and ED-654 (WS/W), piloted by Pilot Officer Newton, returned with the rear gunner (Sgt McFerran) wounded and the mid upper gunner (Sgt Wilkinson) dead. WS/W, the aircraft we had taken to Hamburg eight nights previously, had been attacked by a German fighter. Our crew had been rested that night, so did not take part in the Nurnburg raid.

The crew was due to seven days' leave on the 17th of August, so the morning found us all dressed in number one blues and ready to catch our transport into Bardney for our trains. Unfortunately, ' the powers' nobbled us for a last minute dinghy drill. This was to take place in the giant emergency water supply tank at the side of one of the hangars. So it was that, with just over an hour to spare, seven immaculately dressed and very disgruntled airmen piled into the dinghy and pushed off from the railings to the cheers and jeers of the assembled audience. Our brief was to unpack the various items of life-saving equipment, including the 'tent' and the bright yellow 'coffee grinder' radio, and generally make ourselves comfortable. To me fell the task of winding furiously on the handle of the radio generator so that an S.O.S. message could be broadcast, thus making it possible for the rescue services to home in on the signal and plot our location.

The dinghy in use was not in pristine condition, it having sustained a good number of punctures during its lengthy period of use as a tool for training. The punctures had been dealt with through the medium of the tapered black plugs supplied for the purpose. Because of the large number of plugs in use, the fabric of our craft was far from airtight, and this called for a lot of effort on the part of Reg, who had been given the task of operating the manual bellows supplied for such a contingency. I, being a poor swimmer, was most anxious that he should not fail in his allotted task.

It was indeed most unfortunate for us that, in attempting to settle down in the limited space available, someone accidentally dislodged one of the many plugs, In the stark panic that followed this, the missing plug could not be found, and the dinghy began to deflate rapidly, despite Clem's attempt to save the situation by sitting firmly on the hole. On Bill's order, the hand paddles were quickly unshipped, and we proceeded to paddle furiously for the side of the tank, cheered on by our roisterous audience. Unfortunately, the air pressure soon fell below that capable of supporting our combined weight, and this in turn caused our craft to flounder and go down with all hands.

The time taken in us being fished out of the tank (before we could return to our Nissan hut for a complete change of clothing) caused us to miss the earlier trains we had planned on boarding, so it was late afternoon before I caught a train for Bristol with Reg, who had kindly invited me to spend my leave with him and his parents.

THE BIG TIME

CHAPTER 10

CRASH LANDING

Following my return to Bardney from leave, all of which I had spent in the delightful company of Reg and the Moseley's down in Bristol, I found that 9 Squadron had been highly active during my brief absence. Not only had it successfully attacked distant Milan no less than three times (August 12th., 14th. and 15th), but had also assisted greatly in the destruction of the German secret weapons' establishment at Peenemunde on the 17th., and had paid an unwelcome visit to Leverkusen on the night of the 22nd. The Peenemunde trip had proved to be one of Bomber Command's more remarkable success stories to date, together with the trouncing of Hamburg, and not forgetting Guy Gibson's earlier 'Dambuster' raid. Later in my career, I was to have the honour and the pleasure of meeting Wing commander Gibson, V.C., also Group Captain John Searby, the officer who led the attack on Peenemunde with commendable skill and courage. John went on to gain the rank of Air Commodore before his retirement, and he and I met many times and carried on a lively correspondence on matters aeronautical until his death in 1986.

In addition to these five raids, the squadron had already taken off for a trip to Berlin before my train arrived back at Bardney (on Monday, August 23rd). Fortunately, despite the considerable activity that the squadron had been involved in over the period, not one Nine Squadron aircraft had been lost, although some had suffered slight damage during the Peenemunde attack.

In the late evening of Tuesday the 24th, the station air raid sirens sounded. Only Clem, Dick Jones and I were in the hut at the time, the others having gone to visit the Station Hotel. The three of us decided to go outside and watch the show, expecting that Lincoln would be the target, but were surprised to find a total lack of activity in that direction. Instead, we could faintly hear the sound of aircraft engines high above us, accompanied by the staccato rattle of machine guns. Obviously, there was an air battle going on up there, but we saw no one being shot down, and there were no exploding bombs to be heard. After a brief period, the sound of aircraft faded away, followed by the sounding of the all clear.

Early next morning we were awakened by an announcement coming over the station Tannoy. A german aircraft had scattered a load of 'butterfly' bombs over the runways, dispersals and living quarters, and care was to be taken in avoiding these at all costs.

Each bomb resembled a large can of beans with a short shaft sticking out from one side of the tin. This had attached to it a pair of 'wings' which were deployed when the bomb was released from the aircraft, thus allowing it to float gently down towards the target. Once on the ground, the bomb was fused in such a way that it would explode immediately it was disturbed, and the contents were capable of affecting a much more lethal blast than anything that a mere can of beans could produce.

It was interesting to watch the method used by the bomb disposal squad in dealing with the hazard. An Austin van was backed up to within about fifty yards of the bomb, after which a sturdy rope with a loop at the end was paid out from the rear of the van, with the loop carefully placed around the area on which the bomb was resting. This done, the squad then got back into the van and drove off, dragging the rope behind, thus detonating the bomb with an explosion of sufficient magnitude to produce a medium sized pothole. Because many of the bombs had landed on the runways and perimeter tracks, some damage was caused in disposing of them. However, it was found possible that one runway was reasonably safe for use, so the squadron's aircraft were able to take off for the nearby airfield of Woodhall Spa, from which we were to operate during the next ten days while our own runways were undergoing repair and resurfacing.

From the somewhat crowded venue of Woodhall Spa, our squadron carried out a total of four raids against the enemy: Nurnburg on August 27th.; Munchen Gladbach on the 30th., and two trips to Berlin (August 31st and September 3rd.). We missed out on both trips to the Big City, but managed to log the Nurnburg and Munchen Gladbach flights. These we did in the trusty and well-maintained ED-975 (WS/Y). This Lancaster was the 'property' of Pilot Officer Stout and crew, and had been entrusted to us while they went off on a well-earned spell of leave. The Nurnburg flight was of more than eight hours duration (the longest yet for us), but it, together with the five-hour trip to Munchen Gladbach, proved moderately quiet, although ED-551 (WS/M) with F/Sgt Hall and crew failed to return from the flight. However, the squadron suffered no losses from the two Berlin raids.

the squadron resumed residence at the refurbished Bardney field after the second Berlin trip, and we were immediately placed on the battle order that night (September 5th.). This was to be our second raid on the city of Mannheim in less than a month. Mannheim was one of the more heavily defended

CRASH LANDING

targets visited by us so far, and the duration of our flight over Occupied Europe (6½ hours) again called for a lengthy period of alertness and concentration, particularly on the part of Dick Jones and myself.

Our tactics for dealing with the homeward journey also had to be changed because of the increased use of fighter flares by the Luftwaffe. The flares were like globes of white light which hung suspended in the sky by parachute. These were usually dropped in clusters of five or six, but seldom burned for more than a minute. However, the sighting of them was soon recognised as an indication that an enterprising fighter was lurking in the vicinity, ready to pounce on any unfortunate bomber that showed up in their light. Because darkness was our only friend, the sudden appearance of the flares close to the aircraft called for immediate evasive action, and a speedy escape back to the darkness.

There was no doubt in my mind that our carefully formulated crew tactics were effective. The Mannheim trip (from which we returned safely) had been our seventh to date. Although we had seen a lot of action taking place around us on these raids, we had managed to dodge most of it. Nevertheless, I sensed that crew efficiency and discipline were not the only factors necessary to survive! There still remained the element of luck, and we exercised no control over that. There was so much that could go wrong: a tyre bursting on takeoff; mechanical or structural failure; adverse weather conditions; collisions; having bombs dropped on us from above - the list of possible causes of death and destruction was extensive and frightening.

We found the target of Mannheim to be unsparing in the kind of activity we had come to expect of it: searchlights, flak bursts, flares, a lot of smoke, and a lot of aircraft - including several that were seen burning fiercely as they fell from the sky. Window was again in use, but it was becoming obvious that our worthy opponents were fast adapting themselves to the situation. There was a reduction in the amount of flak coming up, and the searchlights seemed to be concentrating on lighting up as much of the sky above the target as possible, thus increasing the likelihood of our bombers being sighted. Because window had for the present neutralized the German radar system, thus making the directing of their fighters onto us almost impossible, large numbers of single-seater aircraft were being deployed as free lance hunters. The pilots of these relied entirely on interception by sight, and were ably assisted by their practical liaison with the ground defences. Of course, this system of co-operation was only effective in the vicinity of the target, and I envisaged its advantage over us if the target was covered in cloud, as often it was. In such circumstances, we would appear to a high-flying fighter as so many flies crawling across an illuminated opaque screen, and would have difficulty detecting the approach of our attacker as he dived on us from the darkness above. We were to witness this phenomenon later, during the Battle of Berlin, when the target was often found to be covered by unbroken cloud.

As a crew, we were showing promise. Pilot Officer Siddle (he had been granted his commission on the day of our second flight to Mannheim) had a flair for leadership which produced a degree of co-operation and discipline that was not to be found in some of the other crews. (The 'chop rate' amongst new and inexperienced crews appeared to be highest during the first six trips, and we had just passed the magic figure). We were now into the second stage, during which complacency could produce the 'it'll never happen to us' syndrome which was so often accompanied by a slackening of concentration. This was probably the most dangerous of the three segments of a tour, and it was a pity that so many otherwise good crews succumbed so needlessly to careless overconfidence at this stage. The third and final segment of the tour (the remaining ten trips) affected the outlook of a crew in an entirely different way. During the months that you had spent with the squadron so far, you had come to estimate your chances of survival, and had rated them as very slim. Then, having entered number twenty in the log book, you suddenly realised that maybe you might just make it after all, and the resulting degree of caution could in itself be a danger.

The Mannheim trip proved disastrous for 9 Squadron. A Flight lost two aircraft: R-5744 (WS/E), Sgt Knight and crew, and ED-666 (WS/G) piloted by P/O Gill. Both crews had completed less than ten sorties with the squadron.

The following night (Monday, September 6th, 1943) found us again listed on the battle order. This time the target was Munich - again deep inside Germany - and we still had ED-975 (WS/Y) as our mount, although we would soon be returning her to Pilot Officer Stout and crew. I had during the previous few days spent a lot of time in burnishing the rear turret and tuning the guns to a fine pitch of operational efficiency, and was looking forward to the time when we would eventually have a Lancaster of our own, so to speak.

Takeoff was slated for early evening (18:45), and the trip was to take us eight hours and forty minutes in all. Darkness finally closed in on us as we were crossing the English Channel on the outward journey, and we settled down to what was expected to be a long and tiresome vigil. I had taken to flying without fastening my seat belt because I found it impossible to search the area beneath my turret unless I could stand up and peer out over the top of my gunsight. This tactic presented problems for me if the aircraft was engaged in evasive action, but I considered it important that I should be in a position to detect a possible attack on our most vulnerable point before it had time to develop.

As we droned out over the Channel, the silence of the intercom was occasionally interrupted by the quiet, business-like report of a crew member. "Levelling out at twenty thousand feet". Then, "We should be crossing the enemy coast in five minutes, and the Gee's packed up, skipper". This didn't mean that Gee, the navigational aid had developed a fault, but that the Jerries were jamming it. It also meant that navigation from this point on would depend entirely on the expertise of Dick Lodge as he sat out the trip in his tiny, curtained and dimly-lit 'office', sandwiched between the flight deck and the wireless operator's compartment. Immediately aft of the latter crew position was the sturdy armour-plated bulkhead, the door of which was always kept tightly closed in order to provide protection for the forward crew members from the danger that a fighter attack from the rear would produce. The presence of this bulkhead and its ever-closed door came to represent something of a symbol of us gunners from our comrades at arms. To Dick and me, it symbolised the dividing line between companionship and isolation; protection and exposure; aggression and defence - even between comfort and discomfort, since there was no heating in our dark and inhospitable domain. In the circumstances, it is not surprising that, in later years, we gunners were to form our own Association, with an international membership.

Glancing down, I could discern far below the faint line of phosphorescence that indicated the waves beating against the enemy coastline. "Crossing the cost now, Navigator", I reported. "Thank you," came the reply.

The long hours spent in searching the surrounding gloom for lurking shadows could be almost unbearably monotonous at times, and the sound of a voice was all that was needed to ease the feeling of total isolation and loneliness that was so much a part of the tail gunner's lot. From my perspex capsule at the extreme end of the aircraft, there was little to be seen except the receding hostile sky from which I was being transported by the almost invisible platform I

Fig 8. WS/Y down in the field at Minting, Lincolnshire, September 7th, 1943. On return from a raid on Munich. The missing tail section, complete with rear gun turret is hidden behing the hedge.

CRASH LANDING

was riding. The mid upper turret commanded a plan view of the complete Lancaster, but I could only see a small part of the tailplane on either side of my position.

Bill had taken on the habit of calling up each member of the crew (other than the flight engineer, who was usually at his side) at regular intervals of fifteen minutes, but I had noticed earlier in our training that I was not included in this routine, so I had asked him why this was. He had replied that there was no need for him to enquire of my wellbeing because my turret acted as a rudder, and that he could feel its movement on the aircraft's controls.

At times during a raid on enemy territory, I would attempt to relieve the monotony and anxiety by singing to myself over the noise of the engines, having first made sure that my microphone was switched off. My repertoire contained a few Country favourites, but was made up mostly of the hits of the time. Of the latter, there was one that I considered to be appropriate to my particular situation. Featuring the young Anne Shelton, it was entitled "You'd Be so Nice To come Home To", and seemed to sum up exactly the sentiments I was beginning to feel concerning Margaret.

We were now ten minutes away from the target, and the trip had been routine so far. Wind speed and direction predictions had been about right, and we were on track and on time. We had witnessed a few casualties during the outward journey, but had come to expect this. The victims were usually some unfortunates who had wandered off track and strayed away from the collective safety of the main stream, and this usually resulted in them being caught up in the concentrated fire power of a built up area. As a general rule however, the casualty rate was highest in the area of the target and on the homeward leg of the flight. This was because, until then, the fighter force was uncertain of the intended target, thus precluding an organized concentration of resources. Having attacked the target, our next objective (home) was plain, and the Jerry fighters were always quick to seize on the advantage.

Once again I began to experience the now familiar and unpleasant feeling in the pit of the stomach, and the dryness of the throat as we began our run to the target. Although the actual assault on our objective was probably no more hazardous than the rest, it was always a time of intense vigilance and tension, caused largely by the feeling of naked exposure one got when having to traverse an illuminated area which contained so much activity.

Ken was busy giving directions as we lined up on the target with the bomb doors open. There seemed to be just the usual enemy activity: plenty of searchlights combing the sky for customers; one poor sod coned over on the port beam; the expected haphazard mix of light and heavy flak coming up; there were no fighters to be seen so far, but I wasn't complaining about that.

"Bombs gone!". It was all routine so far. Just the wait for the photoflash, then nose down and head for home, weaving like hell.

I was traversing my turret to the starboard beam in search of trouble when we got it. Above and just to starboard, and directly in my line of sight, I beheld a blinding, dull red flash, and heard the deafening "whump!" as a heavy ack-ack shell burst a few yards away.

Our wounded Lancaster at once dropped her right wing to the vertical as if recoiling from the searing heat of the explosion, and it looked like we were going to turn turtle completely. But Bill must have been fighting furiously with the controls, for she slowly levelled out and resumed her normal attitude.

"Crew reports", Bill called out, and began calling each position in turn, beginning with me. "Tail Gunner O.K.", I replied. The check continued. Mid upper, wireless op., flight engineer, bomb aimer - all O.K., but there was no response from the navigator. "Check the nav., wireless op.", Bill ordered. There was a brief silence, then "He's alright, skip. He's down on the floor. Says he's looking for his pencils!".

Next, the skipper asked for damage reports. "Any sign of fire?", he asked. There was none, and Reg reported that all engines appeared to be running normally, but he couldn't be certain because some of his instruments had been hit. "I can see a few holes in the starboard wing", Dick reported from the mid upper turret. "They're mostly outboard of the engines, and it looks like the after end of the fuselage has been well peppered". Fortunately for me, my turret appeared to have escaped damage, although I could see a couple of small holes in the starboard rudder fin.

Bill remarked that the engine and flight controls were responding normally, so it appeared that we had been extremely lucky to have escaped with so little damage.

Once clear of the immediate danger, we settled down to the long homeward flight across the hostile skies of Western Europe. During the hour immediately following on the flak burst, we had investigated the extent of the damage as best we could, and this seemed to be mostly superficial. There were a good number of small holes to be seen, but the riggers

CRASH LANDING

would soon have them patched up - hopefully before we had to hand her back to her regular crew.

As we flew westwards through the darkness, I began to reflect on how we had fared as a crew since joining the squadron. This was only our eighth operational sortie, yet it was the second occasion on which we had been clobbered by flak. During the same period, the squadron had suffered the loss of five aircraft and crews, plus one death and a couple of injuries. Based on a rough calculation, these figures represented a chop rate of little less than a quarter of the squadron's total strength in crews and aircraft. These losses had been realised in the space of just six weeks, and the realisation caused me to seriously doubt the chances of us ever managing to survive a complete tour.

In Bomber Command, the first tour consisted of thirty trips, so that we had a further twenty-two to complete before we could even think about any degree of relaxation. One did not need the mathematical brain of an Einstein in order to arrive at the frightening conclusion that our chances of pulling it off were microscopic. The odds against us were so great that no self-respecting punter would ever have anything to do with them.

We had been airborne for the best part of five hours, and the monotony was beginning to have an effect, so I decided to take a couple of wakey-wakey pills in order to ward off the drowsiness that was creeping over me. As I eased my oxygen mask aside in order to take the tablets. I got a strong whiff of a substance which I instantly recognised as one-hundred octane petrol. I at once reported this to the skipper, and there followed an in-depth investigation into the accuracy of the damaged instrument panel. It was decided that three of the six fuel gauges were functioning normally, but that it was probable that at least one tank (probably one monitored by a suspect fuel gauge) had been holed. Bill and Reg then got involved in a discussion on the transfer of fuel from various tanks to others by means of the cross-feed system, a subject with which I was not familiar. Because we had undoubtedly lost an unknown quantity of fuel, there was also a need for fuel conservation, and this was agreed and adopted.

We had not yet reached the enemy coast, and the fighters were still amongst us, as was evinced by the number of aircraft to be seen spiralling down. One of these had bought it while flying close behind us on the starboard quarter. I was unable to see the fighter, but had seen the tracers strike home shortly before a wing began to burn brightly, casting a revealing red glow in our direction. We slid away from the danger and logged yet another casualty.

We were just crossing the French coast on the homeward leg when it was discovered that our starboard outer engine was showing signs of overheating. During the brief discussion that followed, it was decided that the engine had probably sustained some damage to the cooling system as a result of the flak burst, and Bill ordered it to be shut down and feathered. Because we would be descending for the rest of the flight, the loss of the engine would not greatly affect the performance of an unladen Lancaster, and we would also be saving on whatever quantity of fuel was still available to us. In truth, the need to shut down the engine was a blessing in disguise, and would to some extent serve to conserve our precious fuel still further. Although we were unable to calculate the total of fuel on board, it had been reckoned that, all things considered (the estimated loss through a ruptured tank, plus the saving on the dead engine), we should have sufficient in reserve to make it back to home base comfortably.

At last the English coast passed beneath us, and we were soon within sight of the Bardney beacon. Because we were late, the circuit was almost devoid of aircraft as we joined it, and Bill requested landing instructions over the r/t. As he was doing so, Reg reported that the starboard inner engine was showing signs of losing power. Bill at once requested landing priority, which was granted. As we hurriedly lined up for the runway, the faulty engine appeared to right itself, so we prepared for a normal three-engined landing.

We entered the funnel and lined up for the approach, and as we did so I positioned my turret in the dead astern position in order to avoid the rudder effect. We were now flying at about two hundred feet, and were about one mile from touchdown. Revs and pitches had been set on the three remaining engines, and the order had been given for wheels and flaps to be lowered. Everything seemed to be O.K. from where I was sitting. She wallowed slightly as the flaps were applied, and I could see that Bill was correcting the swing with the rudders as we continued our descent.

The first indication I got that anything was wrong was when I 'discerned an abrupt change in the note of the three remaining engines. There was a lot of popping and coughing taking place, and the aircraft at once swung sharply to starboard, seemingly out of control.

"What the hell's happening?", Bill shouted as he struggled with the controls in an attempt to right the aircraft. "I don't know, Skipper" Reg replied in a voice that lacked the calm and confidence that it usually projected. "We've got red lights showing all over the

CRASH LANDING

place".

"Brace for a crash!"

In the eerie silence that followed the order, I watched the barely discernable horizon drop from my view as the nose dipped sharply downwards and our aircraft began its death dive, then righted itself for a brief moment as Bill fought desperately with the almost useless controls. In the few brief seconds that remained before impact, my thoughts raced furiously as I took stock of our situation. We were without power, and the drag of the lowered undercarriage and wing flaps was adding to the problem. These could not be retracted because the hydraulics were no longer functioning. We could not bale out because we were too low. At less than two hundred feet, a parachute would not have time to open fully before its wearer struck the ground. There just was not anything we could do except sit tight and hope for the best.

"What a bloody awful way to die!", I though, as I tried to prepare myself for whatever the event might bring.

Having sensed that the moment of impact must be near, I forced my back hard against the turret doors, just as I felt the Lanc give a sudden judder, and I heard the sound of tearing metal coming from I knew not where. We were still in a nose-down gliding attitude, but we had hit something a glancing blow - probably a tree or a building. Then I felt the tailplane shake and vibrate violently, and I was forced away for the doors, only to be pounded relentlessly on either side of the head by the oscillating gun mounts. I instinctively raised my arms and clasped my hands behind my head in an effort to ward off the blows. Then we hit once more, and I lost all sense of direction as I felt myself and my turret spinning through space at an alarming rate. There was just one more sickening impact amid all the turmoil and confusion. I felt a severe blow to the back of my head, and this was accompanied by a sharp pain, the seat of which I was unable to determine. There was so much pain. Then, the pain eased, and there was nothing but nothingness; peace; silence; oblivion.

CHAPTER 11

THE HOSPITAL

Gradually, almost imperceptibly, the deathly silence gave way to faint, confused sounds, Strange, mysterious sounds. Metallic sounds. Movement. Distant, unintelligible snatches of conversation. Sight. Vaguely familiar objects in an unfamiliar setting. A feeling of disorientation. The acrid smell of hot metal. Smoke. Pain. The gradual return of reasoning. Surely, there would be no pain after death? Must be still alive.

The restoration of perceptivity brought with it a recollection of recent events. The landing approach. That was it! I was in a bomber. Tail gunner. engine trouble. We were going to crash. Must be down now. Must have been unconscious. How Long? Wonder how the rest of the crew are? No smoke without fire. Got to get out of here. don't panic. Situation calls for clear thinking. What are my injuries? Will I be able to escape without assistance? Is there anyone to give aid? The others must be injured, too. Better get cracking and help them if I can. Got to take stock of things now.

The gradual return of discernment made this possible. Raising my head from its resting place on the reflector sight, I could see that the turret appeared to be lying face down, with the Brownings buried in the soft soil beneath. At least, three of them were. The forth was nowhere to be seen. There was little left of the perspex canopy of the turret. Only the twisted framework remained. I was no longer wearing my helmet and goggles, and my hair was saturated in the blood that poured from a head wound. I was lying face-down with my left leg cradled on top of the empty No 1 gun mounting tray, so that I had taken up the stance of a high kicking dancer. The flying boot was missing, and I feared that the leg must be broken. However, an investigative test disproved this, although I found that retrieval of the limb from the ridiculous position it was in was impossible because of the pain. In addition, the left side of my face was painful and badly swollen, and I suspected that I might have a broken jaw.

The turret appeared to be still attached to whatever was left of the tailplane, because I could see the starboard elevator and rudder to my left. The port section of tailplane was missing, and it seemed that the fuselage had been wrenched off somewhere near the tail, and that this part of the aircraft must be jutting skywards above me, still precariously supported in this position by the remaining starboard elevator and rudder.

The feeble light of the coming dawn made possible the recognition of nearby shapes and shadows. The first of these to capture my interest was a cow gazing into the wreckage of my turret with big, round, questioning eyes. Beyond this most welcome indication of my continued mortality lay the twisted remains of a three-bladed prop, complete with its spinner. Other unrecognizable pieces of debris could be seen scattered around. It looked as if WS/Y would never again get off the ground.

A strong smell of burning hung in the air, but I took this to be coming from the rest of the aircraft, wherever it might be. There was certainly no fire in the part I was in. On trying them, I found the sliding metal doors behind me jammed tight. No getting out that way. My only other means of escape was through the side of the turret, but it was obvious that I would need some help. Some way off, I could see three clumsily-clad men, two standing, the other lying on the grass at their feet.

"When you've got a minute", I called out to them, "could you give me a hand to get out of this bloody mess?". The response was immediate and, as the two mobile members hurried over - causing the cow to amble away - I recognised them as Clem, the wireless op, and Dick Lodge, the navigator. it seemed that there were at least four survivors, but what about the other three, I wondered.

"How are the others?" I asked. "Well, we're all alive, Dick replied, "but Ken and Dick Jones both have back injuries. That's Ken over there on the grass. Reg is badly smashed up, but old Bill isn't too bad. he's got a few bumps and scrapes, but they'll soon have him patched up. he's gone to the farm over there to phone for the ambulances".

"And this idiot [Clem indicated the navigator], he's got a broken arm. Fell down getting out of the wreck and broke it".

"Don't push your luck, Clem," Dick snapped "You came through without a scratch, but you could still land in hospital along with the rest of us. Now let's see if we can get Clayton out of there".

"You'll need an axe", I suggested. "Should be one in the fuselage somewhere". Clem went off to find one.

"I don't mind telling you", Dick said after Clem had gone, "I got one helluva shock when you shouted at us just then. We'd been over to look at you, and we thought you'd bought it. You certainly looked dead to us. Anything broken?"

THE HOSPITAL

"Don't think so, Dick, but I can't say for sure until I get out of here".

Clem returned with the axe and immediately tackled the framework of my turret while Dick Lodge supervised the operation. soon a hole of sufficient size to allow for my exit from the twisted remains of my Frazer-Nash FN20 turret (or should I say Warrant Officer Smith's) had been made.

Once free of the wreckage, I found that I could hobble around, but with some difficulty. Despite this, I decided to reconnoitre the immediate area of the crash. The light was improving, so that I could see that we had crashed near a small hamlet which I later learned was Minting, Lincolnshire, and our arrival had served to supply a local farmer with an instant scrapyard of considerable proportions. During the final seconds of our flight, the starboard wing tip had clipped the branches of a tall oak, and this explained the violent vibration of the tail section. This had in turn caused the fuselage to fracture just behind the mid-upper turret, after which the ragged tail section had dug into the ground, causing it to perform a series of somersaults before half burying my turret in the soft earth. The remainder of the Lanc, containing the other six members of the crew had then bounded over a hedge, striking more trees, and shedding props, wheels and bits of undercarriage in all directions before executing an undignified bellyflop in the next field.

Someone had brought the first aid kit from its stowage in the fuselage, so we had all been suitably patched up. Reg, the flight engineer appeared to have suffered most. Apart from his less obvious injuries, he had suffered a number of facial cuts on being thrown against the instrument panel on impact, and one of his eyes was hanging from its socket. Ken, our bomb aimer, was feeling a lot of pain because of his back injury, as was Dick Jones, the mid upper gunner. Clem, the wireless operator had totally avoided harm by thrusting his parachute pack against the Marconi set and burying his head in it. Dick Lodge, the navigator had also (as mentioned), survived the crash unscathed, but had slipped and fallen from one of the roof escape hatches when leaving the aircraft, in his eagerness to get out in case of fire, and had broken an arm in the process. Thankfully, there was no fire, probably because there wasn't any fuel left to burn.

Bill Siddle had by this time returned to the scene, bringing with him two occupants of the nearby farmhouse. He too had come through the crash with remarkable good fortune, although his blood-bespattered features belied it. In his case, abandoning the aircraft had been a simple matter: he had gone head first through the windscreen on impact, taking with him a portion of the control column to which he had been clinging. Apart from a few cuts and sprains, his chief complaint was the loss of a number of front teeth.

Bill was equally surprised to learn that I had survived the ordeal, having earlier agreed with the others that I had gone for a burton. On reflection, I could understand having been written off. On returning to the turret intent on retrieving the missing helmet and boot, I was shocked at the sight of the mangled position I had occupied a short time earlier. Most of the perspex canopy had been shattered, and there seemed to be blood everywhere. One of my guns was missing, and the remaining three were firmly buried in the soil beneath the upturned turret. The hinged curtain of armour plating which normally travelled up and down with the guns had been wrenched from its fixings, and the turret control column lay drunkenly to one side, apparently broken off at the base. Fractured and kinked ammunition belts hung out through the distorted frames of the canopy.

I found my helmet lying beside the starboard rudder, but the goggles and oxygen mask had been wrenched off, and both were missing, as was the flying boot. It occurred to me that the missing items might be lying somewhere in the path that the aircraft had taken after having struck the first tree, but I was beginning to feel the effects of shock, and was also getting some unwelcome attention from an irate bull, so decided to end the search. No doubt the recovery crew would find the missing items.

By the time I had rejoined the others, someone had recovered a partially-filled flask of tea which had survived the crash, and its contents were being doled out to the more deserving survivors. Someone had improvised a splint for the navigator's arm, and it seemed that everything that could be done to ease the suffering of the less fortunate had been taken care of. All that remained to do was to await the arrival of the ambulances. The farmer's wife came out carrying a tray of beakers and a pot of steaming hot tea, which we gratefully accepted. Soon afterwards, the two ambulances were seen making their way along a road some distance from the farm, and it was obvious that their crews had missed the crash site. Clem hurriedly saved the situation by retrieving the Very pistol from the wreckage and firing off a couple of flares. A few minutes later, we were all being loaded up for the twenty-mile journey that would take us to the RAF hospital at Rauceby, near Sleaford.

Rauceby Hall was a stately country mansion that had been requisitioned for the purpose of providing

THE HOSPITAL

medical care for Air Force personnel in similar circumstances to our own. The hall itself topped a wooded rise within the spacious grounds, and a large temporary annex had been constructed some way down the hill, apparently for the purpose of providing accommodation for the overspill of patients from the main building.

The time was six-thirty, and the reception area was buzzing with activity as we were helped in from the ambulances. The room was already crowded, another crew in similar circumstances having been brought in earlier. As a consequence, the lone Air Force doctor on duty was being hard pressed to deal with the sudden influx of casualties resulting from the night's action.

Although inadequate in number, the collection of nurses and orderlies assisting the doctor wasted no time in dealing with our various bumps and scrapes, and we had all been examined, diagnosed, given treatment and put to bed within an hour of our arrival - all except Clem, who had been checked out as uninjured, and was supplied with transport back to Bardney. I was told that I had suffered concussion, scalp lacerations, severe bruising, and shock. X-rays revealed the absence of fractures, and it had been decided that my wounds would not require any stitches. On having the wound expertly dressed by an attractive but overworked young WAAF nurse, I was treated to a shot of pain-killing morphia and put to bed. Meanwhile, the other members of the crew had been spirited away to another part of the complex. I was anxious to know of their condition and whereabouts, but the drug soon took effect, and I drifted blissfully into a deep and much appreciated state of oblivion.

Some ten hours later, I awoke to find that I was in a ward containing about fifteen beds, all of which were occupied by total strangers. On inquiring of one of the nurses about the whereabouts of the other members of my crew, I was told that they were down in the annex, the section to which cases involving fractures and other more serious injuries were normally admitted.

My ward was just one of the many rooms of Rauceby Hall, all of which had been converted into wards and treatment rooms. This one was on the ground floor, near to the rear of the building, and must have been adjacent to the kitchen, judging from the sounds I could hear coming from that direction. The WAAF nurses were busily engaged in serving the evening meal to the patients, ably assisted in the task by the more mobile of those in their care.

After the meal, I got acquainted with some of my fellow sufferers, and learned that the ward was populated mainly by aircrew types who had either been wounded by flak or bullets, or - as in our case - had been involved in a flying accident. I learned that two of the beds contained members of the ground staff, and this caused me to realise something of the value of these men and the dangers to which they could also be exposed during the execution of their various duties.

Adjustment to the rigours of hospital confinement was eased by the excellent care and attention lavished on us by the overworked and seemingly tireless WAAF nursing staff. I was soon to learn that, apart from their normal ward commitments, their off-duty trips into nearby Sleaford often involved them in shopping for our requirements, with such items as toothpaste, razor blades, newspapers, books, matches and cigarettes being high on our list of essentials. Smoking on the wards was permitted (even by the bed-ridden). The willingness of these girls to carry out tasks in excess of their function was to me more remarkable because of the fact that most of them were of the lowest rank in the air force, whereas their Canadian counterparts, serving in the RCAF establishments all held commissioned rank.

Much of our time was spent in reading, snoozing, or just chatting, with the occasional self-evident lineshoot thrown in. One of the nurses had supplied me with a book of crossword puzzles, most of which I managed to complete during my ten days in residence because, for the first four days, I was compelled to remain in bed. I had taken to complaining bitterly about this - mainly because of the embarrassing inconvenience such confinement forced upon me - but also because I felt well enough to be up and doing. However, the doctor had insisted that I must remain immobile until he conceded otherwise, so that was the end of the argument.

On my insistence, I was being kept well informed on the progress of the other crew members. Their condition was steadily improving, but it was likely that Reg, Ken and Dick Jones would require a longer term in hospital than Bill, Dick Lodge and me, because of the more serious nature of their injuries. All five of them were in the same ward down in the annex, and I was intent on paying them a visit as soon as I was allowed out of bed.

On my fifth day in hospital, it was decided that I was well enough to get up and take an active part in the day-to-day routine of the ward. At first, my field of activity was limited to the immediate confines of the ward itself, and involved me in the serving of meals to the other patients. My progression to the perpendicular was celebrated by the issue to me of the standard 'walking out' uniform of light blue trousers and jacket, white shirt, and bright red tie. Although

THE HOSPITAL

the new garb was a far cry from the elegance of anything tailor-made, I considered it to be a big improvement on the ill-fitting service pyjamas with which I had been hastily supplied on my arrival.

I at once requested permission to visit the others down in the annex, but this was refused on the grounds that I was not yet well enough to be allowed outside. The others were similarly confined, so it seemed that it would be some days before a reunion could be held.

Came the second day of my freedom from 'the sack', and I found myself promoted to the dizzy heights of dishwasher. On taking up this new appointment, I was delighted to find that it provided me with an excellent view of the annex from the large casement window above the sink, and I at once decided that this would afford an excellent means of escape. Prior reconnaissance had indicated the futility of an attempted exit via the main entrance. This I had found to be guarded by a matronly woman of uncertain rank, but of devastating authority. On having found me lurking within her domain, she had wrathfully made it known to me that I was out of bounds, whereupon I was forcefully propelled back to the ward.

That afternoon, on having finished the washing up, I suddenly found myself alone in the kitchen, so quietly raised the window and climbed out. It didn't take me long to complete the walk down the slope and through the trees to the annex. My left knee was giving some pain, and I was surprised to find that I felt distinctly weak and light headed, but put this down to my prolonged stay in bed.

A few visitors were already in attendance as I strolled somewhat unsteadily into the ward containing the rest of the crew. The first that I recognised was Dick Lodge, so I hobbled over and sat down on the edge of his bed.

"Hello, Clayton", he said, extending his good arm to shake my hand. "Up and out already, are you?".

"Up, yes. But don't tell anybody you've seen me out", I replied, then went on to explain my surreptitious presence at his bedside. Dick was sporting a hefty plaster cast, but appeared to be otherwise bright and cheerful, as ever. He assured me that he was feeling fine, but wouldn't be able to plot a course for a week or two yet. I asked him about the others, and he said that they were all improving, but that Reg had got the worst of the deal. The medics had managed to save his eye, but his other injuries would need a lot of treatment yet. Ken's condition was equally serious, and it looked as if both he and Reg would be in hospital for some time yet, as would Dick Jones, who also had quite serious spinal injuries.

Bill Siddle was already decked out in similar attire to mine as he came down the ward to join us. Because he was taller than the average airman, they had been unable to supply trousers of sufficient leg length for his lanky frame, but I managed to stifle a laugh at the spectacle of his approach. He had just been to the doctor's office to get the inside story about the prospects of the other members of his crew. He himself was to be discharged in a couple of days, and was looking forward to some sick leave, which he intended to spend with his wife and family up in Penrith.

Bill told me that, as far as the others were concerned, it looked unlikely that Reg and Ken would ever again be fully fit for further operational flying, and there was some doubt surrounding Dick Jones' future with the crew. He also had spinal problems, and was about to be transferred to a hospital at Hoylake in Cheshire so that he could be near his immediate family in Wallasey.

As things stood at the time, we still had a pilot, a navigator, a wireless operator, and a tail gunner left out of what I had considered to be a first-class bomber crew. It was likely that we would be faced with the selection of two, possibly three new members, and would then be required to train these men to the standard of proficiency we had so far attained.

Afterwards, I walked down the ward to where Ken was, and exchanged a few words with him. Although he was pleased to see me, it was obvious that he was suffering pain, and seemed to be under sedation, so I didn't remain with him for long. Reg and Dick Jones both had visitors with them, so I just smiled and gave them the thumbs-up sign as I passed their beds. Reg was deep in conversation with his girl friend Edna, who had travelled over from Bristol to be with him, and Dick was equally absorbed in talking to Edith, the breathtakingly attractive nurse from county Durham about which he never tired of talking, as I could now understand.

Although there was no way of me knowing it then, I was not to meet Reg and Ken again until some time after the war had ended.

Because I was anxious to return to my own ward before being missed, I took leave of the others and left the annex, turning in the direction of the main building. I was still experiencing grogginess, and my less than perfect perambulatory appointments presented a problem as I launched myself up the steep wooded slope that lay between me and the Hall. By the time I had reached the half-way stage of the journey, I was feeling distinctly weak, and was per-

THE HOSPITAL

spiring freely, so clung to the bole of a tree and waited for the feeling of exhaustion to subside. After resting for a few minutes, I felt sufficiently strong to continue up the hill to the still open window, and was relieved to find, on peering cautiously inside, that the kitchen was still unoccupied. Unfortunately, I then found that I didn't have sufficient strength left to climb back in. On assessing my predicament, I reasoned that the only other means of access was by way of the main entrance. With luck, the dragon guarding that prestigious portal might be absent, in which case my illicit absence from the ward could pass without detection. Having so decided, I made my way cautiously around to the other side of the Hall, taking care to dodge beneath each window as I passed.

Unfortunately, Lady Luck had deserted me, and I found my Amazonian protagonist still holding court as I tried without success to slink past unnoticed. As she fixed me with a gaze that spoke volumes of evil, I cursed my own stupidity at not having realised that there must be other doors somewhere at the rear of the building. Too late! I was immediately subjected to a tirade of verbal abuse of which any Air Vice Marshall would have been justifiably proud, after which I was frog marched back to the ward and promptly put to bed, with orders from the doctor that I should remain there until further notice.

In order to relieve the monotony that afternoon, I engaged in conversation with the fellow in the bed next to mine. Also a tail-end charlie, he was in for treatment to bullet wounds which he had picked up during combat with a Kraut Fokke-Wulfe 190. He had been in two previous 'winding matches' with Jerry fighters, and had shot both of these down. But the last one had been nobody's fool. The enemy had been spotted early, and the standard corkscrew had been ordered at exactly the right time. But, instead of trying to follow the bomber's irregular flight path, the FW pilot had simply kept the Lanc in view and waited until it had taken up its most vulnerable position. This was at the point at which it ceased its climbing turn and began to go into a dive. By this time, the speed had dropped, and it presented a sitting target to the fighter as it topped the climb.

"That bastard knew the standard corkscrew off pat!", my friend assured me. "He knew exactly what we were going to do next, and he just hung around and waited for us to fly through his sights, then he let us have it. Luckily, we managed to find a cloud, and we lost him that way. But not before he had given us one hell of a hammering!".

During the next couple of days, I gave a lot of thought to what I had learned from this conversation, and I decided to discuss it with Bill once we were back on the squadron, with a view to formulating our own tactic. The standard corkscrew manoeuvre was a good one, and presented the attacking fighter with a difficult target to hit. But the effectiveness of the corkscrew depended on the attacking aircraft trying to duplicate the tortuous track of the quarry. If Jerry knew what the next move would be, and conditions were right, he held the ace. On thinking about it, I recalled that some spitfire pilots seemed to have the edge over me during fighter affiliation exercises, and I reasoned that this must be because they knew the pattern.

On the tenth day of my stay at Rauceby Hall, I was finally discharged from hospital, issued with a travel warrant, and given orders to return to my squadron. By late evening, I was back amongst the familiar sights and faces of Bardney.

THE HOSPITAL

CHAPTER 12

RECUPERATION

Next morning I reported to the flight offices, and was told that I had been granted twelve days' sick leave, to be taken immediately. Yet another travel warrant was issued to me, together with orders that, at the completion of the leave, I was to report to the RAF station at Waddington in Lincolnshire for a period of recuperation. Bill had been released from hospital and was on leave, and Clem had also been granted some time off, so I was the only member of the crew still on the premises.

I rode a train to London that afternoon, having resigned myself to spending yet another week or more of unrelenting boredom. Early evening found me booked in at the RCAF NCO's Club in Gloucester Road, SW7. This was an old but attractive period house which had been taken over for the purpose of providing temporary accommodation for lonely Canucks such as I during periods of enforced relaxation. The place was staffed entirely by Canadian girls from some voluntary order or other, and they did much to provide an atmosphere that vaguely resembled home life in our native Canada.

Once settled into my room, I went downstairs to have a look at the register, just in case there was somebody in residence that I knew. There wasn't. Dick Lodge had earlier supplied me with the telephone number of his parents' home in Barking, Essex, so I decided to give them a call, if only to introduce myself and give them some first-hand information on how he was bearing up to his confinement. His mother answered the telephone, and surprised me by stating that Dick was being released from hospital in two days' time, when he would be coming home on leave. He was still wearing the plaster cast, but this would be removed after his leave. She then invited me to come down to Barking and spend a few days with them while Dick was at home, and I was only too pleased to accept the offer.

I spent the next couple of days just wandering around the West End, window shopping, saluting every officer that I met, and getting thoroughly browned off. On the second day, I walked into the Maple Leaf club, intent on grabbing a hamburger and a cup of coffee, and the first person I met was none other than Gerry Rose, son of the boss of the dry cleaning plant I had worked in back in Saskatoon. He had been second in command in those days, but was now a commissioned officer in the Canadian Army. We spent a couple of pleasant hours downing pints and remembering the old times and places that we knew. Gerry was waiting to be posted overseas. Probably to Italy.

I found Dick Lodge's home a most pleasant detached dwelling situated on Longbridge Road, in Barking. The house was occupied by his parents (both retired), and his sister and her husband, who I understood to be working at the Ford factory, just down the road in Dagenham. Dick was making good progress following on our accident, and was looking forward to getting the crew back together again. On being asked, he gave me what information he could on the condition of the others. Dick Jones had been removed to Hoylake for further treatment, and appeared to be improving, but things didn't look too good for Reg and Ken. As things stood, it was likely that we would be able to salvage most of the crew, but it seemed almost certain that we would be losing our flight engineer and our bomb aimer.

The following day we spent in a conducted tour of the Ford factory at Dagenham - a most interesting and educational experience - and the tour took up most of the day. It being wartime, the plant wasn't producing many automobiles, mostly armoured cars and other items of military transport. The factory itself was enormous, and we were shown every stage in the production, from the making of the engine block castings, right through the paint spraying process and final assembly. I had heard it said that a completed vehicle was driven from the assembly line at intervals of two minutes, and I was given the opportunity of verifying this to my own satisfaction.

During the course of my stay with Dick and his parents, I was introduced to a number of family friends. One of these was a young girl named Doris. An attractive and outgoing person, I put her age at about seventeen, and we shared a couple of dates during my stay at Barking. She was a good vocalist, and I spent some time basking in her popularity during the visits we made to the clubs and dance halls in the area. At the end of my leave, she expressed a desire to continue our friendship. My thoughts were on Margaret, back home in Saskatoon, and I didn't really want to get involved with anyone else. But Doris wasn't the type who would take 'no' for an answer, so I gave her my squadron address before leaving.

On the morning of my departure for Waddington, (and because I was not yet fully familiar with the British rail transport system) I thought it best that I should make inquiries of the RTO (Railway Transport Office) concerning what train I should catch in order to get there. The young WAAF Corporal on duty instructed me to catch a train at 14:00 hours from a

RECUPERATION

designated platform at Euston station, and also gave me details of a change of trains that would be necessary in order for me to reach my intended destination before 23:59 hours, the time at which my leave pass would expire.

I was puzzled to find on arrival at Euston that all the trains bore the letters 'LMS', and I remembered that those that I had seen in the Lincolnshire area had been marked 'LNER'. However, since there was no mention of Lincoln in the advice given to me by the RTO (my instructions were to change trains at a place named Crew) I took this to mean that Waddington must be served by a different line, so I boarded my train as instructed.

By the time I had realised the mistake, the train that I was riding was already half way to its first stopping place - Crewe. On discussing my dilemma with a fellow passenger, the cause of the error became clear to me. On requesting directions to Waddington in Lincolnshire, the WAAF corporal must have misunderstood me. No doubt this was due to my Canadian accent, because, as my fellow traveller suggested, she had directed me to Warrington in Lancashire. Due to my ignorance of the geography of the British isles. I was totally unaware of the fact that Crewe lay some sixty miles west of Lincoln, on the border with Wales.

As I was to learn later that night, the British rail system was organized in such a way that travel in north/south direction was fast and efficient, but journeys in a lateral direction necessitated the use of branch lines, and this entailed many changes of trains, with unavoidable delays.

As soon as I detrained at Crewe, I went straight to the RTO office on one of the platforms to request further instructions. The Flight Sergeant in charge proved most helpful in that he laboriously mapped out a new route for me, from which it became obvious that there was no hope of me reaching Waddington before my leave pass had expired. In reality, the earliest that I could expect to arrive at my new posting would be well into the next morning. The F/Sgt then initialled my pass and supplied me with a hand-written and signed note explaining the reason for the error.

Thus equipped, I boarded an eastbound train and began what was to be the most exasperating journey I was ever to undertake. Of the several mixed passenger/freight trains involved, each was unheated, and prolonged and frequent stops were necessary in order to take on passengers, mail and milk churns at each and every whistle stop along the route.

So it was that I eventually reached the guardroom at 'Waddo'. The time was eight-thirty in the morning, and this meant that my leave pass had expired by eight hours and thirty-one minutes. I felt confident that, on presenting my pass to the SP on duty, I would be required to supply a reason for being late, but considered it likely that the RTO's written confirmation of this would serve to alleviate any unpleasantness.

In this respect I was very much mistaken, as I realised on finding myself being bundled into a cell to await an audience with the Commanding Officer, but not before having been formally charged as being absent without leave. Later in the day I was escorted before the Great Man himself, at which time I was pronounced guilty and sentenced to be confined to camp for a period of seven days. I considered this an injustice in my circumstances, and commiserated with respect but firmness on the findings, pointing out that I had been supplied with written confirmation of the blunder from the RTO at Crewe. The CO responded by further ruling that my sentence should be broadened to include 'special duties'.

It transpired that the extra duties assigned would require me to accompany the Duty Officer around the station each day as he carried out his various tasks.

Because the post of Duty Officer was usually assigned to a commissioned man who had for some reason or another fallen from favour, the early formation of a strong bond of sympathy between my fellow unfortunate and me was only to be expected. As a result, he and I soon conspired with might on how best to alleviate our misfortune without inciting the wrath of 'the powers that be'.

One of our duties was to visit the other ranks' Messrooms during mealtimes in order to ensure that the men were being adequately fed. On entering the Mess together, I would loudly call the room to attention and introduce my confederate. Once the clattering of eating utensils and the scraping of chairs had died down and everybody was standing, the Orderly Officer would graciously beg the assembly to be seated, after which he would bawl out "Any complaints?". Complaints were seldom if ever raised, and this was fortunate because, had one arisen, it was unlikely that either of us would have had the foggiest idea of how to deal with it. We were at liberty to personally test the quality of the cuisine, and frequently did so, it followed that we were without doubt the best fed men on the station, at least, during that one week.

RECUPERATION

The matter of accommodation was a sore point with me however, because I found myself billeted in one of the many dormitory blocks that are to this day scattered around the peacetime aerodrome at Waddo. In normal circumstances, this would have presented no hardship because the blocks are well appointed and comfortable, with little expense having been spared in the provision of every modern convenience. Furthermore, I had been given a free choice of accommodation within the designated block, and had selected a private NCO's room for the purpose.

In this case, the snag was that the block to which I had been assigned was otherwise unoccupied, and the heating had been shut down. The British summer was ended, and the nights were beginning to come in cold. On having spent a chilly and most uncomfortable night, I lodged a complaint, but was told that there was no other accommodation to be had. Whilst doubting the truth of this, I accepted it, but requested the issue of extra blankets to help out. The request was refused out of hand by an officious stores attendant. Because he out-ranked me, there was nothing more that I could do.

My battle against the elements was only one of my many hardships however. Yet another was my insolvency. Because I had just returned from leave in London, I was flat broke. My pay was overdue, but my request to visit Bardney in order to collect it was refused because I was confined to camp. During the few free hours that I had to myself, I was unable to have a drink in the Mess bar, and I had no cigarettes. Because I knew no one on the station, the borrowing of a few quid to tide me over a difficult time was out of the question. I was in a situation which precluded me from helping myself, and I could find no one who was willing to help me.

After the first couple of days of enforced discomfort and destitution, I decided to take my problems to a higher quarter, so went to see the station Adjutant. He listened with apparent interest as I listed my complaints, taking care to mention my shortage of cash, and pointing out that I had been posted to Waddington for a period of convalescence after a spell in hospital, inferring that the conditions I was being exposed to were far from conducive to my recovery. Although he appeared to be sympathetic, the Adjutant refused to relax the punishment that had been doled out by his superior, and suggested that I arrange for someone at Bardney to supply my needs. Feeling totally disgusted, I saluted and left the office, without bothering to tell him that I didn't have the price of a phone call on me.

By the fourth day of my confinement (as was only to be expected) I had developed a severe cold, and felt justified in feeling sorry for myself in the circumstances. My resentment at being subjected to such treatment at a time when I was supposed to be convalescing increased my fury and indignation, particularly when I reflected on the biased and unjustified pronouncement of guilt that had been passed on me. I reasoned that the problems facing me were the result of a flagrant misuse of power and lack of understanding by the CO, and I found difficulty in interpreting his reason. Maybe he just didn't like Canadians.

The thought prompted me to consider a transfer to a Canadian squadron. It was known that discipline was more relaxed on those units, largely because of what might be referred to as a national characteristic. Because it was still a relatively young country, Canada was populated by an assortment of multi-national pioneers who of necessity placed great importance on the need to get on with the job of development. This brought about an attitude of relaxed co-operation between the various echelons of the community. A similar principle existed within the Canadian military services, and this made possible a greater freedom of interchange and expression between the ranks, without the loss of respect that the English feared so much. Not that I harboured misgivings concerning my own English crew. Each one of them possessed a quality of courage and determination that I greatly admired. But, because of the crash, the future of the crew was shrouded in uncertainty, and I at once resolved that I would make an immediate request for a transfer in the event of a split.

Meanwhile, there remained a few more days of confinement for me to contend with. The thought of reporting sick did not attract me, because the treatment of a common cold usually guaranteed at least a week in dock, and that would only serve to prolong my stay at Waddington. I was far from impressed by the hospitality of the place, and was keen to get back to a more civilised environment.

As hand rag to the duty Officer, my duties included the accompanying of him during the ceremony of raising and lowering the Union Jack at such times as to ensure that the sun would never set on that great symbol of the British Empire. This chore made it necessary for us to be out of bed well in advance of most of the others on the station, and this was made more difficult because of the fact that we did not have an alarm clock. Yet another hardship resulted from the fact that there was no hot water in the billet I was in. Although shaving was relatively new to one of my tender years, it was nonetheless necessary, and the use of ice cold water didn't make the task any easier.

RECUPERATION

Much of the little spare time that was available to me was spent in lounging around the Sergeant's Mess, just reading the daily newspapers. Because it was wartime, the average national daily seldom numbered more than four pages (sometimes only two), so that reading them took up little more than a few minutes. The rest of the time was spent in listening to the radio and trying to ignore my craving for a cigarette and a pint of ale. I was always the last to leave the comparative warmth and comfort of the mess before making my way back to the billet for the night. In the meantime, I had hit upon the idea of improving my plight to some extent through the adaptation of the window curtains as extra bedding.

Despite the considerable effort ranged against me personally, I somehow managed to survive the abuse I had been forced to undergo at the hands of my captors, and it was with a sense of immense relief that I boarded a service transport bus bound for Bardney on the Saturday evening of September the 25th.

Once in the Sergeant's Mess, I checked for mail, and found a number of letters in my pigeonhole. Looking around the sparsely populated room, I could see that none of my crew were present. There were no ops on for the night, and most of the personnel had taken off for the local boozers. I enquired on how the squadron had fared during my enforced absence, and was told that, in addition to our own mishap, two aircraft had been lost during the period. R-5700 (WS/N), F/Sgt Crabtree and crew, had failed to return from a raid on Hanover on the 22nd of September, and ED-399 (WS/L), with Sgt Ord in charge, had gone missing on an attack on Mannheim the following night.

Back once more in the comfort of my room, I began opening my mail. With one exception, all of the letters were from Canada - two from home, and five from Margaret. In each instance, the content of the letters differed little from the norm. Mother gave the usual run-down on events around Whitfield, and Margaret's considerable contribution centred around plans she was making for our future.

The eighth letter bore a London postmark, and was from Doris. She had certainly wasted no time in contacting me, and it was evident from the letter that she, too intended that our relationship should be far from a casual one. As I read the letters from Margaret and Doris for the second time. I found myself reflecting on the unfairness of my behaviour towards both of these girls. I was forced to concede that I was fast becoming a cad of the first order, although I found such conduct to be alien to my nature and beliefs. I was now at the stage where I was playing them both against each other in the interests of my own selfish desires. And neither knew of the existence of the other. Clearly, there was a need for action on my part, if only to relieve my nagging conscience.

But there was one other aspect that demanded urgent consideration. During the eight weeks that I had served on the squadron, no fewer than eight aircraft had been lost, and this number represented one-third of the squadron's total strength. In the same period, my crew had completed just over one quarter of a tour, and we had been lucky to survive that many trips - all things considered. Losses throughout Bomber command were averaging five or six percent, and this indicated that our chances of surviving a tour were practically nil. The odds against that happening were too great. No matter how you looked at it, I was a bad risk.

Having decided to clean up my act by relinquishing any plans concerning my further involvement in an emotional relationship (at least until my part in the war was at an end), I was then faced with the problem of how best to carry this out in a way which would cause the minimum of distress to all those taking part. My main concern was for Margaret. Although I had deliberately withheld any mention of a wish to marry her, she had been quite open in declaring her intentions, and I had allowed this to continue. As I saw it, my best plan was to give the impression that I was a heartless and uncaring cad who had wasted the past year just leading her on. This would have the effect of instilling in her a hatred for me that was greater than the disappointment she would feel. The relationship between Doris and me had not yet progressed to anything serious. If it did, that situation could be similarly dealt with when the need arose.

That night, I wrote a terse note to Margaret, in which I lied that I had fallen in love with an English girl, and that I wished the correspondence to end.

CHAPTER 13

BACK IN THE SADDLE

The next morning I made my way over the flights, where I found an assortment of aircrew types standing around in the hazy autumn sunshine. Beyond them, out on the field, a Lancaster sped down the runway with its tail up for takeoff, the roar of its Merlins making further conversation impossible until it had climbed out of earshot. It was good to be back amongst the sights, the sounds and the scents to which I had become so accustomed, and there were many faces which I recognised at once. But I couldn't help noticing a number of strangers in the gathering. Replacement crews for those recently lost, these would eventually become familiar until they also became nothing more than a memory. Those that they had replaced would be missed and remembered later.

I found the remnants of the crew gathered at the far end of the briefing hut. The small group consisted of four men: Bill Siddle and Clem Culley, and they were engaged in conversation with two strangers.

Old Bill's sad, sombre eyes lit up, and the familiar broad grin of recognition spread across his rugged features as I approached. The grin had undergone a radical change as the result of this hasty and undignified exit from the flight deck on impact. This totally involuntary act had brought about the unscheduled removal of a couple of front teeth, an event which had done nothing to improve his naturally scruffy appearance.

After having exchanged the customary greetings, I enquired about the state of the crew, and was told that our navigator and mid upper gunner would be back with us in a week or two, but that we would be losing Ken and Reg. Both had been declared unfit for further flying duties because of the extent and seriousness of their injuries, and they were to be replaced by the two strangers present. These were introduced to me as Jock Wilson, our new flight engineer, and Mike Machin, the replacement bomb aimer. As I shook their hands, I noticed that both were Flight Sergeants, so it was unlikely that they were without some operational experience. Jock was a diminutive Glaswegian with an accent as broad as the Clyde, while Mike hailed from Spennymoor in County Durham. As I was soon to find out, the latter possessed a ribald sense of humour, thus making him an ideal substitute for Ken, who had always been adept at defusing a tricky situation by use of a few colourful and well-chosen expletives.

I was later to learn that both men had logged double figures before joining us, and that they had been 'orphaned' through the loss of their respective crews while they themselves had been excused duty. I felt confident that the new men would fit in well with the five remaining originals, and that it would not be long before we were again operational. I reckoned that we would probably be given some time in which to blend together as a crew, and one or two cross country flips and some circuits-and-bumps would afford us the opportunity for the replacements to become familiar with our strategy.

Nine Squadron was operating that night, and we had been detailed to do a night flying test on X-Xray right away, so I hurried off to collect my flying helmet and parachute. Because it was to be our first time up since the crash, the flight was intended as a re-familiarization flip for those of us who had been involved. It had always been policy to get a crew airborne as soon as possible after a crash, thus minimizing the chance development of a condition commonly referred to in Air Force parlance as 'ring twitter'. This was the only effective means by which one's self-confidence could be put to the test, and it usually worked.

We were up and flying in ED-499 (WS/X) within the hour, X was one of the more mature squadron aircraft, having been delivered from A V Roe's Chadderton factory nine months previously. She had completed more than forty trips since then, so could be considered something of a veteran. She was on the battle order that night, and our job was to check her out for the other crew. Because ours was incomplete, none of us were down to operate.

As we climbed out over the patchwork Lincolnshire landscape, I busied myself with the familiar tests on the rear gun turret and its equipment: intercom; oxygen supply; turret rotation; gun elevation/depression; triggers; safe/fire mechanism; electric gun sight; exit doors; manual rotation handle; portable oxygen supply; gun cocking toggle; perspex canopy, etcetera. Everything appeared to be working correctly, so I made my way up to the mid upper turret, checking my ammunition tracks and canisters as I went. Because there wasn't a second gunner with us, I also had to check his position. By the time I had finished, the other crew members had completed their various tests, and Bill had begun to throw the Lanc into a few tight turns, corkscrews and wing stands. Judging by the gravitational forces I felt as I made my way back to the tail (with some difficulty), it was obvious that Bill had lost nothing of his ability to show the loveable brute exactly who was boss.

BACK IN THE SADDLE

After about fifteen minutes, Bill tired of his skylarking, so we turned in the direction of base. On receiving permission to land, we circled left and joined in the circuit. A lot of feverish activity was taking place down on the airfield, and I could see tractors towing long trains of fully-laden bomb trolleys in the direction of the various dispersals, and a profusion of push-bikes, motor cycles, oil and petrol bowsers - even NAAFI vans - added their bulk to the controlled confusion and congestion that was a busy bomber squadron getting ready to go to war.

As we turned into the funnel for our final approach, I fastened my seat belt and swung the turret dead astern for landing, listening to the familiar orders being exchanged between the pilot and flight engineer over the intercom. I was impressed: it was a pity that we had lost Reg, but his replacement seemed to know the drill alright.

As the tall totem poles flashed beneath us at either side, I noted that we seemed to be coming in a little higher than we usually did, but didn't give it much thought. Soon Bill would give Jock the order "Cut!", and the Merlins would suddenly go silent, except for the characteristic popping sound that they always made when the throttles were closed, then the old girl would float stubbornly onwards before settling down gently, just like a brood hen onto her nest.

But not this time, "Overshoot!" came the shout from Bill, and I at once felt the Lanc strain for altitude as Jock hurriedly adjusted the throttles, boost and pitch controls to the required settings for a landing abort. Then, as the flaps were raised and the wheels tucked up into their respective nacelles, we again thundered powerfully into the sky and banked to port. This was the first genuine overshoot we had ever done as far as I could remember. There had been a few 'touch-and-go' practice landings during our conversion course at Winthorpe, but this was not practice. Obviously, some form of emergency must have presented itself, otherwise we would by this time be safely down and rolling along the runway. Maybe Bill had spotted an obstruction - a stray animal; a flock of crows; some idiot taking a short cut on a push-bike, perhaps. Such an occurrence was not unknown. The reason was not long in coming.

"What happened Skip", Jock inquired. "I just didn't get it right", Bill snapped, then remarked, "We'll have to go 'round and try again".

I found the remark amusing. As any schoolboy in possession of all his crayons knows, that which goes up must surely come down again. Gravity would make sure of that. As I saw it, there was no question of us not trying again!

Try again we did, but our second attempt at a landing produced the same result as the first, and our third pass proved equally unsuccessful. By this time it was becoming disturbingly clear to us that old Bill had lost his nerve. Obviously, his cool was being effected by the memory of what had happened before the crash, when he quite unexpectedly found himself at the controls of what he later described as 'the biggest bloody glider in creation'. This was causing him to panic as soon as he got the aircraft into a similar approach situation. Our growing realization that we were in a spot was confirmed when, on our forth overshoot, I observed a procession of fire tenders and ambulances hurrying in the direction of the runway, and I could also see numerous upturned faces gathered outside the flight offices.

As we again roared out over the boundary fence, a new voice was heard to replace that of the WAAF in the control tower. "This is the Wing Commander speaking", it said. "Now just take things Easy, Siddle. Go 'round again, and listen carefully to my instructions. I'll talk you down". Bill acknowledged curtly as we circled the field, and I could sense the mounting tension in his voice. Words intended to restore the confidence of our pilot were coming from the other members of the crews, but Bill remained silent.

Once more we turned towards the runway, to make our approach. "Ease her down a little, Siddle. You're coming in too high". Bill complied. "That's better. Now watch your air speed, and keep her level". Again I saw the totem poles flash past. The height looked right this time. "Now, just throttle back, and keep her steady. You're doing fine", But, once again, just as he felt the power falling off, Bill was seized by renewed panic, and the big bomber was once more made to claw its way skywards, somewhat unsteadily this time.

Obviously, we were now in the midst of a serious situation. The airfield had been placed on full crash alert, and everybody was out watching our predicament. What was more, I considered that the C.O.'s action in assuming complete control had done nothing to ease our plight. I realised that, as Commanding Officer, he had to do something. But why hadn't he, in the initial stages at least, delegated responsibility to the Flight Commander? I found myself wondering if the man had ever tried to do a deadstick landing in the dark with a damaged Lancaster after a nine-hour flight over enemy territory. As things now stood, we were centre-stage. Poor old Bill was in the leading role, and he had forgotten his lines. He was badly in need of a prompt, but not from the Director.

BACK IN THE SADDLE

The show carried on for a further half hour, during which Bill's frustration increased, and the C.O. adopted a less conciliatory tone, issuing direct orders tinged with censure. Finally, on our ninth attempt, we actually succeeded in making contact with the runway in what amounted to a little more than controlled crash. As we bounced for the second time, I thought that we must surely abort the landing yet again, but Bill managed to hold her down next time she hit, with just enough runway left for the pull-up. We turned off onto the perimeter track, and the intercom buzzed with messages of praise and veiled relief from the rest of us. Then, the Winco's voice came over the external radio once more: "Alright, Siddle", it said. "Come on in to dispersal. I want to see you in my office". Bill didn't bother to answer. Instead, he switched the radio off and brought the aircraft to a halt.

"I want the flight engineer to stay with me. The rest of you can get to hell out of here. Jock, I want you to go and check the landing gear and report back to me". We all clambered out and sat on the grass beside the track, watching Jock as he carried out his inspection on the condition of the struts and oleo legs, and checked the tyres for creep. Appearing to be satisfied, he grinned at us and gave the thumbs-up sign before climbing back in and closing the door behind him.

"He's taking her up again to do a few practice landings", said Clem, "but he doesn't want us with him". There at once followed a heated discussion on the possible outcome of Bill's action. it looked as if his flying days were over. It didn't take a Philadelphia lawyer to see that. Bill's intended tack constituted a flagrant breach of discipline, and the C.O. would throw the book at him for having deliberately disobeyed an order. I considered that he would be placed under arrest, and would probably be faced with a court martial. Nevertheless, I could see the reasoning behind his action. If he returned X-ray to dispersal as ordered, this would be an admission of defeat, in which case he wouldn't stand a chance in hell of regaining his nerve. It was likely that he would be declared LMF, and we all knew what that would bring; he would surreptitiously disappear from the scene altogether, after which he would be stripped of his rank and aircrew status and posted to general duties. But if, as planned, he took the Lanc up again, this would serve to demonstrate his remarkable courage and determination, and I for one couldn't see him being branded a coward in such circumstances. His problem was temporary -the result of an unfortunate experience which could have befallen any wartime pilot. He had the will and the courage to overcome it. The missing requirement was a little forbearance from his superior, but it looked unlikely that he was ever going to get it.

We watched X-ray as she taxied to the far side of the field and began her takeoff run. As she soared past us, we all stood up and waved, but our greeting went unacknowledged by the tense figure in the cockpit. The Lanc then circled the field and made what looked like a reasonably good approach. The height seemed right, and Bill held her fairly steady as he brought her down to a bumpy but safe three-point landing, after which he gunned the throttles and lifted her back into the air.

As X-ray again roared past us and out over the perimeter fence, a small canvass-covered Austin pickup pulled up beside us, and the WAAF driver told us that she had been sent out to bring us back to the flights. The lads climbed in the back but I chose the passenger seat so that I could watch X-ray's further progress. As we drove around the track, I saw Bill make yet another good landing, and the Lanc was already turning off in the direction of the dispersal pan when we arrived at the flights. To me, it looked as if Bill had succeeded in making his point. In the space of only a few minutes, it appeared that he had defeated his fear, and his success was due entirely to his own courage and initiative. Now, the one remaining ponderable was the question of the Wing commander's reaction, whatever that might be.

The entertainment having drawn to a close, the crowd around the flight offices was beginning to thin out as we alighted from our transport and walked in the direction of the parachute section. "I bet you won't be risking your neck with him again!", a gunner remarked as I passed "Mind your own bloody business", I retorted elbowing him out of my way.

We didn't see Bill again until after the evening meal. We were all standing at the bar in the Sergeant's Mess when I spotted him beckoning to me from the doorway. He looked the perfect picture of wretchedness and despair as I walked over, so I tried to cheer him up with a few carefully chosen words of praise on behalf of the crew. "Thanks, but forget it", he interrupted. "I want a meeting of the full crew right away. Tell them to meet in my room at the Officer's Mess in half an hour".

The specified time found the six of us crowded into Bill's small but well-appointed semi-private room. The only other tenant was on the battle order for the night, and we could already hear the squadron's Lancasters warming up their engines out on the field as we settled down for what looked like being a serious and sombre get-together. I had a feeling that the next hour or so would have an important bearing on the future of all of us.

Bill got straight down to business. First he gave a condensed report on what the C.O. had said to him

BACK IN THE SADDLE

in the office that afternoon. As was only to be expected, the exchange had been far from congenial, and mostly one-sided or so it had been until the Wingco finally gave vent to his considerable wrath. Bill had then been invited to "give me just one good reason why I shouldn't slate you for a court martial", at which point the intrepid Bill (being of the belief that he was going down anyway, and might as well go down fighting) had decided to pull out all the stops and do some shouting on his own behalf. We never got to know what Bill had said during the exchange. He didn't tell us and we didn't expect him to. But it certainly seemed to have turned the odds in his favour. On having subjected Bill to ' a good bollocking' (thus asserting his authority), the C.O. - in the face of the outburst - had appeared to relent sufficiently to offer a seemingly generous judgement. In short, Bill was to be given one last chance. On hearing this, I considered that the Wing commander had had little real choice in the matter. The squadron had taken a pounding in recent weeks, and he could ill afford to dispense with a pilot who already had several trips under his belt. We were to undergo a short but intensive period of training designed to knock us back into shape, and we could expect to be back on the battle order in a week or so, provided there were no further serious complications.

"However", Bill went on, "it's up to you whether or not we stay together as a crew. I think it only fair that you should be given a choice in the matter, and to hell with officialdom. After today's performance, I can't blame any of you for wanting to chicken out. It was a bloody bad show on my part. But, before you

Fig 9. Crew with replacements, late 1943, Bardney. Standing L to R: Sgt Dick Lodge (navigator), Sgt Clem Culley (wireless operator), Pilot Officer Bill Siddle (pilot), Flight Sgt Gerry Parker (replacement mid upper gunner), Sgt Clayton Moore (tail gunner). Kneeling: Sgt Alan "Jock" Wilson (replacement flight engineer), Flight Sgt Alan "Mike" Machin (replacement bomb aimer).

BACK IN THE SADDLE

Fig 10. Reg Moseley with Edna, his bride, on their wedding day.

I expected there to be an awkward silence during which each one of us would search the other's faces for a reaction. I was inclined to doubt the findings of the investigating body. I considered that this was probably made up of a selection of chairborne has-beens who had long since forgotten all they ever knew about their leaflet raids on Germany in their obsolete Hampdens and Whitleys. More than likely they couldn't even remember what a flakburst looked like. We bomber boys had enough on our plates without having to put up with the pontifications of past relics. As far as I was concerned, their findings should be taken with more than a pinch of salt.

I was mistaken concerning the crew's likely response to Bill's question. "I'm with you, Bill", Clem affirmed. "Me too"., said Jock, "And me", came from Mike. Bill's questioning gaze then focused on me in search of my answer. During my short flying career, I must have flown with thirty or more different pilots, but I couldn't think of a single one that could handle an aircraft the way old Bill could.

"Looks like we got ourselves a crew, Bill", I said.

An hour later, we were all on a bus headed for Bardney village, intent on downing a few celebratory pints in the Station Hotel.

Three days were to pass before we got our next flight. This was partly due to bad weather, but mainly because the squadron was waiting for the arrival of new crews and aircraft. X-ray had not returned from the raid we had tested her out for. decide, there's one other thing I think you should know: A few days ago, I was hauled up before an independent investigation body looking into the cause of our crash. Rightly or wrongly, they found against me, and my log book has been endorsed accordingly. They said I should have known we were short of fuel. I'll leave you to make up your own minds on that score. I think we've got a good crew, and I'd like us to stick together. So, what do you say?" Pilot Officer Gould and his crew had taken her on her last trip (to Hanover) that night (Monday, October 18th). Nine Squadron had been having a rough time of it, so had been given a stand-down between the 8th and 18th, The loss of WS/X was the twelfth since our arrival. In addition, four men had been brought back dead, and three (including Ken and Reg) had been scrubbed from flying because of serious injuries.

BACK IN THE SADDLE

In the meantime, the crew had been supplied with a temporary mid upper gunner to replace Dick Jones, who was still in dock. The new man was Gerry Parker, and American who had been in England attending university when war was declared. He had left the university to join the RAF soon afterwards, and had accrued an impressive number of entries in his log book since then. It was understood by all those concerned that Gerry was only intended as a stand-in for Dick. Although I was impressed by Gerry's past experience, I was keen to have Dick with me in the crew, and Bill had agreed with me on this.

Once the weather had cleared, we were at last able to get some flying in. This consisted of some practice landings, plus a four-hour night cross country jaunt. As was to be expected, we were anxious to have our confidence in our pilot restored, but need not have worried about it. Bill was his old self again, as was evident from the way he carried out the landing in darkness.

The next night (Friday, October 22nd, 1943) we were once more on the squadron battle order.

CHAPTER 14

THE SPIRIT OF RUSSIA

Lancaster CV-340 (WS/Q) was our mount for the trip, so we did an NFT on her before lunch. At the afternoon briefing we were told that our takeoff time would be just after six p.m., and that we would be attacking a city called Kassel, an industrial target deep inside central Germany. As such, we could expect to find it well defended, so it was with the now-familiar feeling of uneasiness mixed with excitement that we lifted off on a flight of about six hours duration. According to intelligence, Kassel had a number of factories producing undisclosed types of 'secret' weapons, and our job was to put them out of business. We had F/Sgt Archer standing in for our navigator.

Lady Luck flew with us on the night. The marking was good and, although we encountered cloud over much of the trip, the target was fairly clear on our arrival, and fires were already to be seen burning beneath us as we went in. The defences were alert and heavy, but our bombing run proved uneventful. We had some trouble with icing on the return flight, but we still made it back to our own base on time. In all, our re-introduction to operational flying had turned out to be something of an anticlimax.

We touched down at Bardney just before midnight, and were pleased to learn that all of the squadron's aircraft had made it back safely, with the exception of just one. Flying Officer Manning and crew, flying in EE-188 (WS/B) had been ganged up on by no fewer than four twin-engined fighters, and the mid upper gunner had been killed and the tail gunner wounded during the battle.

November 2nd., 1943 proved to be something of a red letter day for us, because it was then that we were 'issued' with our own aircraft and its ground crew. Although intended for exclusive use by us, the exigencies of the service were such that 'our' Lancaster would sometimes be flown on operations by another crew if we were on leave or stood down. Similarly, we would be expected to operate in another aircraft if ours was out of action due to unserviceability.

In squadron terms, the assignment of a particular aircraft to a crew marked the acceptance of that crew

Fig 11. Nose of EE-136, The Spirit of Russia. Bardney, 1943.

THE SPIRIT OF RUSSIA

as one which could be relied on to take good care of it, and also indicated the belief held by 'the powers that be' that the chances of the crew surviving were considered to be good. However, the allocation of ex-works Lancasters was usually reserved for crews of higher rank and experience than ours, so it was to be expected that our charge would be of the second-hand variety. After all, we had already subjected one Lancaster to a severe bending.

Because the cost of a new Lancaster was estimated to be in the region of seventy-five thousand Pounds Sterling at the time, we could hardly expect to be issued with a new one. We had managed to survive long enough to qualify for recognition, but our past reputation for recklessness precluded the granting to us of the ultimate accolade. So it was that the Lancaster we got was not new. In fact, it was of near-veteran status, having been handed over to our keeping by Pilot Officer J Lyon and crew after the completion of a tour. Jim, an Australian, was then posted to a training unit for a period of rest, but was to be tragically killed in a flying accident a few weeks later.

Most of the afternoon was spent in inspecting our new charge and getting acquainted with the ground crew. The aircraft bore the registration EE-136, and the squadron letters WS/R. It had emblazoned beneath the 'driver's window' in Ode English Script the most unlikely name of "Spirit Of Russia". Beneath the name were painted several rows of bombs, a record of the impressive number of trips she had so far completed. Although we had no way of knowing it then (otherwise we might have refused to fly in any other aircraft), WS/R was to complete one hundred and nine operational sorties before being withdrawn from active service, and would ignominiously end her days as a practice hulk for fire fighting crews before being sold for scrap.

The reason for choosing the name 'The Spirit Of Russia' was a mystery to us, it having been bestowed on the aircraft by P/O Lyons. One of the rumours circulating on the squadron at the time was to the effect that the cost of her production had been met through a collection made by the people of Leningrad, but recent inquiries made of the Russian Embassy in London have failed to confirm or deny this.

The Spirit of Russia, in common with most other aeroplanes, had her own characteristics, as we were to discover next day, when we took her up for an air test. She had a disconcerting habit of crabbing a few degrees to port in flight, and this was a tendency that Bill had not encountered previously with the type. During takeoff, all Lancasters tended to pull to port because of the fact that all four propellers turned in the same direction, and care had to be taken to compensate for this, particularly if taking off with a full load of highly combustible materials. In the case of WS/R, full rudder trim was necessary at all times, and Bill foresaw difficulties during takeoff.

Nonetheless, we found the Spirit of Russia a delightful aircraft to fly. She was manoeuvrable, and had plenty of power in her well-maintained engines. In the months that were to follow, we were to become jealously fond of our battle-scarred old warrior.

In an attempt to find an answer to the question of WS/R's waywardness, we began making some inquiries around the squadron, particularly of the ground crews. Among the rumours circulating, there was one to the effect that our Lanc had been shot up a few times, and that two tail gunners had been killed by enemy action. It seemed that on one such occasion, the damage had been sufficiently severe as to warrant the fitting of a new tail section, and the problem had been evident ever since.

It was to be several days before we got the chance to take WS/R to war - on Wednesday, November the 10th, 1943. The target was a place called Modane, an important rail junction set high up in the mountainous border region between France and Italy. Some four hours into the flight, we arrived over some of the most picturesque scenery I had ever seen from the air. We found the target area bathed in brilliant moonlight, and this was made all the more effective by the snow-covered peaks rising several thousand feet above us from the floor of the valley in which our objective lay. The Pathfinders had put down excellent markers, superfluous 'though they were in the circumstances, because the ground detail was plainly visible to us, with the steel bands of track glinting in the moonlight between the goods yards and sidings, at the far end of which was a rail tunnel leading into the foot of the mountain.

The defences were so light as to be almost non-existent as we began our bombing run. Because of the lighting conditions, I could see for miles, and of the many aircraft in sight, all were friendly. The bomb doors had been opened, and Mike was giving directions, when I spotted the steam from a train making its way towards the station from about a mile out, so I at once broke into the conversation.

"Tail to pilot. Train approaching behind us. If we go 'round again, it should just be arriving when we bomb".

"Good show, tail. Cancel the run up, bomb aimer, We're going 'round again".

THE SPIRIT OF RUSSIA

As we wheeled between the towering peaks and returned down the valley, I watched the train steam into the crowded marshalling yards and come to a halt. Just why the driver didn't realise that a raid was in progress remains a mystery, but there was no questioning the fate of his train and its cargo. We turned again and were soon on our second bombing run. As the bombs were released, I watched in fascination as one after another of them slammed into the long, ill-fated train. By way of a bonus, the last couple of two-thousand pounders burst in the entrance to the tunnel leading away from the yards.

Just as we were coming out of the target area, Bill reported an unidentified aircraft approaching on a reciprocal course on the port bow. I at once swung my turret to the beam, and was just in time to see a Messerschmitt 210 go screaming past.

"Doesn't seem to be interested in us", I reported.

"Keep and eye on him just in cast", Bill instructed.

"Roger, Cover the rest of the sky, mid upper".

Leaving Gerry to keep watch, I followed the progress of the 210, which was plainly visible against the blanket of snow that stretched out beneath and above us at either side. He appeared to be in some difficulty, because he was losing height steadily. Then, the Messerschmitt did a steep turn to starboard and rammed headlong into the side of the mountain, throwing up large volumes of snow as it hit. There was no explosion or fire that I could see.

The four-hour return flight across France and the water passed without any problems, but we had used up a lot of fuel in negotiating the mountains around the target, so were obliged to lob down in Cambridgeshire, at an airfield known as Gransden Lodge, the home of 405 (city of Vancouver) Squadron, RCAF.

I had hopes of renewing one or two acquaintances from my training days in Canada, but was disappointed to find after debriefing that we had been amongst the last to land, and most of the others had retired to their beds for the remainder of the night. In truth, a good number of 'cuckoos' had nested, and there were no spare beds for us. However, we found that the crewroom sported a large, four-sided fireplace in the centre of the room, so we all sat around it until dawn in a collection of easy chairs, warm, but snoozing fitfully as best we could.

After breakfast, we flew back to Bardney, only to find ourselves victims of the kind of bureaucratic bungling to which we were fast becoming accustomed: we had been officially reported missing! Seemingly, Gransden Lodge control had not reported our presence to Bardney, while Bill had presumed that they would have. We managed to stop some (but not all) of the telegrams from being sent out to the next of kin. Unfortunately, the cable to Canada informing my parents of their 'loss' was one that did get through, and they were thus subjected to a lot of quite unnecessary grief and trauma, particularly since the cable cancelling the first one arrived ahead of the original. As a result, it wasn't until they received my letter explaining the mix-up that they were sure of just what had happened, and that I was indeed safe and well.

Bureaucratic bungling, petty regulations, and an almost total disregard for the welfare of us combatants in the face of the dangers and problems confronting us was beginning to erode my tolerance. Whitewashing the coal in the billet; the imposition of seven-days' confinement on me for allowing myself to be directed onto the wrong train from London; the fact that the crash enquiry body had found fault with the flying ability of the best bomber pilot I had ever flown with, all these I considered to be ludicrous. But they were only a few of the ridiculous rules to which we were subjected by those who, instead of easing our plight, appeared to be devoted to its worsening. A recent order forbade the commissioned ranks to be seen in public with the other ranks, and the service police were under orders to enforce this. Because we were restricted to the use of our own respective messrooms, this rule prevented the fraternizing of aircrews anywhere other than on the flights or in the air. We might well die together in the same plummeting inferno, but we could never share a drink down in the village local.

One other incident that had niggled me was the fact that I had been required to pay the replacement cost of the flying goggles and boot I had lost in the crash. I had been made to sign a Form 664B authorizing the deduction of the total amount from my pay before replacements could be supplied.

Despite the report that we had been listed as missing, our return to Bardney had its compensations. First (and most important), all the Squadron's aircraft had returned safely from the Modane trip. Second, we were given the news that we were to vacate our Nissen hut and take up permanent residence in our respective messes. I had been allocated a double room in the Sergeant's Mess, and on entering it, found a kit bag and other items of personal baggage piled on one of the beds. I turned the air force blue kit bag over and found painted on it the inscription '626828, Sgt Jones, R.E.' This could only mean one thing: Dick had returned from hospital, would be sharing the room with me, and must be somewhere on the premises. It was lunchtime, so I left the room and went down to the messroom.

THE SPIRIT OF RUSSIA

Dick was already seated at one of the long wooden trestle tables, so I collected my meal and sat down beside him. He told me that he had just arrived from Hoylake that morning, and would be leaving after lunch for a spot of well-earned sick leave. He assured me that he was feeling alright, and said that he would be going before a medical board for assessment after he got back from leave. He was looking forward to the leave, but more than that, he was going up to County Durham to be with Edith, the nurse he was forever talking about, and that he intended to take out a special licence so that they could be married during the time that he would be there. As an aside, he added that he was looking forwar to rejoining the crew, probably in December.

That evening, after seeing Dick Jones off, I met the other members of the crew down at the Station Hotel in the village. Over a few brimming mugs of the landlord's best ale, I again brought up with Bill the subject of my lack of confidence in the standard corkscrew manoeuvre, and Gerry (who had discussed it with me earlier) joined in. The resulting debate proved lively, with the others getting involved. Soon ideas were beginning to flow from minds made lucid by the effect that the ale was having. I put forward my belief that the value of the corkscrew in dealing with an attack depended on the enemy pilot trying to follow the tortuous course of his quarry, during which his task was made all the more difficult, not only because of the violence of the manoeuvre, but by the effect that the slipstream produced by four flat-out Merlins would have on his ability to control his own aircraft.

"So, what's wrong wi' the corkscrew", Jock wanted to know. "Why change something that works?"

I went on to relate what I had been told by the gunner at Rauceby Hall, after which I theorized on the likelihood of an intelligent German fighter pilot memorizing the movements of his target and deciding against playing the game our way, as had happened in the case in point.

"If the fighter pilot knows what the bomber's next move is going to be", I continued, "there's no need for him to strain his puddings at all. Instead, all he need do is follow the bomber at a safe distance and wait until it presents a suitable target for his long range cannons".

"And that would be when we reach the top of the climb and level out for the dive", Bill put in.

The others, Bill in particular, warmed to the arguments being put forward by Gerry and me and, after a lengthy and heated discussion, it was generally accepted that the Jerries had in all probability memorized the manoeuvre, and that we should seek to draft an alternative.

Bill listened intently to the ideas before passing judgment. In general, he accepted the need for a new tactic, but was reluctant to dispose of the old one until we had devised and thoroughly tested an alternative. To this end, he had an idea concerning the use of flaps and throttles at the instruction of whichever gunner was in charge of the combat, and he wanted to run a try-out at the next opportunity. The familiar corkscrew would not be used. instead, the gunner would issue orders for the aircraft to climb or dive, and in whichever direction he considered to be best suited to the circumstances.

In the days that followed our discussion, I gave a lot of throught to Siddle's suggestion, as did Gerry. Although it was likely that Gerry would be making way for our own mid upper gunner to rejoin the crew when he got back from leave. I was keen to get the idea set up as soon as possible. The problem was that we were still suffering from the effect of crew deficiencies. We had a temporary replacement mid upper, and we had been given the permanent services of Mike Machin as bomb aimer and Jock Wilson as flight engineer. But we still lacked a navigator, and there was a shortage of these on the squadron. We had been lucky to procure a stand-in for the Kassel and Modane trips, but we couldn't expect to be fully operational until Dick Lodge was back with us.

Despite the temporary reduction in numbers, we still managed to get up once in a while on local jaunts and some daylight training. On one such occasion, we took WS/R up for some bombing and air-to-sea firing practice. On our way back from The Wash, we chanced to meet a lone Hurricane, and the pilot indicated his willingness to play by making a pass at us. Recognising this as a chance that was not to be missed, Gerry and I at once seized on the quite unexpected opportunity to put our new tactic to the test, and set about taking turns at dealing with our playmate.

The Hurricane's first attack came from high up on the starboard quarter, so Gerry took charge. "Climb starboard -Go!" he ordered. With wings at the vertical, Bill made the Spirit of Russia claw for height with throttles wide, and I watched the Hurricane flip on its back as its pilot tried to emulate the climb. "Dive port now", Gerry's voice came over the intercom. This action appeared to have caught the fighter pilot by surprise, he having expected us to continue the climb, but to alter direction to port. The deception worked, and I watched with interest the antics of the Hurricane as it soared above our port beam.

I took charge of the second attack, which was initiated from low on the port quarter. "Dive port - Go!",

I ordered, and watched the fighter turn turtle yet again as its pilot tried in vain to copy the violence of Bill's response to the order. "Now get ready to climb starboard". I had to hand it to the lad - he certainly knew a thing or two about driving an aeroplane, and was soon nearing a position at which he would be able to get us in his sights. At the exact moment I gave the order "Climb starboard". With some difficulty, the fighter strove to follow, so I shouted, "Flaps - Go!"". Again, the Hurricane pilot was taken by surprise, and I watched his aircraft as it streaked beneath our tail, inverted, and apparently out of control.

As we wallowed to regain level flight, I prepared myself for the next pass, but it wasn't to come. Instead, the Hurricane righted itself and headed south, leaving us to return to base. Obviously, its pilot didn't like the way we played.

Thankfully, there were many such incidents, and they did much to ease the tension that attended members of an operational bomber crew. Light relief was of immense value in maintaining morale in the face of the odds, and most crews proved themselves adept at providing it, mostly by means that were frowned upon by their superiors. Low flying; impromptu mess parties; the telling of jokes; the singing of bawdy ballads; dating the local girls, all were considered more effective than the occasional organized football or cricket match, and most (but not all) called for the minimum of physical effort.

Boozing sessions down in the village were popular, but the presence of civilians in our midst called for much restraint on the more raucous revelry favoured by our ilk. To us, tomorrow was an uncertainty, so we lived only for the moment. Although the mess was also used by the female members of the service, the girls were more familiar with our brand of revelry than were their civilian counterparts, and they pretended not to hear our limitless renditions of "That was a Cute Little Rhyme".

There was however one female Member of the Sergeant's Mess at Bardney whose repertoire of such indelicate ditties must have been considerable, she being the only Member with the ability to provide the necessary piano accompaniment. During our many sessions, she would be found seated at the keyboard, straight-laced and unsmiling, as we each took our turn at making a contribution. In return for her services, we kept her well supplied with her favourite refreshment but, on one such occasion, she expressed a desire to be taken on a bombing raid, so she was duly smuggled aboard a Berlin-bound squadron lancaster. Thankfully, the aircraft returned safely.

We overseas servicemen were always in demand at these functions because we brought with us stanzas that had not been heard previously by the English. For example:

There was a young man from Boston

Who bought a baby Austin

He had room for his ass

And a gallon of gas

But his what-nots hung out

And he lost 'em

Chorus; That was a cute little rhyme

Sing us another one, do.

The mess parties, noted for such unique goings-on as foot prints on the ceiling and tyre marks on the linoleum, are all events which have been well chronicled in the past. Airborne entertainment took many forms, but consisted mainly of low flying, and there is little doubt that more than one aircraft and crew came to grief as a result of such high-spirited, low-level jinks. Bill Siddle loved the sport, and his ability to handle a Lancaster at 'zero feet' bordered on the artistic. His choice of victims was varied to include towns, villages, hamlets, main highways, airfields, or quite simply, anything that moved or stuck out from the landscape. On reflection, the sight of a four-engined bomber hurtling towards one with propellers spinning just a few feet from the ground must have generated a lot of anxiety in the mind of the shepherd, farmer, pedestrian or motorist who happened to be in its path

On occasion the prank would be played on one of our own kind. 'Beating up' the airfield of a rival squadron was a good giggle, but usually resulted in a reprisal raid being staged on the airfield from which the perpetrator originated,and an unwelcomed 'tit-for-tat' sequence could develop. Light aircraft such as a Tiger Moth or a Walrus made for good sport, and the tail gunner of a Lancaster always got a grandstand view of the antics these small craft performed while trying or overcome the turbulence set up by the slipstream.

At times, the foolery was extended to involve our own ground control personnel. There is the classic example of the Lancaster pilot who called the watch tower

THE SPIRIT OF RUSSIA

requesting a check on his radio transmitter. On the test being granted the normal procedure was for the pilot to recite the numbers one to ten, then repeat them in reverse order (from ten back down to one). In this instance, the pilot decided to vary the routine, and instead recited the months January to December. He then found himself faced with the task of reversing these, and didn't quite get it right. The duty WAAF then reported the strength of the signal, but (wishing to join in the spirit of things) added, "You missed a month. Are you concerned?", to which the pilot replied, "Not as concerned as you would be!"

The night of Thursday, November the 18th, 1943 marked the beginning of the Battle of Berlin, or 'The Big City' as it was known to us. The squadron was out in strength, but we were once more unable to take part due to there not being a spare navigator available for us. The squadron lost two aircraft: DV-284 (WS/G), Pilot Officer Graham and crew (plus a second Dickie), and ED-871 (WS/Z), Pilot Officer Lees and crew. On the next day, mostly because of our crew deficiency status, we were granted nine days leave, so I entrained for London - the other 'Big City', commonly referred to as 'The Smoke'.

CHAPTER 15

A GENTLEMAN'S AGREEMENT

Standing in the corridor of the crowded London-bound train, I turned my thoughts in the direction of my somewhat uncertain future. The letters that I had been receiving from Margaret had at last ceased to arrive, and I felt pleased that she had not chosen to reply to the last one I had sent. This was to me an indication that the method I chosen had been the right one, and that it had served to get me out of her system for good. Much as I regretted it, there seemed to be no justification in me allowing the relationship to continue. The squadron had lost two more crews last night. That made a total of fifteen crews reported missing or killed during the four months that we had served at Bardney, yet we had only completed one-third of a tour. If the existing loss rate was to continue. I could see no way in which we could expect to survive.

There now remained the question of Doris. She had also been writing to me, and - although her letters made no reference to the formation of a serious regard for me - I considered it wise that I should end the relationship forthwith, and resolved to deal with the matter during my leave.

I was pleased to find Eric Plunket's name on the club register as I booked in. Once settled into my room I telephoned Doris and arranged a date with her for eight p.m. the following evening. Having done this, I met Eric down in the lounge. By then it was too late for us to go anywhere special, so we just had a few pints and a chin-wag in a pub down the round before turning in for the night. Eric only had two days left out of his leave. He was bored out of his mind, so was glad to see someone that he knew, and suggested that we go out and paint the town next night. Remembering the date I had planned with Doris, I at once realised this to be as good a time as any to give her the impression that I was a heartless cad, so agreed to accompany him, and not to bother to turn up for the date. Anyway, I could see that Eric could do with some cheering up. On reflection, I considered the same applied to me, and I knew the wayward Eric was not one to be easily deflected from a campaign once it had been suggested, so what the hell!

It was nearing seven p.m. as we rode the escalator up to the ground level at Piccadilly circus and joined the throng of revel-seekers jostling along the blacked-out West End Streets. We had no set plan of action other than that of finding a suitable public house in which to slake our thirst, after which we intended to simply 'play it by ear' and see what might happen.

Once outside the station, we headed in the direction of Leicester Square, picking our way through the fog and darkness of a typical November night in the wartime metropolis. We hadn't gone far before we heard the sounds of song and revelry issuing from a nearby doorway, so we elbowed the blackout curtain aside and entered.

The Mitre, as it was called, turned out to be a typical West end public house, apparently consisting of just one room which was hardly large enough to accommodate the noisy clientele that was crammed into just about every available square foot of floor space. On finally reaching the bar, we were delighted to find that the beer was still 'on', so shouted our order through the din that surrounded us. Then, each armed with a brimming pint of the amber liquid, we sipped the froth before carefully picking our way out of the jostling throng surrounding the bar and made our way in the direction of a vacant space against the opposite wall. This was fitted with a shoulder-high shelf or delph rack on which we deposited our mugs before attempting to engage in conversation. Our opening exchange was centred mainly on the fortunes and misfortunes of the squadron, but eventually, it drifted to a discussion on the subject of our success or otherwise in the field or romantic associations.

On summing up our respective situations, it became clear that neither of us was having much luck in that department. I told Eric of my recent actions on the matter and found that he was of a similar mind, he believing it unfair of either of us to get seriously involved with anyone in the circumstances. Nevertheless, he was of the opinion that, it being likely that our lives might be short, we should 'grab what we can' while we still had the chance.

The bar was populated mainly by members of the British Forces, with a sprinkling of uniformed 'tourists' thrown in for good measure. The few females present all appeared to be paired off with someone, with the exception of a couple of nice looking young women standing near the entrance. Of these, one was a brunette, and I estimated her age to be about eighteen. The other looked more mature - probably in her early twenties, and she had the most attractive auburn hair I had seen in a long time. This, together with an aura of natural sophistication served to intrigue me, and I found myself attracted not only by this, but by an air of mysterious, yet explicit beauty. She and I had already established eye contact and, although brief, yet intense, I liked the message I was getting. Eric had also become aware of their pres-

A GENTLEMAN'S AGREEMENT

ence, and it was obvious to us both that they were aware of the attention they were getting from us.

"What do you think, Clayton?", Eric asked.

"They could be on the game", I cautioned.

"Nah! They don't look the type to me"

"Maybe you're right. Which one do you fancy?"

"Doesn't matter. I'll leave first choice to you"

"O.K., Eric. You can have the brunette"

"Come on then, Let's get over there before somebody beats us to it"

The Introductions were soon completed, and from these we learned that the brunette was named Rose, and her companion was called Rosanna. They were both single, and had known each other since childhood. Rose lived with her parents, but Rosanna had a small flat near by in North Kensington. This was the first time that they had ventured into the West End together, and it had been their intention to observe rather than take part in the type of entertainment to be found. Nevertheless, they both appreciated our intrusion into their planned evening, and Eric and I were soon being eagerly questioned concerning life in the Air force and in Canada.

As the evening progressed, I found myself responding to the warmth and friendliness of Rosanna's personality. She had a brisk sense of humour, yet she impressed me as being a girl who was capable of great kindness, understanding and affection. Rose was a typical cockney, but Rosanna's speech was more refined, and her features added a degree of dignity to the elegance that could have only resulted from a deliberate and sustained effort at self-improvement. Not that Rose lacked charm. indeed, she was a very attractive girl. But her appeal was physical, whereas Rosanna possessed an aesthetic quality which I found every bit as appealing as her natural attributes.

Getting to know the girls was great fun, and the passing of time went unnoticed as a result of our interest in them. As the traditional call of "Time gentlemen, please", accompanied by the ringing of a hand bell was added to the general hubbub, hurried transport arrangements were made. Eric and I wanted to call a taxi, but the girls insisted on travelling on the Underground, so we offered to accompany them home.

The platforms of Piccadilly Underground station were by then crowded with the people who used the deep caverns as makeshift air raid shelters at night, and we had to pick our way between the sleeping bags and other articles of bedding in order to board our train.

On completion of the half-hour tube journey to Westbourne park, we walked through the darkened streets until we came to the neat row of three-storey terraced houses in which the girls lived. The next day was Sunday, so I invited Rosanna to meet me for an afternoon in Hyde Park, weather permitting. She agreed to this, so I kissed her goodnight at the door to her flat before rejoining Eric for the trip back to the Club.

That night, before I finally slept, I carried out a severe appraisal of myself as a person, and found much that was disturbing. There was I, not yet twenty, yet I had already given two young girls the impression that I was little more that a fickle philanderer, and I now had another innocent person lined up for the run-around. Then I recalled what Eric had said earlier that evening. Life had a lot to offer, and much of it was still unknown to me. Surely I was not to be condemned for wanting to sample some of the good life during whatever time was still available to me! After all, my past would be of little significance to anyone if I was to get the chop, and there was just a remote chance that I might meanwhile provide some comfort and happiness for someone who needed it. The only requirement was that I should be careful not to permit an association to become too seriously involved.

Sunday turned out to be clear and bright, but with a chill in the air. During the afternoon, Rosanna and I spent most of our time together in discussing many topics, and I found myself impressed by her wide knowledge and her ability to converse with intelligence on whatever subject I introduced. She was keen to learn all that she could about my native Canada, but I had to admit that I hadn't seen much of it myself. She expressed a desire to have a holiday there once the war was over, and I assured her that it would be the holiday of a lifetime, but that she would have to be prepared to do a lot of travelling because of the vastness of the country.

Eric had gone back to the squadron (but not before arranging to date Rose again on his next leave), so most of the remaining seven days was spent with Rosanna. She took me on a tour of the sights, but mostly we preferred to watch a good movie, visit a pub, or just sit in a cafe chatting over a cup of tea or coffee. We tended to avoid crowds however, and much preferred a leisurely stroll through one of the many parks when the weather was right. Getting to know Rosanna was easy because of her out-going personality, yet there was ever present a reserve of mystery, promise and intrigue about her that served to draw me ever closer. As the week progressed, I was forced to the conclusion that here was a very special kind of girl - the kind that I would like to spend the rest of my life with.

Saturday, November 27th, 1943 found me back at Bardney, having thoroughly enjoyed one of the most relaxing and satisfying leave periods I had ever had. I learned that the squadron had taken part in two further raids on Berlin during my absence, and had suffered the loss of ED-656 (WS/V) on the 19th. The aircraft, piloted by Pilot Officer Robinson (and carrying a Second Dickie) had crashed on returning to base, and all of the crew had perished, with the exceptions of the two gunners, F/Sgt Mitchell and Sgt Casey.

Dick Jones was also back on the squadron, having been married to Edith on the 13th. I met him in the Mess shortly after my return, and was privately treated to a detailed account of the marriage ceremony and the short but ecstatic honeymoon, which had been celebrated in York and Bridlington. His lucid and detailed account of the proceedings left me with little to imagine, and I found myself possessed of mixed feelings of desire, envy - even jealousy - for my old friend. Nevertheless, I was please to see the effect that the event had produced. I had never known him to be so happy and contented. Because he was anxious to get his tour completed - and because we were still not fully operational - he had volunteered to fly as a spare gunner, and had already notched up a couple of extra trips toward the required number of thirty. On the following day, I also put my name forward as a volunteer.

It was to be December the second before weather conditions allowed the squadron to operate again. Once more, we were compelled to stand down because of crew shortages, but Dick Jones was on the battle order as spare mid upper gunner with Pilot Officer Warwick's crew from A Flight. I was relieved on learning this because I knew the crew to be more experienced than ours, they being into the second half of their tour. In fact their operational standing was indicated by the fact that a Second Dickie would be flying with them that night.

After the evening meal, I found Dick seated at a table in the bar lounge, and he was busily writing a letter. After drawing a pint of beer from the bar, I walked over to join him.

"Writing that last letter home, Dick", I smirked, but not without a feeling of remorse for having said it.

Before making a reply, he smiled and aimed a playful swing in my direction. I side-stepped and sat down in the chair opposite.

"Just writing to Edith", he said, Third one this week. I'm not up to writing letters, but she's worth the effort". At this, he folded the unfinished letter and laid it on the table beside a photograph of her.

I took a swig from my pint, then pulled a pack of cigarettes from my pocket and offered him one. After we had both lit up, I asked him what the target was.

"It's the Big City again", he replied with a grimace.

"Never mind. You should be alright with Warwick. It's a good crew. anyway, Dick Lodge should be back soon, and we want you in the crew where you belong. Gerry's a good man, but I think we should stick together".

Fig 12 Rear gun turret of a Lancaster Bomber

A GENTLEMAN'S AGREEMENT

I then went on to outline the new tactic we had been experimenting with. Dick agreed that it had interesting possibilities, and he expressed his eagerness to get back with the crew so that he and I could develop it further.

On having exhausted the subject of evasion techniques for the time being, Dick again steered our conversation back in the direction of his favourite topic - Edith. Then, in the midst of propounding her qualities, he grew suddenly serious and said, "Clayton, I want you to do something for me". At this he hesitated and added, "I want you to understand that I wouldn't ask this of anyone else".

"Just name it, Dick", I invited him.

"I'm asking you to promise that, should anything happen to me, you'll take care of Edith for me".

My initial reaction to his request was to refuse it because of what my compliance might entail, so my response was slow in coming. Then, on hurried reflection, I considered that, because we were members of the same crew, it was likely that neither of us would survive if we were to be shot down.

"O.K., Dick", I assured him. "You have my word on it", and we shook hands.

Because it was nearing time for takeoff, Dick gathered together his writing materials and left. I downed my beer and joined the other's at the bar. Later that evening I walked across the airfield and took up a position with what was known as "The Press-On Gang At the End Of The Runway" In order to watch the squadron depart for the raid. As each of the heavily-laden Lancasters lined up with the runway and revved up, the assembled collection of WAAF's, ground crew bods and off-duty aircrew waved and cheered in the traditional manner. First of the twenty or so aircraft off was piloted by fellow Canadian Flight Lieutenant "Mitch" Mitchell, with my old friends Plunket and Rogers manning the turrets of W-4964 (WS/J). Named 'Johnny Walker", she bore the world-famous whisky logo emblazoned beneath the cockpit.

Others that I recognised in the gathering gloom were Jack Dickinson, a native of my home town of Prince Albert, and the seemingly indestructible Knox and Travena, gunners of Pilot Officer Argent's crew. Another crew had 'borrowed' the Spirit of Russia for the night, but I couldn't recognise the crew as I watched my familiar old tail turret disappear down the runway and lift off into the night.

At last DV-334 (WS/C) swung into position at the end of the runway. A green Aldis light winked from the nearby control caravan, and the four Merlins roared as P/O Warwick unbridled the eight-thousand horses in his charge. As C Charlie began to roll, I stepped forward from the rest and raised both thumbs as a gesture of good luck to the lone figure of Dick seated in the perspex dome of his turret atop the fuselage. He grinned and waved back at me as the aircraft pulled away, and I watched the white tail light as it bounced along the runway before steadying and rising upwards. When the light was no longer in sight, I turned and walked back in the direction of the billets.

Later, I picked up a mug of cocoa and a plateful of bread buns and Leicester cheese chunks from the Mess and retired to my room to write a letter home. After finishing it, I wrote one to Rosanna and included it in a bundle of nylon stockings for her.

At about six o'clock the next morning, I was awakened by the sound of movement in the room, and turned on my pillow, expecting to see Dick. Instead I saw two men in the uniform of the Service Police, and one of them was standing in front of Dick's open locker. "What the hell's going on?", I barked at the one wearing corporal's stripes. He quickly turned in my direction, obviously shaken by the tone of my outburst.

"I'm afraid your roommate's bought it, Sir," he explained, "and we've been sent to collect his kit and his personal belongings".

I sat up, trying frantically to rub the sleep from my eyes. 'This isn't real', I thought to myself. 'I'm just having a bad dream, that's all'. But the two S.P's were still there when I again opened my eyes.

"You mean he's missing? - failed to return? - I want the details", I demanded.

"I'm sorry, Sir, but we don't have the details. All I know is that we've been ordered to empty his locker. I suggest you contact the flight offices. There should be somebody there who can tell you what you want to know".

Once the S.P.'s had completed their task and left, I got up and dressed while trying to collect my muddled thoughts. My first job was to inform the other members of the crew, then try to find out the truth of what had happened to Dick. 'I'd best have a shave and get down there'. I thought. I opened my locker in order to get my shaving gear, but it wasn't there. In its place was a small canvas holdall which I recognised as the one that Dick kept his in. I decided to postpone my ablutions for the present, and went down stairs to find a telephone. When I finally contacted Bill in the Officers' Mess, I told him what had happened.

"I know, Clayton", he replied. "The C.O. told me a few minutes ago. And he isn't missing, he's dead, I'm afraid. They were shot down near here by a Jerry bandit on the return flight. Two managed to bale out, but the others were all killed, including Dick".

I stood at the telephone transfixed, unable to speak, unable to fully grasp the significance of what had been said. Not missing - dead. Only two survivors. Jumped by a bloody Jerry. I could picture Dick struggling to get out of his turret and down to the escape door. Maybe he had been wounded. Maybe he had been killed in the attack. So many questions. No answers.

"Hello. You still there, Clayton?" It was Bill's voice coming over the telephone again.

"Yes, I'm here, Bill. What about the crew? Should I tell them?"

"No, I'll do that later. Just you get your breakfast and get down to the flights. I'll see you there".

I replaced the receiver and climbed the stairs back to my room. Once there, I resumed the search for my missing shaving kit, but without success. Dick and I had never been fussy about the privacy of lockers, hence the mix-up. There was no real mystery concerning the disappearance of my shaving gear. It had probably been in his locker, and that was now empty. As I continued the search, I found Dick's pen, ink and writing tablet in a zip-up valise. Inside was the still-unfinished letter to Edith that I had seen him writing down in the Mess. The sight of this reminded me of the callous remark I had made when I found him writing it that evening, and I was at once overcome by a feeling of shame and remorse for having said it. We had all developed the habit of thumbing our noses at the grim reaper, but my remark had been proved prophetic. The valise also contained a number of letters that Edith had sent him, plus some snapshots of herself, together with a lock of blonde hair.

As I studied the photographs - one of a smiling and attractive young woman in a smart two-piece, the other showing her wearing a crisp nurse's uniform - the full importance of the discussion I had held with Dick on the previous evening came back to me. He had asked me as a friend to take care of Edith should anything ever happen to him, and I had agreed to comply with his request. Furthermore, we had shaken hands on it, and that mattered to me. Although it was in no way legally binding, it was a gentleman's agreement, and I at once realised that my conscience would dictate my compliance, regardless of whatever the implications might be. Quite apart from anything else, I had just lost a friend and a member of my crew in circumstances that could only be described as disastrous, and I felt that I owed something to the memory of him.

I placed the letters and snapshots back in the valise and returned it to my locker, having decided that my first task would be to send them to Edith, together with a letter of condolences from myself and the other members of the crew. I resolved to write the letter that evening, but was at a loss as to how I should word it, not having had to write such a missive previously. Deciding on the content of the letter was to occupy my thoughts throughout most of the day.

Down at the flight offices, I learned that Pilot Officer Warwick's aircraft had not been the only casualty of the previous night. In addition to it, DV-332 (WS/D), Flight Lieutenant Wells and crew, had failed to return from Berlin. The aircraft had completed a total of nine raids before going missing.

Bill asked me if, in view of our loss, I was prepared to accept Gerry parker as a permanent mid-upper gunner, and I agreed that we should take him on as a full-time member of our crew.

During the days that were to follow, Gerry and I continued to perfect our new evasion technique, and practiced it whenever the opportunity came up. Once having considered that we had it working right, we requested a camera gun session with a Spitfire, and this was granted. We had been detailed for some bombing practice at Wainfleet, so arranged to rendezvous with the fighter somewhere over The Wash afterwards. This we did, and we were delighted at the effect that our tactic seemed to be having on the fighter pilot as he tried in vain to get a bead on us. After having used up our film footage, we turned the Spirit of Russia around and headed back to Bardney, and I was slightly bemused to see that the Spitfire was following us. In fact, it landed behind us and followed as we taxied to our dispersal.

I was first to alight from the aircraft, and was immediately confronted by a red faced pilot wearing a battle dress tunic with the rank of Squadron Leader on it.

"I want to speak to the pilot and the gunners" he announced in a tone that left me in no doubt of his intention.

Once these had been assembled outside the aircraft and identified, the Squadron Leader launched himself into a tirade, the stringency of which closely resembled that of a severe reprimand.

A GENTLEMAN'S AGREEMENT

"In fairness", he began, "I suppose I should congratulate you on your performance. I've never seen a Lancaster flown like that before. To be honest, I was inverted for most of the time".

He then went on to complain - in words that are best not repeated - that his film footage was useless because of the total absence of anything on it.

"You used flaps, throttles, the lot. The one thing you didn't use was the standard corkscrew manoeuvre as laid down", he forcefully pointed out.

"But Sir", I protested. "It worked, didn't it?".

The Squadron Leader didn't reply. instead, he climbed back into his Spitfire, gunned the Merlin and moved out of the dispersal, leaving us to shield our eyes from the resulting cloud of dust, our derisive laughter drowned by the noise of the engine.

WS/Y, the aircraft we had written off on our return from Munich, had been replaced by the spanking new DV-293, with which we were entrusted for a couple of daylight training flights while our own Spirit of Russia was undergoing a spot of refurbishment. When WS/R finally rolled out of the hangar with a couple of new engines, we took her up for an air test, and were delighted at the renewed power she had. She still lacked the ability to fly in a straight line, but we had by that time become accustomed to this abnormality, and had in fact become devoted to her, as often happened when a crew was assigned to an aircraft of their own. That night (Thursday, December 16th., 1943) another crew borrowed her for a flight to Berlin, and managed to bring her back unscathed, although the squadron lost two aircraft on the night - those flown by Pilot Officers Bayldon and Black. P/O Bayldon's crew took with them WS/Y. Nevertheless, she had completed eighteen operations during her twelve-weeks stay with the squadron. P/O Black and crew went down with EE-138 (WS/B), an A-Flight aircraft.

The average bomber squadron usually consisted of two Flights, lettered A and B. The aircraft were lettered alphabetically from A to Z, so A Flight was allocated aircraft letters A to M, while B Flight had N to Z. It didn't necessarily follow that each squadron had twenty-six aircraft on strength, the average complement being eighteen to twenty, depending on losses and the availability of replacements. To date, A Flight seemed to be having a run of bad luck, it having lost thirteen of its number during our term of service with the squadron, whereas B Flight (the one to which we were assigned) had lost only eight.

Three days later (on Monday, December 20th), Dick Lodge, our regular navigator, turned up on the squadron, fully fit after the crash, and eager to get back into harness. It appeared that he had been unexpected because, although ops were on that night, we had already been stood down due to crew shortage. Dick was immediately placed on the battle order, and was to fly as navigator to Pilot Officer Argent and crew in ED-700 (WS/O), while I had volunteered to accompany Pilot Officer Lasham in ED-721 (WS/S) as tail gunner. The target was to be Frankfurt, but I wasn't particularly worried about the welfare of either Dick or myself on this occasion. Lasham had a good crew, and I knew that Argent would be ably protected by Knox and Travena, two of the best gunners around.

For me, the six-hour trip was mainly run-of-the-mill, with the opposition being what I had come to expect. I observed a few aircraft being shot down, and it was apparent that the Luftwaffe was out in force, but we didn't encounter any of their fighters. Flak and searchlight activity was heavy, but we completed our bombing run without incident, and had an untroubled return flight. The Frankfurt raid was my eleventh sortie.

At the de-briefing, I learned that just one squadron aircraft had so far failed to return, but details were sketchy at that stage. However, on noticing that none of the P/O Argent's crew were in the room, I became concerned about our navigator's whereabouts, and began to ask questions. It was believed that someone had landed at another field, as we had done on the Modane trip, but I could get no information on what aircraft and crew was presumed to be missing.

At last the details began to trickle through to the squadron. The first message was to the effect that P/O Argent and crew had failed to return. Then a message came through from Group stating that WS/O had come down in the sea off Great Yarmouth; that the crew were in the dinghy and were being picked up by Air/Sea Rescue, but that an as yet unnamed member of the crew was dead.

It was to be mid morning before the picture became clear. Pilot Officer Argent's Lancaster had been attacked simultaneously by two twin-engined fighters (a Messerschmitt 210 and a Junkers 88). The aircraft had suffered severe damage during the combat, but had managed to escape. Unfortunately, the tail gunner, Sergeant Knox had been killed during the exchange. The remaining six members of the crew, including our navigator, were unhurt, and had survived the enforced ditching. However, all were suffering from the effect produced by their four-hour exposure to the rigours of the North Sea in mid winter.

A GENTLEMAN'S AGREEMENT

As a result of his experience, Dick was to be denied further flying for the next ten days while he recovered from the ordeal. Because of this, we had Flying Officer Hearn with us as navigator on the night of Thursday, December 23rd., when we carried out a further attack on the Big City. As mentioned previously, F/O Hearn's aircraft had been attacked by four fighters during the Kassel raid, and this had resulted in the death of the mid upper gunner and the wounding of the tail gunner. F/O Hearn's task in navigating us to Berlin and back demanded some skill because of the devious route put out by the Bomber Command planners, a feature of which was a series of feint passes at some German cities, each proving successful in preventing the effective organization of the defences.

It was becoming increasingly evident that the Jerry night fighter force was experimenting with the hunter pack technique, probably because of the disruption caused to the German radar detection system by our use of window (although the new and improved SN-2 equipment had of necessity been introduced as a means of combating this). It was certain that the bomber had little chance of surviving the pack formation, as had been proved by the experiences of Hearn's crew and that of P/O Argent. There were also instances of bombers returning from a raid with evidence of their having been fired upon from the under side of the aircraft, with the pattern of holes indicating that the fighter's guns had been fired vertically. There was much debating taking place amongst the crews about this, but no one had as yet come up with the truth - that a resourceful Krout armourer had hit upon the idea of mounting the cannons in the cockpit of the fighter in such a way that they fired more or less upwards. This enabled the fighter pilot to position his aircraft safely within the bomber's blind spot before opening fire. In such an attack, the fighter pilot held all the aces: his presence was undetected; the underside of a Lancaster or Halifax bomber in straight and level flight presented a target that was difficult to miss; time could be taken in ensuring accuracy of aim, and this was guaranteed through the absence of the turbulence that the bomber's slipstream would provide, as would apply in the case of an attack which was initiated from dead astern.

Berlin, together with Essen and the industrial towns of the Ruhr, was looked upon by most crews as the ultimate test of one's nerve and skill because of the strength of the defences. The Big City differed from the Ruhr targets in just one respect: A trip to Essen or cologne, although it could prove hectic in terms of the opposition to be met, usually lasted little more than four hours, of which about ninety minutes would be spent in enemy air space. Berlin, being inside Germany, demanded long hours of concentration, alertness, and the suffering of severe cold on the part of the crews involved. In addition to the heated reception one could expect from the city's considerable defences, there was always the guarantee that the fighters would be in close attendance for most of the six or more hours spent over Germany and the occupied areas of Western Europe.

Despite the trepidation I felt at being ordered to visit Berlin for the first time, the outward flight passed without incident. the presence of fighters within the stream was savagely demonstrated by the number of bombers that I saw spiralling down in flames along the route to the target. The fearsome spectacle of a fully-laden bomber meeting such a fate was one never to be forgotten. The slow, agonizing downward spinning, flame-engulfed hulk; the pieces breaking away; the holocaust when it hit the ground. I observed and reported six such disasters during our flight to the target.

On reaching Berlin, we found the city to be almost totally blanketed in cloud which was effectively illuminated by the searchlights beneath it. This presented the area as a sheet of opaque perspex across which the bombers could be clearly seen as they crawled like army ants across the brightly lit cloud tops. The gunners were sending up a box barrage, and I saw a couple of single-engined fighters lurking beneath us as we began our bombing run.

At last the bombs were gone, and we had taken our worthless picture of the cloud cover before turning north into the night. Suddenly the gathering darkness glowed red as another Lancaster stopped one a few hundred feet above us and began its death dive. The skipper took immediate evasive action, throwing us into a steep dive to port. But the stricken Lanc followed us, and Bill asked me for instructions on its location and what further action to take in order to avoid a collision. I watched and waited unable to decide on which way we should go. The doomed aircraft was obviously out of control, and it was difficult to predict which direction it would take next. The port wing was blazing furiously, also a large section of the fuselage aft of the wing. It was directly behind us and getting uncomfortably close despite our dive, and I could make out details of it as it began to break up about a hundred yards astern.

Fearing the danger of the aircraft exploding, I realised the need for immediate action on my part if we were to avoid being brought down with it.

"Level out to starboard, NOW!", I shouted into my microphone, having detected a slight course alteration to port by the stricken bomber as it continued its death throes. Even as I spoke, the fire in the after

A GENTLEMAN'S AGREEMENT

part of the fuselage flared, and I could clearly see inside the cockpit two dark figures silhouetted against the flames as they struggled to make their escape. The Spirit of Russia winged over to starboard at once, and I fought against the forces of gravity in order to stand up and watch the wretched Lancaster as it disappeared from sight beneath my turret. As we began to level out, the falling aircraft again came into view, permitting me to see that the port wing had broken free, leaving the still burning fuselage to spin drunkenly downwards. Once clear of the danger, we resumed course, while I watched the ill-fated Lanc continue its downward plunge. The fire had spread from the fuselage to the starboard wing by this time, and more bits were beginning to break off, but I didn't see any parachutes come out, nor had I been able to read the aircraft's markings. 'Poor devils', I thought as I watched it strike the ground far below us, 'there but for the grace of God go us!'.

Some four hours later, we touched down at Bardney.

Although the Battle of Berlin was proving quite costly to the hard-pressed aircrews of Bomber Command and the Pathfinders, Nine Squadron suffered no losses on the trip, although a total of fifteen heavies were knocked down. On Wednesday, December 29th., we again took off in WS/R for what was to be the squadron's last sortie of 1943. Once again, the target was the German capital and, although it was to be my thirteenth trip, it proved to be reasonably trouble free, despite the feeling of fear born of superstition that stayed with me throughout the flight. Again, all of the Nine Squadron crews returned safely, thus indicating the degree of efficiency attributable to the squadron's air and ground crews. However, command's tally amounted to twenty aircraft lost, which was about the going rate for such a raid, but the overall trend was moving steadily upwards.

Cartoon by J J Jamieson

Fig 13. In Fighter affiliation excercises the attacker generally expected to win

CHAPTER 16

ROSANNA

1944 was just one day and twenty minutes old when WS/S lifted from the Bardney runway bound for yet another raid on Berlin - my third. On this occasion I was flying as stand-in tail gunner with F/Lt Hadland and crew. The most outstanding feature of the trip was a large hole in the cloud covering much of the capital. Through this we glimpsed a lake which we were able to identify, thus making sure that we were in the right place at the right time. Nine Squadron lost just one aircraft on the raid: JA-711 (WS/A - yet another A Flight Lancaster), flown by Pilot Officer Ward and crew.

Three days later, on Wednesday, January 5th, we at last got our regular crew together, complete with Dick Lodge, who was by then sporting with pride the small embroidered patch of the Goldfish club in recognition of his having survived a spell 'in the drink'. This time we took the Spirit of Russia to the Polish port of Stettin on what was to be the longest operational flight we would ever undertake - nine hours and thirty-five minutes of danger, darkness and extreme cold.

The route was a devious one, and included a faint at Berlin which, together with a spoof raid on Berlin by a squadron of Mosquitoes, succeeded in fooling the German defences into thinking that the capital was again to be attacked. We found Stettin to be mostly clear of cloud cover, and were able to press home the attack without meeting serious opposition. Because of the lateness of our takeoff, dawn had broken by the time we got out over the North Sea on the homeward leg. As we gradually lost height in order to ease the cold that we had suffered for so many hours, we chanced to fly over a British merchant ship, and I noticed that somebody on the bridge was flashing an Aldis lamp at us. Dash-Dash-dot, dash-dash-dash, dash-dash-dash, dash-dot-dot I read and tried desperately to remember my earlier training in order to decipher the coded message. I did manage to get most of it, then filled in the blanks so that it would make sense. Fortunately, it consisted of just two words, so that my limited Morse code reading ability was not over-taxed.

"Ship astern flashing the message 'Good Homecoming', I reported to the flight deck. The skipper responded by rocking our wings in reply, and I found myself reflecting on the courage of those who's lot it was to go to sea in unarmed merchant ships. Their contribution to the war effort was crucial, and theirs was a special brand of courage that was to be admired.

We touched down at Bardney just before ten a.m., feeling fragile after our long and exacting flight. After debriefing, we learned with a mixture of elation and dismay that we had been granted a period of seven days' leave, but that someone in Admin had blundered, and that our leave period had taken effect from 23:59 hours the previous night - just eleven minutes before we had taken off for Stettin. In redress, we were given the option of either taking the remainder of our leave at once or having it deferred until a later (unspecified) date. Our preference for the bird-in-hand alternative prompted us to cut and run, with the result that we were all entrained and bound for our various destinations before nightfall.

It was getting dark when I arrived at King's Cross, so I took the Underground to Gloucester Road, where I booked myself in at the club. In next to no time, I was bedded down for twelve hours of well-earned sleep.

I rang Rosanna next day, intent on arranging to meet her that evening in the West end. We were undecided on where best to spend the evening at such short notice, so I suggested that we revisit the place in which we had first met - the Mitre public house. she at once agreed, and we spent a delightful but noisy evening in furthering our understanding of each other before I eventually accompanied her back to her flat.

Although chilly, the weather remained fine and pleasant throughout most of the week that I was on leave. Because our mutual interest centred mainly on each other, Rosanna and I spent much of our time together just strolling arm-in-arm in one of the many parks, seeing a show or film, or calling at a restaurant or cafeteria when the need arose. She was a most interesting conversationalist, and I found myself stimulated by her witty yet fluent knowledge of whatever topic of discussion that came up.

On one evening towards the end of my leave, we were together in Hyde Park when she brought up the subject of superstition, and wanted to know if I or any of the crew carried a good luck charm on operations. I replied that Gerry Parker flatly refused to fly without his beloved golliwog, but that he was the only one known to indulge in such occult beliefs.

"Wouldn't you like to carry one?", she asked.

"All depends on what it would be", I replied.

"Well, what do the others on the squadron favour?"

ROSANNA

I replied that a memento of the wife or fiance was the most popular, with a photograph, headscarf or an article of clothing being among the more favoured.

"Mind you", I added fiendishly, "with reference to articles of clothing, it is claimed that the more intimate the article, the greater its power of safeguarding the carrier".

Rosanna smiled at this, then asked, "Are you referring to knickers?"

"Yes", I replied. "But there's just one snag: according to popular belief, any such provider of good fortune is without its magical powers unless it has first been removed from the person of the donor by the recipient".

Her laughter rang out across the park, and I felt relieved at the way in which she had responded to my pretentious proposition.

"I've got nothing but admiration for your technique", she giggled, "and I've got to give you ten out of ten for originality".

Darkness was beginning to close in, and the park was almost deserted as I gently steered Rosanna in the direction of a nearby thicket. It was some time later that we emerged, she holding my arm, me feeling inside my pocket the silken texture of my newly-acquired amulet.

Rosanna accompanied me to King's Cross at the end of my leave, and there was something special about our parting kiss and the way we clung to each other, even as the train began to move.

There were no vacant seats, so I took up a position along with a number of other uniformed passengers standing in the long corridor. As my train gathered speed through the goods yards and past the tall tenements perched high above the cutting, my thoughts were only of Rosanna. The more recent, intimate development of our relationship had brought home to me the realisation that this was so much more than a mere flirtation - a means of repelling all thoughts of mortal combat for a brief period. With Rosanna I had a future. Love, companionship, tenderness and understanding. A prospect so different from the hatred, the violence and the uncertainty of war. There was no doubt in my mind that we were in love, and my one desire was to spend the rest of my life with her. Ultimately I began to recognise the importance of my survival, no matter what the odds against it might be. The future held so much promise for me - for us - if only I and the crew could continue to dodge the unthinkable as we had done in the past. I knew the chance to be sparse - too much to hope for, in fact. Now I had something to live for, as opposed to something to die for.

Not much had happened on the squadron during my leave. No raids had taken place since the Stettin trip, so we hadn't missed out on anything. The weather clamped down on activities immediately on our return from leave, so that, for the next couple of days we could do little else than hang around the flights or support the bar. Such lack of activity always proved to be a difficult time for those closely involved in the conflict.

The ever present element of uncertainty that nagged at the minds of a bomber crew was real, although it was never expressed. One was afraid of revealing to anyone - in particular those of his own crew - that he knew and experienced real fear. I felt certain that it was present in all of us, but that we had somehow learned to control it, knowing that failure to do so would be looked upon as cowardice. Over a period, I had come to recognise the various ploys used by people of varying temperament in dealing with the problem.

There were those who fronted an air of exuberance and good cheer, and these were of considerable value to a crew, their attitude providing an element of light relief which was frequently displayed during a time of crisis. Of my own crew, I considered Gerry Parker, Jock Wilson and Mike Machin as being followers of this ruse, together with former members Ken Hill and Reg Moseley.

Bill Siddle, our pilot, and Dick Lodge, the navigator, both projected an aura of quiet, serious professionalism which not only served their individual requirements, but gave to the other members of our crew a feeling of secure confidence, and I reflected that Dick Jones, our late mid upper gunner had fitted well into this category.

Of the other methods in use, some individuals attempted to overcome their fear by deriving what comfort they could from over-indulgence in the consumption of alcoholic beverages during free periods, or by their frequent participation in sexual conquests. A few others (but not members of our crew) experimented with drugs, and some became involved in crime. Those who failed to effectively provide their own resistance to the problem became its victims, and were quietly but quickly removed from the scene, as was to happen to some members of the crew during our period of active service.

On attempting to identify the method I had chosen in dealing with the problem, I was forced to conclude that it embodied a combination of most of those I had recognised, with the exception of the drug taking and involvement in dishonest behaviour.

Preventing the mind from dwelling on the more morbid aspects of the conflict was paramount, and this was more difficult during periods of enforced leisure. During such times, I tended to involve myself in any form of social activity that was going. On the squadron, this consisted of impromptu Mess parties, visits to a local inn with friends, or with members of the crew, or the writing of letters. Efforts were made, during periods when operational flying was restricted, to get us into the air whenever weather conditions were favourable, and such jaunts presented us with the chance to take part in airborne activities which were, to say the least, blatant infringements of airspace and recognised aerial conduct. The much welcomed periods of leave were the most effective means of restoring morale because one was then remote from the trappings of war. Even London, with it's ever-present threat of an air raid, supplied an environment that resembled normality, with people getting on with their lives as best they could in a world gone mad with hatred and violence.

After two days back on the squadron, during all of which time we were prevented from flying because of the weather, we were at last listed for a raid on Braunschweig, a town about a hundred miles east of Berlin. Once again we had an uneventful flight, although we saw a lot happening all around us to indicate that some of our friends were having a rough time of it.

Losses in the Battle of Berlin had been averaging about six percent of late, and this figure was disturbingly high for anyone hoping to complete a tour. There was no question of the Germans not having adapted to the effect that window had given earlier. For one thing, they had changed the wave length of their radar systems, so that we were now obliged to drop strips measuring almost twice the size of the originals. The increasing efficiency of the German air defences was borne out by the loss rate suffered on the Braunschweig raid. This had been more than seven percent, but the figure included just one of the Nine Squadron's aircraft, ED-721 (WS/S) - the Lancaster in which I had flown to Berlin as spare tail gunner (With F/Lt Hadland) on January 2nd. This time, it had been manned by P.O Argent and his ill-fated crew, one of which was F/Sgt Travena, thus bringing to a close the saga of the Knox/Travena partnership.

There was a lot happening throughout Bomber command during the period. although the chop rate was steadily mounting, so too was the degree of success we were having in hitting the enemy where it hurt. The techniques being developed by the innovative Pathfinder Force were beginning to show promise, and a lot of crews were showing an interest in joining Air Vice Marshall Bennet's 'Blue eyed Boys'.

Of the squadron crews showing an interest, Squadron Leader Mitchell had already joined Eight Group (PFF), taking with him my old friend Eric Plunket, so I was in a sense receptive when Bill called a crew meeting to propose that we might also make the move. The vote went in favour of the proposal, and the application was lodged the next day.

Following on the Braunschweig trip, there was a five-day period during which little flying other than training took place. during one of these flights, we took part in formation flying training for the first time. As was later to emerge, this was in preparation for the introduction of the RAF's heavies to daylight attacks on enemy territory - a technique which I was not looking forward to. We had heard accounts of the Yanks being forced to watch their buddies being blasted out of the tight formations that the American Eighth Army Air Corps favoured,and I much preferred the RAF's present go-it-alone tactic carried out under cover of darkness. After all, the Yanks were getting a severe pounding despite the fact that the Fortresses and the Liberators of the 8th carried many more guns (and of much greater calibre) than we had on offer, and I - together with more than a few others in our midst - held a preference for the existing strategy.

Once we had tendered our application for membership of the Pathfinders, little time was wasted in processing it, and acceptance was confirmed almost immediately. We were told that we could expect to be included in the next available navigation training course, and that this would be commencing in a couple of weeks. According to the information we had so far managed to get, membership of PFF would be an entirely new ball game. Emphasis would centre on a crew's ability to navigate within precise limits, with timing to within a tolerance of plus or minus ten seconds at the target being the maximum error allowed. We also learned that each member of the crew would receive an automatic bump up in rank on completion of the training.

Shortly after hearing the news, we were detailed for a cross country flip. The route took in the English Lake District, so Siddle at once seized on the chance to 'beat up' his home town of Penrith. As a result, the fifteen minutes we spent in dislodging slates and frightening old ladies and pets alike was talked about for years afterwards. It was said that even the Crown Hotel in the High Street suffered slight damage, and that the hens had stopped laying for a week. However, an official complaint was never lodged against us, it being probable that the town's dignitaries had been able to positively identify the facial features of old Bill as the Spirit of Russia roared a few yards above the rooftops of that otherwise halcyonic holiday resort.

On January 20th., operations were again called for. This time, the Spirit of Russia was to be flown, not by us (we were to be stood down), but by F/Lt Hadland and crew.

Hadland was again short of a tail gunner, so I volunteered for the job. However, I was made to question my wisdom on learning that the target was again to be Berlin, but drew some comfort from the knowledge that I would be protecting the hind quarters of our trusty old aircraft, not to mention those of Group Captain Plessance, the Station commander, who had decided to come along for the ride. Due largely to luck and the proficiency of F/Lt Hadland and his crew, I was not called upon to defend WS/R, and we returned safely to Bardney just before midnight. The trip marked the completion of my sixteenth sortie, and - because of the number of spare trips I had made - placed me ahead of the other members of the crew in the number of trips I had logged. It was also my last operational flight in the Spirit of Russia, although we were to take her up for some bombing practice at the Wainfleet range a couple of days later, just prior to our departure from the Squadron for pathfinder training. I felt sorrow at having to leave her. Over the months that we had flown in her, we had become fond of our battered old war bird, Then or course, there was the equally unpleasant task of leaving all the many friends I had made during our stay with the Squadron.

We were detailed to drop four small smoke bombs on the range, using a clover-leaf pattern, thus ensuring that our run-up was from a different direction each time. This made it necessary for Mike Machin to calculate a new release point each time in order to allow for wind direction. Our first drop was made on an easterly heading, and we were pleased to observe the smoke burst fairly close to the large white cross laid out on the ground as we turned starboard to commence our northerly approach. The result was the same, so the bomb doors were again closed as we put about to do a run from the east. This time something went wrong, because there wasn't a smoke burst to be seen. Presuming that the bomb must have been a dud, the bomb doors were once more closed, and we lined up for our final (southerly) run-up. Mike ordered the bomb doors open again, and we released our fourth bomb soon afterwards. Like the other two, this produced a puff of smoke in close proximity to the cross, so we turned for base.

Soon after our return, both Bill and Mike were called to the C.O.'s office, where it was pointed out that a smoke bomb had been dropped on one of the buildings at the bombing range, and that it had come from our aircraft. A lot of people, including the wing commander, were perturbed about this, and an immediate explanation was required.

After a period of heated argument and a lot of deliberation, the truth was finally arrived at: the bomb which we had considered to be a dud had in fact been a good one, but that it had failed to come unstuck from the bomb rack until after the bomb doors had been closed, this meant that it had been allowed to fall when next the bomb doors were opened. In accordance with Sod's Law, the errant missile had thus been released from our aircraft at the precise instant necessary for it to score a bullseye on the building. The effect of this was further exacerbated by the fact that the unfortunate edifice just happened to be the canteen, and that the incident had occurred during the morning tea break. Consequently, the small wooden hut was packed to capacity when the bomb came in through the roof. It was most fortunate that no serious injuries had resulted, although a number of personnel had been forced to undergo treatment for smoke inhalation.

The next three days were spent in getting ourselves prepared for our impending transfer to PFF, and I took advantage of this by collecting my kit and packing it in readiness, and in the writing of an unusually large volume of letters - a task to which I was in the habit of showing neglect. I appreciated the receipt of letters, particularly those from home, but letters from me were sparse, partly through laziness, but largely because of the limit imposed on their content by the restrictions of censorship.

As was ever the case, finding myself with so much free time allowed my thoughts to dwell once more on the subject of survival. During the half year that we had served with bomber command, I had come to appreciate the improbability of it. In numbers of aircraft and crews failing to return during the period, Nine Squadron had been almost completely wiped out. In addition to the seventeen aircraft and one-hundred and twenty-one aircrew reported as missing, a further five aircraft - including our own - had crashed. These mishaps had resulted in fourteen deaths and a number of injuries, and the bodies of two members of aircrew, both of them gunners, had been brought back from raids, together with two wounded men - again both gunners.

Now we hoped to become members of the Pathfinder Force, an elite and highly specialised Group made up of screened, volunteer crews who had already proved their courage and professional ability. Because I had in the past spoken to members of the force, I was not under any delusions concerning the increased degree of danger with which we would be faced. I learned that, for the first few trips at least, we would not be dropping markers, but would be going in along with the leading crews for the sole purpose of drawing the enemy fire, thereby easing their task of getting the primary markers in the right place. It was true that we would be dropping a bomb load, but our primary function would be that of making up the numbers.

After I had finished writing my letter, I went on to compose what was traditionally known as the 'last letter home', and addressed it to my parents. I then placed it amongst my earth-bound belongings, knowing that it would be sent on in the event of my demise. The preparation of such missives was standard practise amongst most aircrew members, and the letter varied in content, depending on the personality of the individual. In mine, I laid stress on the fact that being reported missing didn't necessarily mean the worst, and I privately hoped that this would serve to bring about a gradual and less traumatic acceptance of the truth.

At twenty minutes past three o'clock on the afternoon of Sunday, January the 23rd., 1994, we took WS/R up for what was to be our final flight in her. It was a one-hour flip, during which we dropped a few more smoke bombs on the Wainfleet range, this time without undue concern to the personnel on the ground. I had arisen that morning to find that I had the daddy of all headaches. The condition had given periodic trouble since the crash, but I tended to consider it the result of the strain we were all experiencing because of the pressures of the job, plus my increasing dependence on ale and other liquid anti-depressants. Like most aircrew, I was concerned that the complaint might be sinusitis, a fault which usually put paid to a career in flying, so I was therefor reluctant to take my problem to the Squadron Medical Officer.

However, this attack had been particularly severe, and I knew that it wasn't a hangover because I hadn't indulged on the previous evening. Furthermore, I noticed that there had been moments during the flight when I appeared to be wearing blinkers, a symptom which I recognised as indicating tunnel vision. it was my concern for this phenomenon which I found most sinister because of the effect it would have on my ability to perform my duties as an air gunner. Because I believed the headache and the sight defect to be interrelated, I decided to pay a call on the M.O. that afternoon in the hope that he might prescribe a remedy for the head pains, thus dispensing with the sight defect.

I just managed to catch the Medical Officer before he shut up shop for the day, Nine Squadron's M.O. had something of a reputation for being slightly eccentric. A jovial chap in the uniform of Flight Lieutenant, and sporting pilots wings plus a number of campaign medals, it was said that he had been doing alright as a bomber pilot until someone up top discovered his true profession, as a result of which he had been brought down to earth with a bump and presented with the desk job, much to his annoyance.

"And what's wrong with you, lad?", he asked as I walked into his surgery. I told him about the headache, but withheld any mention of my sight problem.

"There's always bloody something!", he exclaimed, making use of what he had himself established as the unofficial Nine Squadron motto (His Majesty's contribution had been worded 'Per Noctem Volamus').

I had heard previously about the unorthodox methods the M.O. used in dealing with minor medical complaints, as a result of which the Squadron was considered one of the healthiest in the Command, but I was totally unprepared for what was to follow.

"Here", he said. "Try a few of these", whereupon he opened a drawer in his desk and presented me with a handful of loose pills. "I just made them last night. Let me know if they do you any good".

After leaving his office, I retrieved the pills from my pocket and inspected them. From their appearance, it was obvious that they were indeed home made. I tossed them away and made my way to the Mess, where I bought some aspirin and retired for the night.

Next morning I awoke to find that the headache was gone. Later that afternoon, we boarded a train for the PFF Navigation Training Unit at RAF Station Upwood in Cambridgeshire.

ROSANNA

CHAPTER 17

PATHFINDERS

The first segment of the course at Upwood consisted of time spent in attending lectures and taking copious notes. In the main, the instruction was aimed at the pilot, the navigator and the bomb aimer, with the result that the lessor members of the crew proved to be something of an embarrassment, they being surplus to requirement. In an attempt to alleviate the problem, a number of subsidiary lectures on various topics had been prepared. One of these was delivered by a Canadian air gunner of the rank of Flying Officer, and his subject dealt with the methods of evading capture in the event of being shot down on the other side. Because he had once suffered this indignity, but had eventually been smuggled back to England by the French Resistance movement, his qualifications were beyond question. Other of his attributes included a wry sense of humour and a propensity for the deliverance of loquacious prose.

After parachuting into France, our hero had made his way to a lone farmhouse. Some time after knocking on the door, he was confronted by an elderly Frenchwoman in night attire, and the lady was understandably rattled at finding what appeared to be a visitor from outer space standing at her door in the small hours of the morning. Making use of what limited knowledge he had of the French language, he had hastened to inform her that he was from Canada, but was greatly disappointed to learn that the lady had never heard of the place. Fortunately she had heard of England, so he was at last made welcome, and was later passed over to the Resistance for repatriation.

The lecturer then went on to describe the experiences of a colleague who had been captured by the Germans', but had later escaped back to England. On being exposed to the usual interrogation process, the intrepid airman had hit upon a plan whereby he could 'take the mickey' out of his captors by divulging details of a 'new' heavy bomber that the RAF was about to introduce into service. The aircraft, which he described as being the ultimate weapon in destructive capacity, was to be the new Huntley-Palmer with Peak-Frean engines. In return for this information, he was given VIP treatment. At least until the Jerries discovered the true identity of the British biscuit manufacturers, after which he was subjected to treatment which was not strictly in keeping with the terms of the Geneva Convention.

The flying training was meant to end with a long cross country exercise during daylight, and this was to be flown from the nearby aerodrome at Warboys. Bad weather prevented our takeoff until almost lunchtime, and the skies were still totally overcast when we eventually got into the air and climbed above the unbroken cloud that seemed to cover all of Britain. All things considered, the exercise was being performed under ideal conditions since we would be compelled to rely entirely on instruments in order to locate our objective on the east coast of Northern Ireland.

At the completion of more than an hour in the air, we had failed to get a visual fix because of the cloud cover, and were having to place our trust in an H2S set, the reliability of which was suspect. Because I had reasoned that my part in the exercise would be minimal, I had brought along with me a book in order to ease the boredom. Glancing up from the page, I saw a lone Mosquito aircraft climbing towards us from astern, and I watched as it drew level with us on the starboard quarter.

Once in position, the Mosquito pilot dipped the wings a couple of times and began to gesticulate in a manner which I took to be a friendly greeting. I waved back, whereupon the Mosquito did a sharp about turn and proceeded to fly back in the direction from whence it had come.

"Did you see that Mosquito?" I asked of Gerry.

"Yeah," he replied. "Friendly sort of guy, wasn't he?".

I went back to reading the book. Soon afterwards, the silence was again broken by Gerry.

"That Mosquito's comin' back again, Skipper. Comin' alongside on the port beam this time. Think he's trying' to tell us somethin'".

There was a brief pause while the Mosquito took up a position off the port wingtip.

"He seems to want us to follow him", Bill announced "I think we'd better do what he says. There must be something wrong".

As we turned in pursuit of the Mosquito, a lengthy discussion began on the likely reason for our recall, and we were particularly puzzled as to why no attempt had been made to contact us on the radio. Our bewilderment was ended on receipt of an impassioned message from Dick Lodge, our navigator:

"Sorry Skipper, but I'm afraid it's all my fault. It seems that I gave you the wrong heading from base, and

PATHFINDERS

we've been flying a reciprocal course ever since".

Bill's response to the news was couched in terms which are not considered suitable for publication.

"And where the hell are we now?", he asked, having given full vent to his considerable displeasure.

"Don't know for certain, but I reckon we must be somewhere out over the English Channel. I'm trying to get a fix now".

Almost an hour was to pass before the Mosquito finally led us down through the still continuous cloud cover. Prior to this, Dick had managed to calculate our approximate location, and this had put us somewhere off the Kent coast. In fact, as we broke through the cloud, we found ourselves directly over a large airfield which was immediately recognised as one of the emergency landing fields which had been set up for the purpose of accepting incoming aircraft that were in trouble. The one we were now over was known to all in Bomber Command as Manston. Radio silence at last having been broken, we were granted permission to land, or 'pancake' as was the term used in radio parlance.

During the return flight I reflected at length on the effect that our navigator's blunder might have on our chance of gaining membership of PFF. Accurate navigation was of prime importance to the Pathfinders, and Dick, having dropped a colossal clanger had in my estimation put paid to any hope we might have. Nonetheless, I had also admired his professionalism. It was the first time that we had been lost, but his action in sending us in the opposite direction to that intended was the worst gaff he could have made in the circumstances. On summing up our prospects, I was forced to conclude that we didn't have any, and that all thoughts of accelerated promotion could be forgotten.

After landing at Manston, we learned that our progress during the flight had been monitored on the British radar system by an alert and resourceful WAAF to whom we were greatly indebted. On noticing the trace of a lone and unescorted aircraft flying out over the channel in the direction of France, she had at once realised the nature of our error, and had wasted no time in alerting her superiors. This had resulted in the Mosquito being scrambled with orders to go out and bring us back. We were also told by the Mosquito pilot that we had actually been ten miles inside the French coast before he finally succeeded in getting us turned around. The realisation of this caused me to feel alarm. During the whole of the flight, my guns had been totally unprepared for use in action.

Meanwhile, the weather had turned really nasty, with the result that we were unable to get off again for the return flight to Warboys until the afternoon of the following day. During our enforced and unscheduled stay at Manston, we had held a crew conference during which it was generally agreed that we were in deep trouble, and that our future with PFF looked far from promising. Doubtless we would be faced with a thorough enquiry on our return, and our one ace in the hole was the previous showing of operational efficiency during our period of service with Bomber Command. But even this brought no comfort when I reflected on the fact that, during that time we had written off a Lancaster; that Bill had been made to shoulder the blame for the crash, and that he had lost his nerve on his next flight.

The expected hearing began almost immediately after our return, but the presence of any crew member other than Bill and Dick was not required. As a consequence, I and the other four were subjected to a couple of hours of nail biting tension. At last the waiting ended with the appearance of our pilot and navigator at the bar. Looking sombre and subdued, they both ordered drinks before strolling slowly over to join the rest of us at our table. As they approached, I tried to read their expressions as an advance warning of what was to be expected, but failed to detect anything other than unrelenting gloom.

Not being one to miss out on the opportunity to engage in theatricals, old Bill sat down, took a long drink from his pint, then positioned the tankard carefully on the table in front of him. Still looking sombre, he then proceeded to study our worried expressions for what seemed like an eternity. Then, slowly, almost imperceptibly, the faint glimmer of a smile began to spread across his rugged features, and he gently raised a thumb to us. With the exception of himself and Dick, we all stood up and cheered.

"That's enough of that!", he admonished. "We're not out of the wood yet. Thanks to our showing on ops, they're giving us one more bite at the apple. They're letting us repeat the exercise, but we've got to get it exactly right this time, otherwise we've had it".

Two more days were to pass before the weather again made flight training possible. At twenty-five minutes past eleven on the morning of February the second, we took off in a Warboys Lanc (X-Xray) for our flight of vindication. This time everything went like magic. Although weather conditions were far from ideal, we made our landfall on the east coast of Northern Ireland well within the required time limit, and Dick was able to present on our return a flight chart that was beyond reproach.

On the following day we were posted to 83 Squadron, PFF, which was at that time based at Wyton in Cambridgeshire. Prior to our departure from Warboys, we were given our individual assessments by the Officer in charge of training, and were delighted to learn that we had all fared remarkably well despite our blunder. in fact a number of us - myself included - had been assessed as being above average. We were then issued with badges to signify our membership of the Path Finders' Force. These took the form of the brass albatross worn as a cap badge by commissioned officers, but was to be worn by us on the left breast pocket flap of the Number One Blues uniform. Prior to receipt of the badge, we were required to sign a declaration stating that we would not permit ourselves to be photographed while wearing it, and that it would not be carried or worn during operational flying.

We found RAF Station Wyton to be a large peacetime airfield with excellent runways and accommodation, and I at once became aware of the multi-national element within the aircrews that made up the squadron. As a result of this, there was ever present a business-like atmosphere, yet I found conditions around the flights and in the Mess to be relaxed and unassuming. Everybody just got on with the job, and there was ever present an air of friendliness between the ranks that was not to be found on most other squadrons and stations that I had served on.

Tuesday, February the 15th, 1944 was to be the beginning of our active service with PFF, when we took up JB-309 (OL/N) for a night flying test prior to taking her to war that night. N was a seasoned Lancaster, having been delivered from the Chadderton factory in October of the previous year, but we found her and her equipment to be in excellent condition. For the first time, I was seated inside the modified and greatly improved FN-120 tail gun turret. Although the space available to me was still somewhat limited, the layout of the perspex canopy was much improved, thus making possible a less restricted view of the sky around me, and this had been further enhanced by the removal of most of the perspex from the front of the turret. I had been issued with the standard pilot's seat pack parachute, so the small seat cushion (normally a feature of the FN-20) had been removed, together with the minute piece of armour plate intended as a means of affording some degree of protection to the 'family jewels'. Because there were within the air gunners' fraternity some who complained that the plate was not in any case of sufficient dimension to give complete protection, it's removal was not entirely regretted.

The flight was to be the first of six trips as 'Supporters', and it was with some trepidation we learned at the briefing that our target was again to be 'The Big City' (Berlin).

Because we were to go in with the leaders of the pack, our takeoff was set for the early time of nine-thirty p.m., and our load would be made up entirely of high explosive and incendiary bombs. All things considered, there was no denying the fact that we were being thrown in at the deep end for this one.

The outward flight proved no more traumatic than any of the previous Berlin raids in which I had been involved. Again, weather conditions were a problem, mainly because of the cold, and we were forced to come down below our designated operational height when condensation trails were seen to be forming behind us. These were a dead give-away to any fighter that happened upon them, and both Gerry and I had strict orders to report these to the skipper whenever they appeared, whereupon Bill would bring us down a hundred feet or so. I was also having problems with my microphone due to the condensation of my breath. This quickly turned to ice, thereby making conversation with the rest of the crew almost impossible. Because of the importance of me being able to give clear orders during a possible attack, I had to dislodge the ice at frequent intervals during the flight by giving my oxygen mask a sharp rap with my gloved hand. At a later date, the vexing problem was to be overcome by the extension of the heated clothing to include a small heater within the mask itself, an improvement which was to earn the gratitude of many.

This was the first time we had gone in with the primary marker aircraft, and we found the German capital unusually quiet as we began our run-up. As on previous occasions, there was almost total cloud cover in the area, but this time there was nothing to indicate that the city had a defence to offer. Darkness reigned, there being no searchlight beams to be seen anywhere in the area and this, together with the marked absence of a flak barrage led one to believe that we were nowhere near our intended objective. I was later to learn that the Jerries often 'played possum' in this way, hoping that the Pathfinder crews would go on to drop their marker flares over one of the many decoy targets that had been laboriously and skilfully constructed in the vicinity of the more important German cities. Berlin was not without one of these, and there was no doubt that more than a few crews had in the past been fooled into dropping their markers on these 'cardboard' cities.

But our marker crews were not to be duped this time. The H2S set was behaving well, and Dick was confident that we were on track and on time. We already had the bomb doors open when we saw the first target indicators go down just ahead of us. That was

PATHFINDERS

the signal for all hell to break loose around us.

Suddenly the city beneath took on the visual impact that we had all come to expect of it. On came the scores of searchlights as if by the throwing of a single switch, and I again sensed the feeling of naked exposure as the sky around and beneath us became flooded with the all-revealing illumination that I hated so intensely. In almost the same instant, the flak barrage opened up with deadly accuracy, and I again heard the familiar 'whump' of the shells bursting near us and the metallic rattle of the shrapnel against the aircraft as we flew steadily onwards on the bombing run. This was the part of a raid that we all feared the most. There was nothing we could do except sit it out and hope to God that our luck stayed with us. Dead astern, somebody's luck let them down, and their aircraft suddenly exploded in a ball of white heat and coloured marker flares, indicating that it had been a Pathfinder. Off to starboard, two others were going down, one in flames, the other with no sign of fire, but apparently out of control as it spiralled down in the direction of the opaque cloud tops. In all probability the controls had been damaged, or maybe the pilot had been killed or injured. Whatever the cause, I was too busy to reflect on it. I had seen a twin-engined fighter silhouetted against the clouds as it passed from port of starboard a couple of hundred feet beneath us, so the situation required that I exercise the utmost vigilance, otherwise we too might join our unfortunate friends in their death dive.

At last the bombs were released and the snapshot had been taken for posterity, thus freeing us for evasive action as we winged over to head for the comforting darkness beyond the city. There now lay ahead of us the three-hundred miles flight over enemy territory that would take us out across Holland to the comparative safety of the North Sea. Indications were that it wasn't going to be an easy trip. Even though we were in the forefront of the attacking force, the German fighters were already in the bomber stream, as was evinced by the number of aircraft we could see going down on either side of us and astern. I was having to report such sightings every few minutes, and it was clear that the Gerries were having a right old turkey-shoot.

Bill had issued an order for all non-essential crew members to assist in scanning the sky around us for signs of a possible attack, and both Gerry's turret and mine was constantly on the move. Our vigilance paid off, and we spotted two fighters during the return flight. Gerry let go a burst at the second one (an ME-109), but we managed to lose him in the darkness before he could launch an a attack on us. I was later to have a word with Gerry on the matter of his having opened fire first. This was a policy favoured by a lot of gunners, but it was one with which I disagreed strongly, not only because the sight of his tracer bullets had served to betray our position to the enemy.

The seven-hour, forty minute flight ended with the touching down of OL/N just after five a.m. on the 16th. On arrival at dispersal, we inspected the aircraft, and were not surprised to find that she had picked up a couple of flak holes, but nothing serious had resulted. Although we were to complete a number of training flights in her during our service with the squadron, the Berlin trip was to be the last operational flight we would complete with this aircraft. However (and despite our having got her shot up), JB-309 was destined to survive the war intact.

Later in the day, I awoke to find that I again had a severe headache, and that I had also fallen victim to the common cold, so decided to pay the M.O. a visit. On presenting myself at his surgery, the Medical Officer (a Squadron Leader) examined me briefly and diagnosed coryza (common cold), thereby confirming my own belief. I was immediately consigned to the Station Sick Bay, but was severely admonished by the M.O. for having failed to bring my toothbrush and shaving fear with me on reporting sick. After collecting these from my billet, I reported as instructed, and was promptly put to bed, where I was to remain for the next four days. Again, I had deliberately refrained from making any mention of the sight defect which accompanied the blinding headaches from which I had been suffering so frequently of late. I was by then beginning to suspect that the condition was in some way connected with the crash.

On February the twentieth, while I was still indisposed, the crew was detailed to take part in a raid on Lelpzig, taking with them a spare tail gunner in my place. Next day, Jock Wilson and Mike Machin called at the sick bay to tell me about the trip. They had flown in ND-494 (OL/G), a fairly new aircraft which they had borrowed from A Flight for the purpose, but had disgraced themselves by getting clobbered by flak. None of the crew had been injured, and they had experienced little difficulty in getting back to base, but the unfortunate Lancaster was found to be in need of more than a few patches. In addition to this, the squadron had lost two aircraft; ND-448 (OL/S) and ND-505 (OL/T). These had been piloted by Flying Officer Field and Pilot Officer Langford respectively. Apart from the loss of two valuable and experienced crews, these aircraft had only been on the squadron for just over a month. OL/T had spent a total of just twenty-seven hours in the air.

Soon after my release from the sick bay I was given the good news that the crew was to go on seven days leave. In keeping with unofficial Pathfinder policy, a Lancaster was laid on for the purposes of providing transport for those leave-takers whose destinations were difficult to get at, so Bill and a couple of the others caught a free ride home. Because I was of course travelling to London, I didn't qualify, so caught a train instead.

February of 1944 didn't provide the kind of weather conditions that favoured a romp in Hyde Park, so Rosanna and I spent much of the seven days in visiting the cinema or seeing a live stage show, with a popular variety theatre in the Edgeware Road being high on our list of favourite venues. We usually attended the first house in order to make time for a meal or a visit to a pub afterwards, and it was during these breaks that we became involved in serious discussions on our present and future prospects. I was very much aware of the extent of my attraction to Rosanna, and was keen to proceed with plans for our future. But she refused to respond in the way that I had hoped that she would, saying that it would be unwise of us to make plans in wartime. I was compelled to accept that her mature realism regarding our situation made sense, particularly when I recalled the tragic death of our mid upper gunner just two short weeks after his marriage to Edith. As always, the memory of this reminded me of the solemn pledge I had made to him just hours before his death, and the solemnity of it served to indicate to me the ignoble way in which I was prepared to dismiss the commitment I had made. Supposing his young widow was carrying his child - just what would her prospects be? Here I was, intent on planning a future with Rosanna at a time when I should instead be listening to the dictates of my conscience.

Despite my disappointment, the week passed pleasantly. Just being with Rosanna was all that I needed to ease the tension that always dogged me on the squadron, and it was an ideal means of preparing me for whatever lay in store. During the whole of the week, I had not once suffered a headache. Coincidentally, neither had Rosanna, to whome I now owed a few more pairs of nylons.

On our arrival back at Wyton we were presented with the good news that we had again been allocated our own aircraft. This was ND-464 (OL/S), but she was not a new aircraft, having served first with 405 Squadron for a time prior to being transferred to 83 Squadron.

We wasted no time in getting acquainted with our new charge, there always being plenty of flying training to do on PFF. We took 'S' up on no less than nine occasions during the next twelve days. Seven were cross country flips laid on for navigational training, but we also got in a spot of fighter affiliation, and Gerry and I got some shooting practice by letting off at a drogue towed by a Martinet. Although we did our level best to cut the drogue down, we failed miserably, thus forcing me to surmise that perhaps I had just been lucky back at the gunnery training school in Canada.

The cross country flight we did on March the fourth provided us with some entertainment and not a little concern. Bill Siddle was in one of his playful moods, so he decided to take part in some more low level flying. As we neared base on the return flight, Bill spotted a gaggle of six American fighters lined up for takeoff from their field, so he decided to go down and queer the pitch for them. The group was made up of three P-51 Mustangs, two P-47 Thunderbolts, and a P-38 Lightning. The leading Thunderbolt was about to begin its takeoff run when we came thundering down the runway in the opposite direction at 'zero' feet. As we completed the pass, old Bill banked hard to starboard and executed what he affectionately termed 'a split-arsed turn off the watchtower' before going around again to attack the runway. After a couple of these passes, our American buddies began to tire of our antics, probably because they would be having problems with engines overheating. As we again roared across the grass in the direction of the watch tower, an irate American 'Loo-tenant' raced out to meet us on foot furiously brandishing his fists as we screamed in his direction. As we approached him, the poor man had no option other than to take a belly-flop on the grass to avoid certain decapitation. As we passed over him, he rose to his feet and set off chasing after his cap, which was by then being bowled across the grass in the wake of our slipstream.

It was at this time that Jock, the flight engineer suggested that we had best set course for our home base because we were beginning to run low on petrol, so we called a halt to the game and pointed the nose towards Wyton. That was when we made our big mistake. No sooner had we cleared the field than the fighters all took off and came after us. There then followed the most spectacular mock dog fight that the local populace had ever witnessed, with six assorted American fighter aircraft giving one lone Lancaster a bad time as they dived on it from all directions. Despite their unwelcome attention, we continued on a straight course for base, and requested landing permission as we approached.

The fighters were still milling around us as we lowered our wheels and lined up with the runway for a landing. But the six American pilots had other ideas. We had prevented them from taking off from their own airfield, so they sure as hell weren't going to let us land on ours. With the other five in close attendance, the twin-boomed Lightening took up a

PATHFINDERS

position close beneath the nose of our Lancaster and refused to budge despite frantic gesticulations directed by us at its pilot and his five buddies. Sensing the folly of trying to carry out a landing under such circumstances, Bill then decided to abort the attempt and request assistance from our control tower.

"We'll huvtl get doon fast, Skip", Jock warned, "We've no' got much petrol left".

Bill was already in contact with base, and the resulting exchange made interesting listening. After he had explained the gravity of our plight, we were instructed to stand by while control tried to do something for us. As we continued to circle the field with the Yanks in close attendance, a lot of activity could be seen to be taking place down below. Four Mosquitos were being hurriedly scrambled for takeoff, and these were soon in the air and heading for the melee. Fortunately for us, the ploy worked. Soon the Yanks were too busy dealing with the new arrivals to pay much attention to us, with the result that we were able to sneak in for a landing beneath a sky that was filled with wheeling and dodging fighter aircraft. The intervention of our compatriots had not come a moment too soon however. As we turned off the end of the runway and began to taxi along the perimeter track, our Merlins spluttered and grew silent, forcing us to request the assistance of a tractor to get us back to our dispersal while we reflected on the cost to the taxpayer of our little escapade.

Fortunately for all those involved, the C.O. was on leave at the time, thus making possible the avoidance of what would surely have been an unpleasant investigation.

Fig 14. Path Finder Award. Signed by Air Vice Marshal Don Bennett.

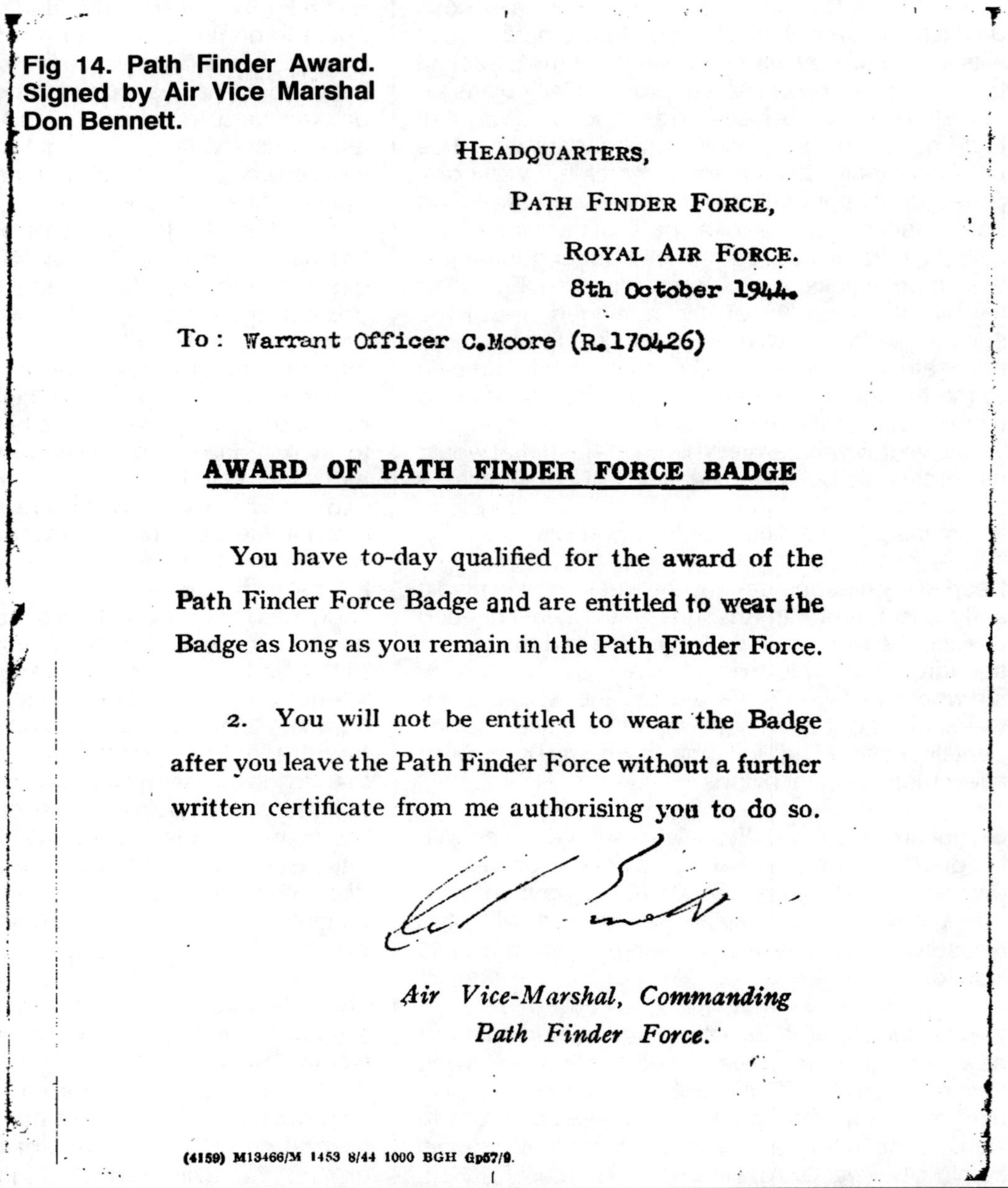

HEADQUARTERS,
PATH FINDER FORCE,
ROYAL AIR FORCE.
8th October 1944.

To: Warrant Officer C. Moore (R.170426)

AWARD OF PATH FINDER FORCE BADGE

You have to-day qualified for the award of the Path Finder Force Badge and are entitled to wear the Badge as long as you remain in the Path Finder Force.

2. You will not be entitled to wear the Badge after you leave the Path Finder Force without a further written certificate from me authorising you to do so.

Air Vice-Marshal, Commanding
Path Finder Force.

(4159) M13466/M 1453 8/44 1000 BGH Gp57/9.

CHAPTER 18

JETSTREAM

Wednesday March the 15th, 1944 marked the end of a two-weeks' training period for the squadron, and the resumption of operational duties. On that night, the squadron staged a raid on Stuttgart, and the crew joined in with OL/S for the seven hour flight, which proved uneventful. In our role as supporters, we were this time required to assist the 'backers-up' - the crews whose job it was to replenish the original marker flares before they had time to burn out. This meant that we were not in the forefront of the attack, and we found the German defences somewhat overloaded with attacking aircraft by the time we arrived over the target. On this occasion, the weather was good, as was the marking, and all 83 Squadron aircraft returned to base safely.

Three days later, we took ND-390 (OL/U) on a cross country trip lasting two hours. Shortly after our return, we were told that ops were on that night, and that we would be taking OL/U because OL/S was in the hanger getting some attention paid to it.

We learned at the briefing that the target was to be Frankfurt, and that we would be taking off at nineteen hundred hours for the five-hour trip. Again our role was that of supporters, and we would be going in with the leaders once more, as we had done on the earlier Berlin trip.

Everything went more or less according to plan. We had no difficulty in locating the target, and the markers looked good as they went down. After we had disposed or our bombs and turned from the target area, all the indications were that it was going to be a well concentrated raid. The main force pounced at once, and the pot was really boiling as we set course for the return flight.

During the homeward part of our flight over enemy territory, it became increasingly evident that the German fighters were once more amongst us. A lot of aircraft could be seen on fire, and both Gerry and I were kept busy reporting sightings. Off to port I saw a four engined bomber which had strayed over a built-up area as it spun earthwards, completely enveloped in flames. As it neared the end of its fall, the fierceness of the flames that surrounded it served to illuminate the ground beneath it, and I watched as it plunged into the saw-toothed roof of a large factory, where it started an equally large fire.

As we forged on through the darkness, searching for a possible attacker, the quiet voice of Clem, the wireless operator, came over the intercom.

"I've picked up an aircraft on fishpond", he informed us. Fishpond was an extension of H2S, and gave a reasonably clear indication of what was happening between us and the ground. Such detail showed up on a small screen in the radio compartment, and a good operator could usually differentiate between friend and foe by turning detective. Because of its superior speed, the blip produced by a fighter was easily distinguishable from that of a more ponderous bomber.

"I think it's a fighter. He came up fast behind us".

"Where is he now?", I asked.

"Underneath us, but slightly to port, and he's slowed to our speed".

I stood up in my turret and peered out over the gun sight, but couldn't see him.

"Instructions, gunners", came from the cockpit.

"Corkscrew port, GO!", I ordered.

As we winged over into the dive, I again stood up in the turret in an attempt to catch a glimpse of the fighter, which I figured would be popping up into view somewhere to starboard.

"There he goes!" shouted Gerry. "High on the starboard beam, and he's trying to turn in on us. Up starboard, GO!".

Gerry had given the order for evasion, so I left him to get on with it, at the same time thinking that it might be a good idea if we were to show some fight this time. There was little doubt that the sight of a shower of tracer bullets coming in his direction would have a demoralizing effect on the Jerry pilot who, after all, had spotted us, and was out to get us. I recalled that more than a few gunners were of this belief, and that some of them insisted on having more than the prescribed percentage of tracers in their belts for that reason. Having a go once it was obvious that the fighter had seen you made sense.

I wrenched my turret around just in time to see the ME-110 go streaking past into the darkness. It was standing on one wing, and had side-slipped into the night before I got time to open fire.

Thankfully, we didn't see the Messerschmit again, and it was to be much later that I realised it must have been a Schrage Musik aircraft with upward firing cannon, and that it had probably been on the point of opening fire on us when we began our dive. It was only when I learned of the existence of such an aircraft that I came to appreciate the vigilance of Clem in having saved our bacon that night.

Our next operational sortie, On Friday, March 24th., 1944, was to be the last of my six trips to Berlin. Our mount for the night was to be ND-400 (OL/Q), a recent replacement for R-5868, the Lancaster now on permanent display in the RAF Museum at Hendon. Unfortunately, ND-400 was to be lost one month later on a trip to Schweinfurt.

A visit to the Big City was always a daunting prospect, but this was to be the worst. Our problems began on the outward leg, when we found that the information on wind speeds supplied by the Met Office was far from accurate. Dick, our navigator was quick to realise that something was wrong, and he directed us to carry out a series of time-wasting dog-legs in order to compensate for the strong winds that were pushing us on to the target ahead of time. Despite this, we still arrived too early, only to find the raid in full progress, since most of the other crews had not questioned the error.

It was after we had dropped our bombs and turned for home that the real trouble started. Now we were heading almost directly into a wind (later to be recognised as the Jet stream) which Dick estimated to be more than a hundred miles per hour - almost twice the predicted speed. As a result, our rate of progress was almost halved, and we were being blown off course by the hurricane which was attacking us from a north-westerly direction. Fortunately, the skies were reasonably clear above us, and Dick was able to take a few star shots with the sextant, thus enabling him to plot our position. From this he was then able to get a fairly accurate estimate of the true wind speed.

The clear skies would also have provided the defending fighters with an advantage, except for the fact that they too were faced with the same problems that we had. Not so the searchlight and flak batteries, however. For them, the conditions were ideal., and the degree of co-operation between the two forces was to be admired. Because of the mixup, many bombers were straying over heavily defended areas where they were being shot to pieces by the ground defences.

After we had spent more than an hour in doing battle with the elements, Bill's voice came over the intercom:

"Pilot to navigator - are you sure about this course we're on?"

"Not entirely, Skipper, but it's the best I can do. These wind speeds are all to hell. Why?"

"I think we're a long way south of track. There's a devil of a lot of searchlights and heavy flak up ahead. I could be wrong, but I think I'm looking at the Ruhr".

"Can't be".

"Then you'd better come up here and have a look for yourself".

There followed a pause while Dick unplugged his intercom and oxygen supply in readiness for making his way forward to the flight deck, where he reconnected himself to spare sockets.

Fig 15. Flight Sgt Dick Lodge (navigator)

"You're dead right, Skipper, that's the Ruhr. Let's get to hell out of it".

Soon after this, Bill was given a course correction, and our Lanc heaved over and turned to starboard. Now we were flying straight into the face of the hurricane as we skirted the northern edge of the Happy Valley.

After a few minutes we altered course to a more westerly direction in order to aim north of the trouble spot for Holland and home. As we rounded the Ruhr valley, I could see from my turret the slaughter that was taking place out on the port beam. During all of the time that it took us to clear the area, there was scarcely a minute during which I couldn't see at least two aircraft going down in flames together. It seemed that everybody was lost, and they were all sticking firmly to the duff winds that Group was insisting to be correct. The German defences were having a ball, and the lads were paying the ultimate price because some chair-bourn boffin refused to admit his error.

Dick was only one of the many navigators who had calculated the correct wind speed, and the information had been radioed back to Group. But, because the information was so unprecedented, each of the numerous reports was considered exorbitant, so was ignored. Winds of such speeds had never before been encountered over western Europe. As a consequence, the entire force was strung out all over central Germany. Those crews which, like us, had elected to ignore the broadcast winds and work to their own findings had a chance. The considerable remainder were in deep trouble. Lost, well behind schedule, and with fuel stocks running dangerously low, they blundered on in bunches, straight into the waiting ground defences, where they were picked off one by one.

When the tally was finally arrived at, it was learned that a total of seventy-two bombers had been lost during the action. 83 Squadron had not contributed to this number however, and we all looked upon this as a reflection of the undoubtable efficiency of the crews (the navigators in particular) rather than luck.

The carnage we had witnessed that night was uppermost in our minds when, two nights later, we were briefed to do a raid on Essen, right in the heart of the Valley itself. S was not yet available, so we took with us JB-402 (OL/R). She had been with the squadron for four months, and was to continue in service until failing to return from a trip to Mailey-le-Camp in May. This was to be our last trip in the role of supporters, it being the sixth such duty that the skipper had completed.

The Happy Valley had a reputation for being inhospitable to the extreme, and there was always an audible intake of breath throughout the briefing room when the curtain was drawn aside to reveal the tape running to and from one of the several industrial towns or cities in the Ruhr. Essen was looked upon as being a particularly nasty place since it contained within its boundaries the Crupps Works, a most important part of the German war effort, and one which they fully intended to defend to their utmost.

Although short in duration, a visit to the industrial heart of Germany was guaranteed to provide a good deal of entertainment of the kind that most of us (myself included) found undesirable. It followed that I wasn't looking forward to the experience. Takeoff was set for 9:20 p.m., and the flight was to take just four and a half hours. Despite my dread and diffidence, the trip turned out to be something of an anticlimax. We found the target defences to be no more impressive than others we had visited, and we didn't see a single fighter during the whole of our flight. This was due largely to some clever flight planning by Butch Harris and his boffins. We had gone in over Holland, thus giving the impression that we were aiming at a target in central Germany. The German controller had just managed to assemble his forces in the area of our supposed track when we turned south and headed for our true objective, thus throwing the airborne defences into a state of turmoil. Our attendance, plus another by the Americans earlier in the day, served to create a lot of problems for Herr Crupps who, it is alleged, suffered a stroke on inspecting the damage next day. 83 Squadron again survived unscathed from it's ninth consecutive loss-free attack on Germany.

We didn't fly again until March 30th, when we took the refurbished OL/S up for some fighter affiliation. Ops were once more on that night, but we were stood down, having completed four trips in the past two weeks.

The target under attack that night was Nuremburg, and the raid proved to be one of the most costly that the RAF was to launch during the whole of its war against Germany. Although 83 Squadron was again to survive without a single loss, no fewer than ninety-four bombers were to be shot down during the running battle with the Luftwaffe, whose revenge for the Essen blunder was complete and without mercy. Much has since been written by historians and statisticians on the slaughter which resulted, and the reasons put forward have ranged from misfortune, through adverse weather conditions, to downright incompetence on the part of the planners. Whatever the reason, the result was the temporary abandonment of the bloody campaigns in which we had all been involved - notably the Battle of Berlin. Perhaps this was in preparation for the coming invasion of western Europe. Perhaps not.

It was at about this time that the promised crew promotions on being accepted for PFF duty began to filter through. Bill Siddle was made Flying Officer, and the others each progressed one rung up the ladder from their previous position. I was promoted to Warrant Officer, 2nd. class - a rank peculiar to the Royal Canadian Air Force. This involved the removal of my stripes and the re-positioning of the brass crown on the cuff. The promotion also entitled me to be addressed as 'Major'.

I was aware that my pending attainment of the rank of Warrant Officer (1st Class) in a few months' time would make me top dog in the Sergeants Mess. It would also bring nearer the possibility of a commission, and this would place me at the bottom of the heap in the Officers Mess, a prospect which I anticipated with some misgivings. Most of my friends were in the Sergeants Mess, and I liked it that way.

Of the many characters that the Mess could boast, there was one that surpassed all others in his ability to dispose of large quantities of ale without losing his faculty for speech. Paddy Blanche by name, the diminutive Irishman was to be found most evenings clinging desperately to the bar while he good-naturedly regaled all those present with colourful accounts of his various exploits as an air gunner on 37 Squadron out in Egypt. His favourite narration was of the time he and his crew had crash landed a Wellington in the desert, after which they had spent a couple of days trudging through the sand before reaching their base at Shallufa. At the end of one such evening, I volunteered to assist Paddy up to his room. On entering, I found that some comedian had deposited the contents of the many fire buckets on the floor, supposedly in an attempt to make Paddy feel at home, and I spent the next hour shovelling up the sand and returning it to the buckets while Paddy laid on his bed snoring like a badger.

Because of the loosening-up effect of alcohol on one's mental processes, entertainment in the Mess was seldom without debate and philosophic discussion. Topics were wide and varied, but the subject of our involvement in aerial conflict was rarely mentioned because of the unexpressed fear we all had of examining the prospect too closely.

During one such evening, the subject of aircrew life expectancy was forcefully launched into by one of the less optimistic members of the group at the bar. The Battle of Berlin had cost the command close on five hundred aircraft and crews, and the more recent Nuremburg fiasco had dragged morale down to rock bottom. There was no doubt that we were all aware of this, but no one was really up to voicing an opinion - apart from this one barrackroom sceptic.

"Let's have a look at the situation", he suggested. "Losses are averaging five or six percent now - eleven percent on Nuremburg, and they'll rise even higher as Jerry improves his defences. Then, there's the invasion coming up soon, and that ain't going to be no picnic. Just work it out for yourselves: anybody that's done more than twenty trips is living on borrowed time, but we're all expected to do thirty for a tour. Alright, this is war, and we're all in it. But I'd like to think I've got a chance, and I haven't. Not at these odds".

Our prophet of doom was really warming to the subject now. As he continued, we all sipped at our pints, shuffled our feet uncomfortably, and tried our best to smile.

"We're all condemned men just waiting for the chop", he went on. "There'll be no wife and kids waiting in a vine covered cottage for any of us when this is all over. And we can forget all about the cane, the spectacles, the false teeth, AND the pension, because we won't be around to get them".

Like the others in the group, I was beginning to feel embarrassed by our friend's outburst, so I polished off my pint of ale and left for my room. As I climbed the stairs, I reflected on what had been said, and found myself forced to accept that the man had only given voice to my own private thoughts on the matter. We had a first-class and efficient crew, but the odds against us were just too great. One night soon, our luck would run out. The equation was simple:

$20 \times 5\% = 100\%$.

The Essen trip had been my twenty-second, and I still had another eight to do to complete the tour. I was already into borrowed time.

$30 \times 5\% = 150\%$.

April the seventh, 1944 signalled a brief and much welcomed respite from the battle fatigue that was undoubtedly having such an adverse affect on myself and the other members of the crew. At this time we were granted another week's leave, and for me at least, it couldn't have come at a more convenient moment. Although it was seldom expressed, I felt certain that fear was lurking in the minds of us all, and that rest was the only effective cure. Tempers had been on a short fuse of late, and I had been experiencing concern over the effect that the strain of battle was having on the members of our crew. Previously rare differences of opinion had been surfacing, and I had witnessed a particularly nasty incident one evening when Bill Siddle and Dick Lodge had come to blows during a heated argument on crew strategy. The incident had escalated to such an extent that Jock Wilson and Gerry Parker had joined in the fray, and the remaining three of us were hard pressed to calm the situation before it got out of hand. I was both concerned and saddened to see this conflict within such a small and interdependent group of men, and it only served to deepen my own sense of despair for our future as a team. Fortunately, once some semblance of order had been restored, the more rational elements within the crew came to recognise the true reason for the flareup, and constructive countermeasures were thus made possible.

Once settled in at the Club in London, all my cares fell away, leaving me to enjoy another happy and pleasant week in the company of Rosanna. There was no question that she provided just what I needed to ease the tension that had been giving me so much trouble in recent months. Her companionship made me aware of just how wonderful life with her could be, but for the war. Although the thought was uppermost in my mind, I avoided broaching the subject of a future for us, because I already knew her views on that. Perhaps she was right, I reasoned to myself. All things considered, I must seem like a bad risk to her. After all, she was of more than sufficient intelligence to appreciate the unlikeliness of my survival, and had probably written me off in her mind, as I had done in mine. It was unfair of me to expect that anything permanent could come out of the relationship. In the meantime, she seemed happy to let things drift as they were, and I was sufficiently selfish to concur. Who could tell? I might just get through this bloody war. If I did, then I could - and would - ask her to reconsider. In the meantime, I was content to just take what was on offer. I was not yet out of my teens, but I knew something of the good things that life could provide, and considered that, in my present circumstances, I couldn't be blamed for wanting to experience them. True, I was of a generation which forbade such behaviour, but - what the hell!

The pattern for the leave period resembled that of all the others I had spent since making Rosanna's acquaintance, but was soon at an end. On the evening prior to my return to the squadron, Dick phoned me from his home in Barking to tell me that he had bought a second hand motorcycle, and had spent his leave repairing it, with the intention of taking it back to Wyton, where he hoped to sell it at a profit. He intended to ride it up the next day, and invited me along for the ride. I at once agreed to his suggestion, so arranged to meet him at his home in Barking the next day.

After a brief crash-course on riding pillion (I had never before ridden a motorbike) we set off for a pleasant and thoroughly enjoyable trip up to Wyton, where we arrived safely just before nightfall.

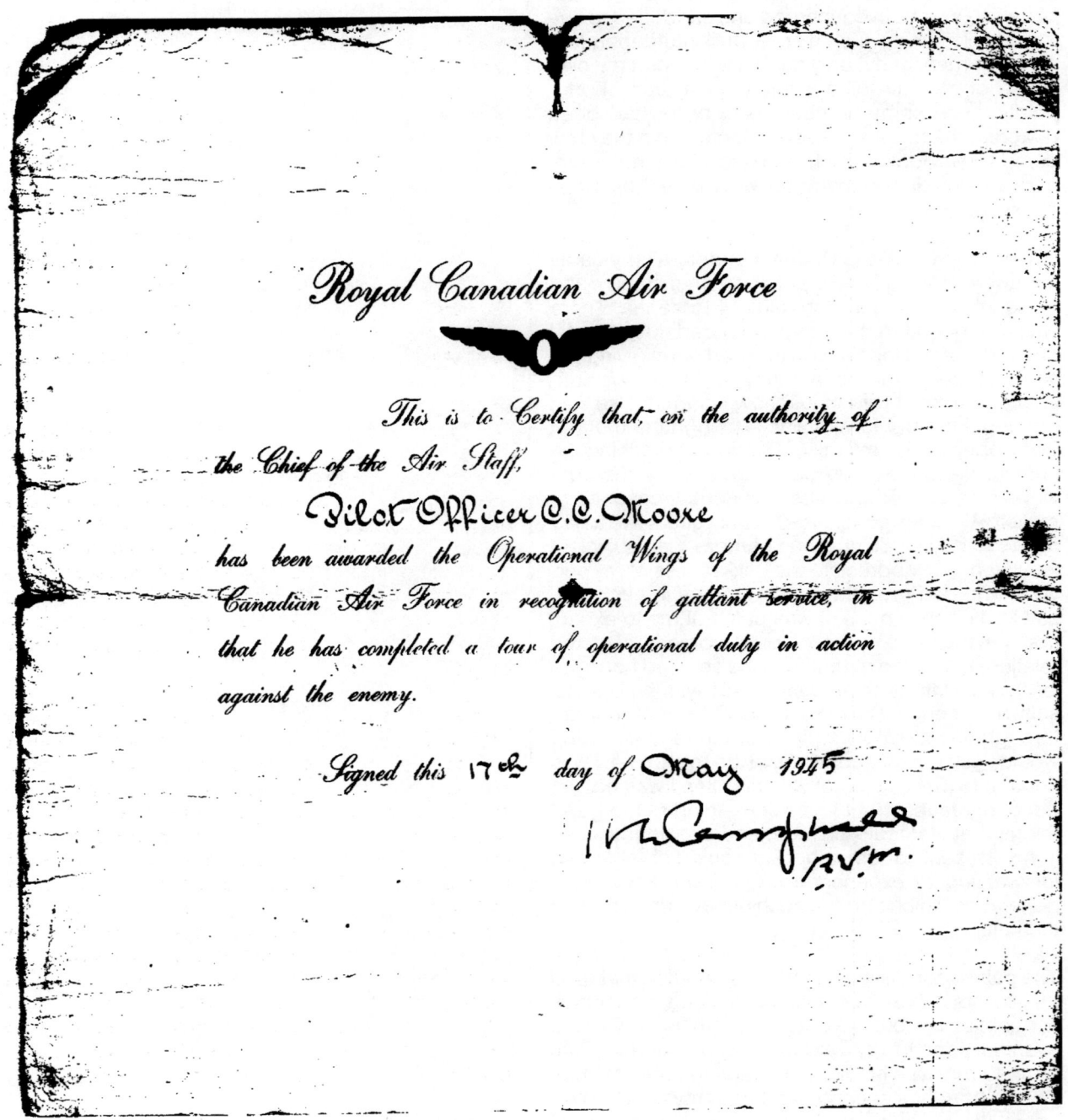

Fig 16. Operational Wings Award Royal Canadian Air Force

CHAPTER 19

THE CURTAIN GOES UP

On Monday, March the 13th., we returned from leave to learn that 83 Squadron had lost two Lancasters during our absence. Both A Flight aircraft, they had failed to return from a raid on Aachen on the 11th, ND-389 (OL/A) had been piloted by Pilot Officer McConnel, while ND-395 (OL/E) had been in the care of the highly experienced crew of Flight Lieutenant Denny.

Next morning we flight tested OL/S in preparation for ops that night. During most of the day I had been troubled for the first time in my flying career by an unshakeable feeling of premonition and doom. Finally, with the briefing over and two eggs under my belt, I settled into my turret as the pre-flight engine tests began. There was a lot of cloud in the darkening sky, and it was raining, but I thought it unlikely that this would prevent us from taking off. Meanwhile, the feeling of abject fear remained with me, and I found myself hoping and indeed praying that an engine would suffer mag drop, or that some other item of equipment would fail the test, thus preventing us from taking part in the raid, because I simply didn't want to go on it.

As if to give credit to the undoubted efficiency of our ground crew, OL/S passed all the many tests, causing me to turn my attention once more to the sky above us. It still looked black, but some of the other aircraft had already moved out from their dispersals, and I could just make out their dark shapes as they slowly made their way to the main runway. The order 'chocks away' had been given, and I could hear the sharp hiss of our brakes as Bill made ready for taxying to begin. But, before we got the chance to move, I saw two Very cartridges lighting up the sky off to starboard signalling to all that the raid had been aborted.

"Ops are scrubbed!". Gerry had beaten me to it in announcing the good news. The conventional cheer of derision and mock disappointment went up from the crew as the engines were silenced, and the wheel chocks were replaced. Soon we were all standing in the rain awaiting the arrival of transport to take us back to the flights. My sense of relief was almost overwhelming, and I realised for the first time what it must feel like to a condemned man who has been reprieved from the gallows. Clem was the first to voice his feelings, and I was not in the least surprised to find that the others had been similarly affected by premonition. Instead of being resigned to taking part in another run of the mill attack on fortress Europe, we had each been convinced that we would not be returning from this one.

Most of the following week was devoted to frenzied activity on the part of everyone on the squadron as we prepared to move the whole shooting match north to Lincolnshire. 83 Squadron was being transferred from Eight Group to Five Group where we would join 97 Squadron as the Group's Special marker Force at an airfield named Coningsby. It was widely rumoured that the move was something to do with the impending invasion of Western Europe, and was part of the reorganization put forward by General Eisenhower, who had been appointed Supreme Commander of the Allied Expeditionary Forces. Whatever the reason, thousands of irate aircrew, ground staff and WAAF's were loaded into a large convoy of trucks and characbancs for the long journey north, while the pilots, flight engineers and station bikes flew first-class in the Squadron's Lancasters.

Coningsby was a large pre-war aerodrome, and as such was well capable of housing the hordes of personnel and equipment that it took to make up two squadrons of heavy bombers and a flight of Mosquitos. Accommodation was excellent, as had been the organization of the move, with the result that everybody was soon settled in, and the squadron was ready to resume operational flying within a matter of hours, much to the displeasure of those who considered that more time was required for the process of getting acclimatized.

I and the other members of the crew had been looking forward to a foray into the village in order to explore the boozing facilities, but the war intervened on the first available evening for such pursuits. Instead, at about the time that the local bar maids would be draping the towels over the pump handles, we were racing down the runway, bound for Paris. We were riding Queenie again, and she was laden this time, not with markers, but with high explosive bombs and parachute flares. On this trip, the marking was to be done by Mosquitos, and the flares we were carrying were to be used to illuminate the rail marshalling yards at La Chapelle, a heavily populated northern suburb of the French capital. Jock Wilson had gone on special leave, so we had with us sergeant Arnold as flight engineer.

At the earlier briefing it had been forcefully pointed out that the dropping of bombs on any of the residences surrounding the yards would result in the most severe disciplinary action being taken against the crew or crews responsible. It followed that our brief called for exceptionally accurate bomb aiming from a height well below our usual altitude of about

THE CURTAIN GOES UP

twenty thousand feet. The purpose of the many flares to be dropped was to ensure that everybody got a good view of the area, thereby avoiding serious damage to the surrounding dwellings - broken windows excepted, of course.

Apart from the need for precision, weather conditions had to be good over the target, since cloud cover would have caused a late cancellation. But the Met men had got it right, and we found Paris almost totally clear of cloud when we arrived just after midnight. Enemy opposition was moderate, although there was a lot of light flak coming at us as we swept in low over the brightly lit city on our bombing run. The flares had turned the night into day, making ground features plainly visible. As a result, such landmarks as the Eiffel tower, the Arc de Triomphe and other tourist attractions were easily recognised. We got it right the first time across the city, and I watched our bombs as they blasted a path of destruction throughout the length of the railyards.

Next day we got the news that all the squadron aircraft had made it back, and that we had won yet another aiming point. There was some bad news, too. somebody 'up top' had decided that the Paris trip, together with all future 'softening up' targets would only count as one-third of an op. There was even talk of basing a tour on the number of hours flown on operations, instead of the number of trips. The news raised a lot of eyebrows - and tempers. As one plaintiff put it, attacking a target was like going over the top with bayonets fixed, and few swaddles were ever expected to do that too often. "They're getting blood", he stormed. "What more do they want?"

For us at least the following week was mainly taken up with short daylight training flights, although the squadron had taken part in a raid on Munich on Monday, April the 24th., from which one of our aircraft failed to return. This was ND-469 (OL/C), and it had been in the charge of Pilot Officer Pezaro.

The longest flight that we carried out during the week was a daylight cross country. As was my habit during such trips, I had carefully prepared myself for the expected boredom to which those members of a crew whose reason for going was the provision of ballast were usually subjected. So it was that I had taken care to arm myself with a flask of coffee, a couple of bars of chocolate, a pack of woodbines, and a paperback novel before we climbed into the warm spring sunshine and headed south.

One hour and two coffees into the flight, I was just beginning to enjoy the interesting bits of the paperback when my attention was diverted from the printed page by the sight of something low down and dead astern of us. Glancing up from the book, I was at once confronted by the unmistakeable full frontal of a Junkers 88 climbing towards us. My reaction was instant. The book and the beaker of coffee went flying as I grabbed the control column, brought my guns to bear, and depressed the triggers.

Nothing happened! My trusty and well-tuned Brownings failed to fire because they hadn't been cocked and ready for action! In almost the same instant, the JU-88 pilot - who must have witnessed my impulsive reaction because of his close proximity to me - winged his aircraft over to starboard and screamed off in a steep dive, thus displaying to me for the first time a pair of RAF roundels painted on the underside surfaces of the wings.

In the same instant that I recognised the markings, it dawned on me that I had been confronted, not by an enemy but by a playful and somewhat foolish pilot from some RAF research unit or other. No doubt the JU-88 had been captured intact, and it was probable that the pilot only wanted to give us a close up view of the plane he was flying. In the circumstances I considered it most fortunate for all concerned that his approach had been observed by a rather inefficient tail gunner who was totally unprepared for the visual impact and panic that the sudden appearance of a potential killer could produce.

On the night of Wednesday, April the 26th., 1944, we took OL/S on a near nine-hour flight to the ball bearing factories of Schweinfurt. Jock was still away, so we had in his place Flight Lieutenant Robinson, DFM as a worthy substitute flight engineer.

Again, the flight was without incident, except that we got slightly off course on the homeward leg and blundered straight across the middle of Frankfurt. As was to be expected, the Jerries waited until we were well within the range of their flak batteries before launching the kitchen sink at us, and we spent a hectic few minutes dodging and weaving through the most impressive fireworks display we had witnessed in a long time. Next day we visited the squadron intelligence section, where we learned that, man-for-man the Frankfurt defences had outnumbered us by at least two hundred to one.

We thus considered that we had indeed been fortunate to have survived. had we not, the squadron's losses for the night would have been four. ND-449 (OL/J); ND-400 (OL/Q) - (the one we had taken to Paris six nights earlier) and JA-928 (OL/W) didn't make it back. With these aircraft went the three valuable and experienced crews of Squadron Leader Collett, Flying Officer Pennington and Flight

THE CURTAIN GOES UP

Lieutenant Martin respectively.

The Schweinfurt raid marked the last of our attacks on the Reich for some time, and the start of the softening up raids in readiness for the invasion. There had resulted such an outcry on the proposal for counting each of these targets as one-third of an operation in the log book that the idea had been dropped, much to the delight of us all.

I needed just six more trips to complete my tour, and was hoping to have these logged before the show got started. I knew that the RCAF was keen to have its operational aircrew rested after a tour, and I was looking forward to a few months of rest at a training establishment, although this would being about a change of crew should I be returned to operations afterwards.

Two nights later, on April 28th., the assault on the invasion targets began in earnest for us with a raid on a place named St Medard en Jalles, near Bordeaux. This was followed three nights later by a visit to St Martin Du Touch, and many other strange sounding names were to be logged during the run up to the invasion. To the uninformed, the appearance of these unfamiliar locations in one's log book tended to indicate that the owner was having an easy time of it, but this couldn't have been further from the truth. Most such targets were important road, rail and communication centres, airfields and defence installations, all of which were heavily defended, so that quite a few crews had good reason to log such entries with pride. On the night of May 3rd/4th, JB-402 (OL/R - used on our trip to Essen) was lost on one such sortie when Squadron Leader Sparks (our Flight Commander) and seven experienced men -some of them equally high ranking and decorated - failed to get back from Mailey le Camp, a German military camp.

On May the 5th - my twentieth birthday - we took off in S and headed west for yet another daylight cross country training flip. it was a bright spring morning,and our route took us out over the picturesque hills and mountains of Wales. The challenge presented by the sight of a small Welsh mining village nestling in an otherwise peaceful valley was one that Siddle just couldn't pass up, so down we went. The roar of our Merlins as we skimmed over the rooftops and pit winding gear must surely have been audible at the coalface, and there was no doubt that those on the back shift lost most of their sleep as a result of our disregard for the sanctity of rural peace and tranquillity.

It wasn't until we tried to leave the area that our troubles began, for we then discovered that our Lancaster was being prevented from gaining height by a strong downdraught coming at us from the hills on all sides. With the assistance of the flight deck occupants, Bill steered us around the village in tight circles,gaining a few feet of height on each circuit. halfway up the hillside, we happened upon an unfortunate shepherd with his flock, and I watched in horror as his sheep were sent rolling down the steep hillside in our slipstream. But my concern for the animals changed to amusement when the prostrate shepherd emerged from beneath my turret, rose to his feet and angrily hurled his crook at me. A few anxious moments later, we thankfully cleared the hills and headed back in the direction of base.

Our next foray into France, on the night of May the eighth provided us with some interesting entertainment. We took off at 21:15 hours to attack a German airfield just inside the coast, flying in ND-551 (OL/V). V had been on the squadron since February, and would survive until June the 22nd., when she would fail to return from a raid on Wesseling. On this occasion we were briefed to mess up the runways at a place called Lanveoc. We had no difficulty in finding the target, and went straight in through moderate flak and a few searchlights to drop our load. The sky in the target area had a scattering of clouds in it, but we got a good view of the field, which was well lit up with flares, and I got a brief glimpse of the destruction wrought by our load as it splattered across the runways. Having got the photograph, we banked and went into a shallow dive to port on a course that would take us back out over the sea. The manoeuvre couldn't have been better timed if I had ordered it myself, because it was only then that I came to realise that we were under attack. As we turned I was presented with the full underbelly plan view of what was unmistakeably a Focke-Wulf 190 as it soared skywards less than a hundred yards from my turret. Unbeknown to me, the fighter had been in the act of launching a deadly attack from beneath us as we had turned, thus robbing him of what would have been an almost certain victory.

"Dive port, GO!" I yelled into my microphone, watching the fighter which was now silhouetted against some searchlights.it was already banking to make a second attack. "One-ninety, port beam, high. Stand by for attack", I informed Gerry. "I see him" came from the mid upper turret.

I could feel my jaws droop under the pull of gravity as Bill tightened the turn,and my arms felt like lead as I battled with the controls in an effort to bring my guns to bear. So far we were winning. The F/W was still unable to get a bead on us, despite its increased rate of turn, which had the effect of placing it on its back. But the fellow at the controls obviously knew a thing or two about flying an aeroplane, because he was gradually getting the upper hand, and I could

THE CURTAIN GOES UP

see that he would soon have us in his sights again. Although he was still beyond the range of our Brownings, I knew that his cannons could reach us even now, so decided that it was time for corrective measures. "Climb port, GO!", I ordered, then realised that this wasn't such a good idea after all, because it was the next move in the standard corkscrew manoeuvre. The Jerry pilot had been expecting us to do this, and soon recovered, lining us up in his sights. I remember thinking to myself, 'if he opens up now, he just can't miss!' The though caused me some concern, so I decided it was time for drastic action.

"Flaps, GO", I barked. It was my hope that this would cause the attacker to overshoot. At least, it would serve to shorten the duration of the attack. He had his aircraft righted, and was probably at full throttle in an attempt to close on us once again. In the split second that it took Siddle to respond. I sat almost transfixed by fear, waiting for the deadly volley of canon fire that I knew must surely come. The fighter was bearing down on us, and I had him firmly framed in my sights. I was just on the point of opening fire when things started to happen fast. Bill applied what must have been full flaps causing the Lanc to lift vertically and to slow dangerously near to stalling speed. The F/W grew large in front of me, then screamed above my turret, its pilot trying desperately to avoid a collision. In what couldn't have been much more than a millisecond, he was beyond the upward reach of my guns, which were still silent, but I heard the distinctive rattle of Gerry's twin Brownings as the fighter roared past, a few feet above us.

OL/V was beginning to vibrate, indicating that she was nearing a stall so I gave the order for flaps to be raised, then enquired: "Did you hit him, Mid upper?"

"Don't know for sure"

"Where is he now?"

"Can't see him, He'll be up ahead somewhere"

"Good show, gunners [this from Siddle]. Keep your eyes peeled, everybody". Fortunately we didn't see him again.

Next day, back at base, Bill took me aside and told me that he had recommended that both Gerry and I should be rewarded for our part in the action. If granted, this would mean a DFM for Gerry and DFC for me, because I was now a Warrant Officer, first class. Although I considered such an award to be deserved in Gerry's case. I had serious doubts concerning my own entitlement. After all, I had so far completed no less than twenty-seven sorites without having fired a single shot in anger.

The day also brought another snippet of good news for us: We had qualified for another aiming point certificate as a result of our previous night's work. But there was bad news, too: ND-818 (OL/T) had failed to return from Lanveoc. She had been under the command of Flying Officer Whitford, DFC, and his highly experienced crew had also included one Pilot Officer and three Warrant Officers. On hearing the news, I couldn't avoid wondering if they had been jumped by the same F/W that had given us such a rough time. It's pilot was nobody's fool, and had come within an ace of downing us.

The question as to why we hadn't been attacked again by the fighter remained open to speculation. Perhaps the pilot had lost us after the overshoot, or maybe he had decided to leave us alone and go in search of easier game. Or it could be that Gerry had damaged the aircraft. We would never know.

By may the eleventh, Jock Wilson, our regular flight engineer had returned from leave, during which he had been married to Mary, the NAAFI girl from Bardney. So it was that ND-464 (OL/s) was once again in familiar hands for an attack on an enemy military depot at Bourg Leopold (in Belgium) that night. All squadron aircraft returned safely from the raid. On the eighteenth, we were given the excellent news that the crew had again qualified for a seven-days leave period.

According to intelligence reports circulating at the time, the Germans were developing a number of 'secret' weapons, and it was generally believed that these would be launched against the British capital. A directive had been issued advising personnel to avoid the London area when on leave unless such a visit was necessary in order to call on close relatives. In other words, the presence of sightseers and tourists in and around the city in large numbers was not to be encouraged.

Although Rosanna was not yet a close relative, I had every intention that she would be one day, so I boarded a train for King's Cross. I considered the risk of having a bomb dropped on me to be no greater than that taken when delivering the things on Germany. Anyway, the Luftwaffe wasn't visiting London quite so often now. It appeared that the hammering we had dished out to such places as Berlin, Hamburg, Essen, etcetera had effectively placed the Germans on the defensive. This was good news for the British populace, but not for us in Bomber Command. Our job was becoming increasingly difficult and dangerous, and would continue to worsen until we succeeded in winning the upper hand. The German night fighter force was expanding despite our concentrated attacks on its aircraft industry, and this, together with the improvement in

THE CURTAIN GOES UP

ground-based defensive systems, was having a detrimental effect on our endeavours. Our loss rate was mounting steadily, so that there were few of us left with the confidence that we could survive. I had so far logged twenty-eight attacks, most of them on heavily defended targets in Germany itself. This meant that I had only two more to complete in order to qualify for two weeks end-of-tour leave, if not an extended rest period. We were an experienced and efficient crew, but would our luck hold out? It would only take that one flak burst or well-placed cannon shell to end it all for us.

My week in London passed quickly but pleasantly. It was springtime, and the weather was kind to us and the many servicemen and women who packed the capital in search of respite and recreation. In the main, it was evident that the 'stay away' directive was being flagrantly ignored. The parks were resplendent with early blooms and foliage, and Rosanna and I made good use of the warm sunshine and surroundings on offer to us. I had become interested in rowing, so a couple of our afternoons had been spent either on the Serpentine lake in Hyde park, or on the River Thames. I thoroughly enjoyed the exercise that the sport provided, and the peace and tranquillity of the lake or river afforded us the opportunity to converse freely, well away from the jostling hordes of land-trapped pleasure-seekers.

We often spoke of our families and friends, and on more than one occasion she mentioned a family friend who was serving in the Italian campaign. Married, his wife was still in London, but their young daughter had been evacuated to Wales in order to be away from the bombing, and Rosanna had spoken of the despair and loneliness that this had caused the young mother. I was concerned for Rosanna's safety in view of the pending secret weapons attack on London and, although I gave her no indication of the real danger, I advised her to consider a move away from the metropolis. But she refused, saying that she felt it right that she should stay and take her chance along with all the others.

Like most people, I believed that the time for the invasion of Europe was near. The evidence of this was to be seen everywhere. In past weeks, the lanes of Lincolnshire had been packed with military vehicles of every description, all of them involved in exercises, much to the annoyance of the farming community in particular, and to the disruption of rural life in general.

At this time, my brother Tom was serving in the Royal Canadian Electrical and Mechanical Engineers. I had been just five years of age when he and Charlie, another brother had left home to set up in a new and thriving farming community at Debolt in western Canada. Tom had succeeded in starting a lucrative blacksmith business there, while Charlie had acquired some land and started up in farming. In the intervening years, largely because of the vast distances that separated us, I had not seen Charlie, and had only met Tom once. Tom had disposed of the business at the outbreak of war in order to join the Canadian Army, and had arrived in England with the Canadian First Contingent soon afterwards. For much of the intervening three years, Tom had been in the thick of the fighting - Dunkirk, North Africa and Italy. Now he was stationed at Aldershot, and I decided that this was a good time to pay him a long overdue visit, so I boarded a train bound for Hampshire.

On arrival at the camp, I called at the Guardroom and made known the reason for my visit. After some considerable time, I was told that brother Tom's unit was out on manoeuvres, and that it wasn't expected back in camp for at least two days. My leave period was almost at an end, I was left with no alternative but to return to London for a last day with Rosanna before reporting back to the squadron. Although I wasn't to know it then, I had missed my last chance of ever seeing brother Tom again.

After spending the last day of my leave with Rosanna, during which time I again begged her without success to consider a move out of London, I made my way back to Coningsby. There I learned that the squadron had lost only one aircraft during my leave, that of Warrant Officer Lane, who had been operating against Brunswick on the 22nd., in ND-963 (OL/H).

During the week following on our return to the fight, we were again subjected to a programme of intensive training, with emphasis placed mainly on bombing, air firing and fighter affiliation. Then, on the night of Thursday, June the first, we took OL/S for an attack on a a railway junction at Saumur. Although our aircraft scored another aiming point on the raid, it appears that the attack was largely ineffective, it being left to 617 Dambusters Squadron to complete the task a week later.

We were not called upon to fly again until three days after the Saumur trip. Then, just after five p.m. on the evening of June 5th., we were ordered into the air for a hurried night flying test on OL/S. Fifteen minutes after take off, we were back at dispersal, surrounded by bomb trolleys, bowsers and ground crew bods. An hour later, we were sitting down to our pre-flight supper, and the Mess was buzzing with speculation on whether or not this could be 'it' - the opening of the invasion.

THE CURTAIN GOES UP

The briefing was very late, thus indicating that the trip must be a short one because of the limited period of darkness available to us. Then the curtain was pulled aside to reveal the target, and our suspicions were confirmed. We were to attack some shore-based naval guns at a place called La Pernelle on the French coast. Strict orders were given concerning the need for pin-point accuracy and timing, and it was stressed that we must not fly below a specified height, and that bombs must not be jettisoned in the Channel under any circumstances. When asked if, in his opinion, it was the beginning of the invasion, the briefing officer refused to pass comment, other than to say that he didn't know any more than we did. But to us, all the indications were there. This was a maximum effort and, although we had carried out similar raids across the Channel before, this was the first time that we had been warned not to jettison any bombs in it, and the reason for this was obvious to us.

We took off at 00:30 hours on June the 6th., 1944 on a flight that was to take us just four and a quarter hours. Although the large numbers of aircraft with us was a good indication of the importance of the target, we saw nothing other than this to support our suspicions. The weather was good, and we went straight to the target and dropped our bombs and markers with only moderate opposition, then turned for home. The return flight took us on a more direct route over the Channel to our landfall at The Needles, and it was during the Channel crossing that we began to detect the first significant signs of activity. As we neared mid-Channel, the navigator reported that he was picking something up on his H2S set.

"Must be a convoy of ships, but it looks like a bloody great island, and it shouldn't be there".

Cheers came from the other members of the crew, and Bill had to call for silence. I found myself thinking that brother Tom was probably down there somewhere, and I wished him luck.

As we neared England, the dawn was beginning to show, enabling us to see hundreds of aircraft heading out in the opposite direction to us. Fighters. Light and medium bombers. then, as we flew up England, the sky above us was filled with Fortresses. There was no doubt now, this was IT.

CHAPTER 20

ON WITH THE SHOW

By early afternoon I was down at the flight offices, having first had lunch in the Mess. I had found the Mess hall filled with high-spirited aircrew celebrating the recent BBC broadcast in which it had been announced that the Allied Invasion of western Europe had begun. Although I welcomed the news, my delight was tinged by concern for my immediate future. Like the other members of the crew, I had now completed a tour, and was therefore entitled to at least an extended leave period, if not a spell on a training unit as an instructor, and I was determined to get it. The granting of the concession was not only the policy of the RCAF, of which I was a member, but of the Royal Air Force as well, and my fear was that this new development might interfere with the tradition.

My fear was justified.

"Forget it", Bill suggested when I announced my intention. "The invasion's on. The Squadron's on full alert, and all leave has been cancelled. Besides", he continued, "We've volunteered for a second tour. Are you coming with us?"

I could see little point in refusing, so agreed to go along with the idea, at least until things had settled down a bit. At last, the tide seemed to be turning for the Allies. For the first three years of the conflict, Britain, together with her commonwealth compatriots had stood alone against the might of the oppressor. For much of that time, airpower had been the only effective strike weapon that could be used against the common enemy, and it - under the tenacious control and direction of 'Butch' Harris - had been used well. The oppressor was now on the defensive, not just in the skies over Germany, but on most other fronts as well. The late but welcomed intervention of the USA, together with Hitler's tactical and political blunders, had stopped the mighty Wehrmacht in it's tracks. Now, ground once lost was being clawed back. Rommel had been driven out of North Africa; Italy had surrendered, and Allied land forces were at last assailing the shores of Western Europe. Together, we - including the Russians - were on the winning side, and the feeling was great. German resistance was beginning to crumble everywhere, and the German people knew it. We in Bomber Command and Pathfinders had spent three years carrying the message to them, and the many friends I had seen going down bore witness to the ferocity of the bloody conflict we had endured.

Maybe things would get better now, I thought. Maybe we might be lucky enough to survive a second tour. Surely the war must come to an end soon, and it would be a shame to pull out while we were winning.

My second tour began a few hours later when, at thirty minutes past midnight on Wednesday, June the seventh, the squadron lifted off for a hastily called attack on the rail marshalling yards at Caen.

Because of the considerable confusion caused by the swift and unpredictable arrival of the Allied armada, we encountered only moderate opposition over the target area. This was to be expected in the circumstances. Because of the vast area of coastline to be defended against possible invasion, the German resources in guns and troops were scattered and sparse, and would remain so until these could be concentrated in the area of the attack. In the initial stages of the invasion, we could expect to be called upon frequently to attack these important road and rail centres so that the transportation of vital enemy troops and equipment to the front could be delayed.

The attack on Caen turned out to be a fairly easy one for us, and it was the first operation I could recall during which I had not seen a single aircraft being shot down. Nevertheless, the squadron did lose one - ND-467 (OL/B), manned by Flying Officer Kennedy and his crew, which was made up of two Sergeants; two Flight Sergeants, a Warrant Officer, and Lieutenant Van-Horn, who, it would seem, was a native of Holland.

Three nights later, on the tenth, we were called upon to carry out yet another attack on a transportation target. This time it was on Orleans, situated about seventy miles south/south-west of Paris. Again we had an easy ride. We took ND-933 for the trip, and the squadron came through the attack unscathed.

On the morning of June twelfth, I got nobbled by Group Captain Evans-Evans, the Station commander, for a daylight outing in ND-966 (OL/C). Known to most of us as "Evans Squared", the Group Captain was a typical RAF 'old boy' of enormous proportions, complete with the traditional ginger handlebar moustache. Although it was not unknown for him to be found on the battle order with a scratch crew, he usually went about his business in a spitfire which he had somehow acquired for his personal use, having first had the cockpit modified so that it could accommodate his ample frame. He was nonetheless anxious to keep his hand in as a Lancaster pilot, and it was for this reason that I had been selected to make up a crew for him that day.

ON WITH THE SHOW

After a short gunnery exercise over the wash, we headed south, to an American bomber base at Alconbury, near Huntingdon. It appeared that the Group Captain had some business or other to conduct there, so we landed and parked our Lancaster outside the control tower.

The engines were switched off and we all piled out, to be met by a group of American airmen intent on having a good look over our aircraft. I engaged in conversation with an air gunner, and learned from him that they were all waiting for the return of the station's aircraft from a raid on Germany. He wanted to know what it was like to fly alone over enemy territory in darkness without an escort. I replied that I preferred this to their method of attacking a target in daylight, flying in formation, and thus being prevented from dodging at attacker as we cold. The debate continued, during which he pointed out our inferior fire power and our lack of a system of collective defence, plus the danger of collision in the dark.

The American and I had agreed to differ on the friendliest of terms by the time the expected appearance of the returning Fortresses took place. As they joined the circuit for landing, my friend grew silent, anxiously counting their number, it was obvious to me that they had been subjected to a severe trouncing. More than one had a prop feathered, and as each touched down on the nearby runway, the amount of damage that it had suffered could be clearly seen. Personnel carriers were by now making their way out to the dispersals, together with a couple of ambulances. One of the latter was already removing casualties from a Fortress that had not yet reached its pan, but had stopped just off the runway to effect the transfer.

As the crew transports began to unload their cargoes of weary airmen near to where I was standing, I was struck by the look of fatigue, fear and relief on the battle begrimed faces of the men as they passed on their way to debriefing. Silently they walked, unsmiling and grim faced, each registering shock at the significance of his recent experience. It occurred to me that they had probably witnessed in the cold light of day the killing of men who were known to them personally. Friends and messmates whose identity would have been evident from the markings on the aircraft as it went down. Maybe it had been alongside in the formation when it was cut from the section by cannon shells. In my minds eye I pictured the big silver plane dropping slowly out of the formation with smoke and flames streaming out behind it, setting fire to the clothing of those who had managed to bale out. Or maybe the bomb load had been detonated by a flak strike, causing the doomed aircraft to bring one or more of the others down with it. I had heard that the Luftwaffe fighters were now experimenting with the dropping of small bombs amongst the tightly-packed formations from above with some degree of success, and that a new tactic, involving a concerted head on attack by cannon-firing fighters was also showing some promise.

As I continued to observe the passing procession, my American friend pointed to one of the men approaching us and asked if I recognised him. My first impression was that the man was older than most of the others - probably in his mid thirties. He was carrying a bulky parachute, and his flying helmet dangled from its lead at his side. His battle begrimed face bore the same tired and frightened look as the others around him, one of which I noted was carrying a large cine camera. The subject of my scrutiny sported a well groomed black moustache, but his equally dark hair had been flattened and disarranged by the wearing of the flying helmet. As I continued to study his features, a flicker of recognition at last came over me "It can't be him, but by God, he sure looks like Clarke Gable", I retorted.

"Right first time, Buddy! He got caught in the draft, so he's over here doing his share with the rest of us".

It was lunchtime, so I was treated to a slap-up meal, together with Gerry Parker (who had also been detailed by the Group Captain for the flight), after which Gerry and I shot a game of pool, and I bought some Sweet Caporals for Rosanna and me. Meanwhile, the Group Captain had gone for a local flip in a Fortress, so it was late afternoon before we boarded our Lanc for the return flight to Coningsby.

I had thoroughly enjoyed my brief visit to Alconbury, and was particularly impressed by the free and easy attitude displayed by the many Yankie airmen I had met. Although life on a Pathfinder squadron was a big improvement on that which I had experienced at Bardney, there remained a trace of class distinction which I found difficulty in accepting because it precluded the degree of co-operation between ranks that I considered to be important to the job we had to do. As was to be expected, Gerry parker, being a native of the USA, was equally impressed by what he had witnessed during the visit, and told me that while at Alconbury, he had made tentative enquiries concerning a possible transfer. Because Gerry had already completed twenty-two trips with us, and had proved himself a worthy member of our crew, I was concerned at the possibility of losing him, and asked him to consider carefully before making such a move.

Much of the following ten days on the squadron was taken up with cross country training flights and bombing practice. Old Bill was particularly fond of the cross country flights because of the opportunity

ON WITH THE SHOW

they provided for him to partake in terrorizing all and sundry with his daring low level exploits. Not that we ourselves had any fears. There was no doubting Bill's ability to place a thundering Lancaster to within a few inches of where he wanted it to be.

Late one afternoon, after having returned from one such flight, I was making my way up to the flight offices. I had just read in Daily Routine Orders that Andy Mynarski, my old friend of training days back in Canada, was missing, so I was feeling somewhat unsociable and unprepared for what was about to happen. According to the report, Andy had just been promoted to the rank of Pilot Officer, and I knew that he had been posted to 419 (Moose) Squadron at Middleton St George, up in county Durham. As I was walking past the Admin Block, I was assailed by a small dog of uncertain breeding which ran out at me and fastened its teeth into my trouser leg. Despite my wretchedness at having had the bad news, the well-aimed kick I delivered to the animal with my free leg was not severe, but of sufficient force to send it yelping back in the direction of the office from whence it had come. Thinking that I had effectively dealt with the problem presented by the quarrel some quadruped, I continued on my way, only to be stopped in my tracks by a blood-curdling shout from behind. Turning, I was at once confronted by the furious and red-faced Wing Commander 'Dixie' Deane (Squadron C.O., no less), whose dog, I was forcefully made to understand, I had just kicked.

He at once invited me to visit him in his office, but the invitation was far from cordial, and I swear that, once inside, the dog (which sat at one end of the desk) had a satisfied smirk on its face as the C.O. began his tirade.

From what I was told during the altercation that followed, it became clear to me that the Wing commander held a much higher regard for the family pet than for me, and that my action in having tried to protect myself against its unwanted attention amounted to a crime just short of treason. In his opinion, such conduct warranted punishment, and it was therefore ruled that I should be made to repaint the picket fence outside his office. Although I could think of nothing in King's Regulations (Air) in support of the C.O.'s action, I decided to submit to his judgement, so armed myself with a brush and a bucket of paint and got on with the job. I later learned that the Wing Commander's affection for his pet was such that the animal was frequently allowed to accompany him on local jaunts, and that an oxygen mask had been specially adapted for the dog's use during high altitude flights.

In the early afternoon of June 21st., the entire squadron took part in a two-hour formation exercise involving a couple of hundred Lancasters. The news was circulating that the RAF was to take part in daylight attacks on the enemy, in addition to the customary method of bombing during darkness. The prospect was one that I found daunting, particularly in view of the loss rate being suffered by the Americans despite the recent introduction of long-range fighter escorts.

During the course of the exercise it became obvious to me that a lot of training would be needed before our pilots would become proficient in the execution of the new technique. In particular I noticed that the simple implementation of a change of course presented problems, and to my mind, was downright bloody dangerous, with aircraft side-slipping and bobbing around in an attempt to maintain station within the formation.

As an air gunner, I was very much aware that I was little more than a very small cog in a very large wheel, and was therefor neither qualified nor privileged to question decisions reached by those in command. Nevertheless, that didn't stop me from expressing my views, as I did with some distinction in the mess common room later that afternoon. I was delighted to learn that I didn't stand alone in my beliefs, but that even some members of the crew agreed with me.

During the debate it was pointed out that, although our losses remained high, our success rating in terms of the degree of damage we were inflicting on the enemy was on the increase, and it was therefore widely agreed that we should avoid getting involved in daylight bombing. I considered that my recent visit to the American air base served to add weight to the belief that we should leave day bombing to the Yanks, and I found much support for me in this.

As one of my concordants put it, there was little similarity between the Flying Fortress and the Lancaster. The Fortress bristled with guns of a much higher calibre than the few we carried, and was therefore more capable of defending itself. Because of the extra armament and personnel on board, its bomb load was of necessity less than that of the Lancaster, which was capable of carrying almost its own weight in bombs, armament, fuel and crew. It followed that the Fortress, together with its sister ship the Liberator, was more of a gun ship than a heavy bomber. It was true that the daylight bombing technique ensured the attainment of a greater degree of accuracy than that of our methods, but the Yanks were paying a high price for their success, and it could be assumed that our losses in daylight would be even higher, at least until the Luftwaffe's ability to defend German airspace had been greatly reduced. In recent months, the American bombers

ON WITH THE SHOW

had been withdrawn from attacks on targets deep inside Germany because the loss rate could not be sustained. With the recent introduction of the Mustang and other long-range support fighters, the Americans were again reaching far into Germany, and their contribution to the eventual victory was to be admired and appreciated. But they were trained and equipped to carry out daylight attacks, and we were not. It followed that we should be left to get on with the job we were best at.

However, not all of the crew were against the prospect of daylight bombing. Gerry for one had finally decided to apply for a transfer to the American 8th Army Air Corps. This he was entitled to do because of his American citizenship. I again tried to dissuade him, but he remained adamant, pointing out that, although he and I were both Warrant Officers, my rate of pay was well above his because I was in the RCAF, while he was on the RAF rate for the rank. One other incentive was the likelihood that he would be promoted to officer rank on the acceptance of his application. Faced with this, I had to admit that Gerry had a point, and that I would be wasting my time in trying to talk him out of his intended action. In general, the remaining members of the crew were prepared to accept whatever 'the powers that be' might throw at us.

Our heated argument was brought to an abrupt end by a Tannoy announcement calling on a number of crews, including ourselves, we were told that ops were on that night, and that the designated crews would be taking part. Briefing was scheduled to take place at seven p.m., so we guessed that the trip would most likely be a short one, probably to the invasion area once more, imagine our surprise when at the briefing it was learned that we were to be sent to the heart of the Ruhr to attack an oil target at Wesselling, Cologne.

We lifted off in OL/S forty minutes before midnight, and managed to dodge much of the action that was taking place around us during the approach. It wasn't until we began our run-up to the target that things started to get hectic. To begin with, there was a lot of heavy flak coming up at us, and there was no doubting its accuracy. Then, just as we were lining up for the bombing run, we got coned in the searchlights, and the Jerries started firing up the beams at us. Having decided that discretion made more sense than valour, the skipper ordered the postponement of the straight and level bit, and proceeded to throw us all over the sky in a manner that threatened to do more damage to our Lancaster than the Cologne defences could inflict. After about a minute of this, during which time I had banged my head against the top of the turret a couple of times, Bill decided that the tactic wasn't working, so put us into the screaming dive manoeuvre. This produced the desired effect, and we soon found ourselves free of the flak and searchlights, but only because we were by then well out of the target area. This made it necessary for us to go around again in the hope that Lady Luck would be more kind towards us this time. To this end we succeeded, and the run-up proved uneventful. Not so for some of the others, however, and I was again made to witness the horrendous sight of a couple of Lancaster being blown apart and falling into the inferno beneath.

Once rid of the bombload, we headed west, soon to be hidden from sight by the darkness that I found so comforting. The tracking of a bomber by electronic means had not yet advanced to the stage which would enable a fighter pilot to launch an attack without first establishing visual contact with his quarry. First he must find us, and this was one advantage that we had over the poor bloody Yanks on their daylight raids. They were there for all to see.

Shortly after leaving the target, I detected a malfunction in my gun turret. Bill was in the habit of executing a gentle weave whenever we were over enemy territory, and I now felt that the turret was wobbling each time the aircraft banked. My suspicion was confirmed when I positioned the turret on the beam and sighted one of the canopy frames against the nearby rudder fin. The turret was undoubtedly loose, and I reasoned that the mounting must have suffered damage during the violent evasive actin that we had been forced to take over the target. I at once reported the fault to the skipper.

"Is it serious?", he asked.

"I'm afraid it might easily part company, Skipper".

"Then you'd better get out of there and come forward".

"I'd like to stay here while all these fighters are around, Skipper", I countered "I've got a seat pack parachute, so I'll be able to bale out if the turret does come off, and I'll be alright in that respect. But you'll know what's happened if you don't hear from me".

"O.K. But I want you out of there as soon as we cross the enemy coast".

I stayed in the turret until we were out over the water on the way back. Apart from not relishing the idea of going down in 'the drink' without a dinghy (particularly since I was a non-swimmer), I didn't want to be in the turret during the landing, just in case. In the event, Bill sat her down to a landing which was so smooth as to be uncharacteristic of his standards, and I was thus able to present the ground crew waiting at dispersal with the proof of my complaint.

On the following afternoon I visited the armoury, and was told that all but two of the bolts which secured the turret to the rotating service joint had sheared off, and that it was improbable that the turret would have remained in place on the airframe during any further violent evasive action. I also learned that the squadron had lost two aircraft during the rad: JB-180 (OL/T) and ND-551 (OL/V), flown by Sqdn/Ldr Dunn and F/Lt Walker respectively.

Later that evening I found a letter waiting for me in the Mess. It was from Edith, Dick Jones' widow. In it she asked how the crew was getting along, and I was at once overcome by shame and remorse when I realised that I had only written to her once during the six months since I had sent his effects off to her. In that short time I had almost forgotten about Dick, and the realisation of this at once brought home to me the terrible effect that war could have on one so closely involved in it. Friendships now seemed so fleeting and of little importance to me. So many of the friendships I had formed during the past two years had come to an abrupt end. Harvey Renaude had failed to return from his first trip. 'Cowboy' McKinnon was gone, as was Andy Mynarski. And there were others, and I couldn't even remember their names. Then or course, my own crew had not been unscathed. We had lost Ken Hills and Reg Moseley through injury, and finally, Dick had paid the supreme price for his patriotism.

As I read through the letter I was impressed by the lack of complaint in its content. There was little doubt that the death of her husband so soon after their marriage must have been a terrible blow to a young bride, yet no mention was made of her feelings, apart from the remark that, on attending Dick's funeral, she had requested that the coffin be opened so that she could see and touch him for the last time, but that this had been refused.

The letter went on to reveal that she had left the York hospital, and had taken up a full-time residential nursing post at a small geriatric unit at Middleton St George, near Darlington. It was there that Andy Mynarksi had been stationed, and I regretted having missed the chance to introduce Edith to him. She seemed to be enjoying her new job and the spirit of friendship to be found within the unit, and mentioned the nearby air field, and the fact that a number of the nurses frequently attended parties in the Officers Mess. It was the closing sentence of the letter -seemingly written as an afterthought - which I found most disconcerting. The news that she was pregnant to Dick was something that I had never expected to hear, and I could only regard it as tragic. I tried to imagine how she would manage to bring up a child alone and without the care and support that Dick could have provided. Then I remembered the pledge I had made to Dick only hours before his death. Although I sensed an obligation to honour the commitment, it had been made in the private belief that there was little if any likelihood of it ever becoming necessary that I should comply, and I felt that fate had tricked me into an impossible situation. I had no intention of getting involved in marriage until my war service was at an end, and it was my resolve that Rosanna should figure prominently in any such plans I might have. Despite all that, my heart went out to Edith at this time, and I found myself overcome by the reality of her predicament - and mine.

That evening I stayed in my room and composed a long letter to Edith, in which, as requested, I supplied details of the activities of the crew during the period that had elapsed since I had last written, but I avoided mention of the troublesome circumstance with which I was faced. As I wrote, the thought troubled me that I should suggest a meeting between us sometime in the near future, but I closed the letter with only the suggestion that we should endeavour to correspond more frequently. In private, I hoped that she might remarry, thus relieving me of my sense of shame and personal dislike.

The next four days were taken up by a lot of daylight formation exercises in which most of the squadron's aircraft took part. It was also at this time that Gerry Parker was granted his transfer, thus leaving us again in need of a replacement mid upper gunner. The position was immediately filled at my suggestion by Flight Sergeant Paddy Blanche, whose bar-room notoriety has been mentioned earlier. Despite his fondness for a tipple, I considered him to be an efficient gunner, and his experience was without question. Furthermore, his propensity for dry wit and buffoonery was exactly what the crew was in need of. He had been without a permanent crew for some time, and appeared keen to get involved once more in something that resembled a permanent relationship.

It was also during the temporary lull in operational flying that I was approached by the B Flight Gunnery Leader and invited to become his Deputy. The post was purely unofficial and called for the person so honoured to assist in the supervision of B Flight gunners and their armament. Although the position carried with it no increase in pay or rank, I considered it a challenge. My duties were to include frequent spot checks on the condition of the guns and turrets of all the flight's aircraft, and my findings were to be reported to the Flight Gunnery Leader, who, together with his A Flight contemporary, was in turn accountable to the Squadron Gunnery Leader. I fully realised that in accepting the post I had be-

ON WITH THE SHOW

come little more than a general dog's body to one who didn't relish the task of cycling around the perimeter track in the rain, but welcomed the authority it afforded me, so I took the job on.

Meanwhile, more than three weeks had passed since the invasion of Normandie but, although the beachhead had been secured and Caen had been taken, the Allied forces were being denied the rapid inward advance that had been hoped for. This was due mainly to the fierce and courageous resistance being put up by those German forces which had managed to reach the area, and it was probable that we in Bomber Command would be needed for some time yet as a support force.

There was one other development in the conduct of the war which threatened to place a considerable demand on our operational activities in the immediate future: The Germans had launched their 'flying bomb' attacks on London and the south east, and it was more than likely that we would be called upon to attack the launching sites. No doubt these would be small and well hidden, but we were confident of our ability to seek out and destroy them.

I was soon to get first-hand experience of the havoc that these ingenious products of modern technological warfare could produce. On July the sixth, exactly one calendar month late, we were granted two weeks' end of tour leave. The 'doodle-bugs' (as the Americans called them) had first been introduced on Tuesday, June the 13th, and the advice that personnel should avoid visiting the Greater London area had again been stressed.

I at once boarded a train bound for King's Cross.

CHAPTER 21

COMMISSIONED RANK

By late evening I was settled into my room at the RCAF Club at 111 Cromwell Road, SW7, having unpacked my luggage and stored the contents. In addition to my uniforms and other articles of clothing needed for a two-week stay, I had brought with me a few more pairs of nylon stockings for Rosanna; the Sweet Caporals I had purchased at the American Air Force base, and a substantial supply of chocolate bars. The latter I had saved from the standard issue of two bars which we received before taking off on a raid, and these were intended as a supplement to the meagre sweets ration to which civilians were limited. I had telephoned Rosanna on my arrival, and it had been agreed that she would meet me at the Club the following afternoon.

Our meeting was blessed with a clear blue sky and warm summer sunshine as we left the Club and walked along the Cromwell and Gloucester Roads in the direction of our favourite haunt - Hyde Park. As always, we had a lot of things to discuss, and we had almost reached Palace Gate before I discovered that I had forgotten to bring any cigarettes with me.

The purchasing of a pack of cigarettes in wartime Britain was never easy, and called for a lot of pre-planning and psychology. The drill was to locate a likely looking shop and wait until there were no customers in it. Once the conditions were exactly right, you then entered and made known to the disinterested shopkeeper the nature of your need, having first assumed your most pleasant demeanour. If you got it right, it was not unknown for a packet of the precious weed to be secreted from beneath the counter and tendered to you, particularly if you happened to be clad in the uniform of one of His Majesty's forces.

We had selected one such establishment, and I had walked in, closely followed by Rosanna. I had already made known our requirement, and was anxiously awaiting the shopkeeper's response, when the sound of an approaching aircraft was heard. The engine noise was unfamiliar to me, it being a raucous, throbbing sound unlike any piston-driven engine I had heard before. The shopkeeper was also listening intently to the sound, and I calculated that the aircraft must be almost directly overhead when the engine suddenly ceased its guttural throb. The deathly silence that followed was at once broken by the urgent shout of warning from the proprietor as he dived from view beneath the counter.

"Flying bomb! Get down!", he screamed, in a voice that reminded me of Corporal Kosick and my days at Edmonton.

I didn't hesitate, but headed for the floor boards pulling Rosanna down with me. As I did so, I noticed that the shop door was standing open. It seemed that Rosanna had neglected to close it when she followed me in. A few seconds later, the eerie silence in the street outside was shattered by a whacking great bang and the sound of falling bricks and masonry somewhere down the street. My ears popped; the tape striped shop window rattled in its frame, and the door was violently sucked shut by the vacuum created by the backlash of the nearby explosion. We rose to our feet and hurried outside, to be met by a thick cloud of choking dust rolling up the street from the newly created bombsight. Through the airborne smoke and dust we could see dim figures hurrying in the direction of the incident, and the cries and screams of the injured mingled with the running footsteps of the would be rescuers, some of which were already clawing at the rubble and shattered glass with their bare hands. At that moment, a Red Cross ambulance which happened to be going down the street pulled up at the edge of the rubble, and I watched the driver and assistant, both female, hurry to take part in the rescue.

Help was by then coming from all directions, and I could see no point in us adding to the resulting confusion, so I re-entered the tobacconist's shop, again, followed by Rosanna.

The shopkeeper, who appeared to be a part-time member of the emergency services, was already reporting the incident by telephone when we returned to the shop. After completing the call, he turned to me.

"I believe you wanted cigarettes", he said as he produced two twenty packs of Player's from beneath the counter and handed them over to me. I produced a couple of half crowns from my pocket and laid them on the counter. He pushed the coins back at me.

"You can have those for nothin", he said.

"But I don't understand, Sir".

"The fact that you left the door open has saved my shop window from finishing up out on the street when the bomb went off", he explained with a broad smile. Indeed, as we resumed our walk in the direction of the park, broken glass crunched beneath our feet, and we noticed that a lot of shop windows had been shattered by the blast.

Half an hour later, Rosanna and I were deep within the warm summer splendour of Hyde Park, with its colourful profusion of carefully tended flowers and smooth lawns, and this, together with the song of the birds, provided a sharp contrast to the devastation we had witnessed earlier.

The park offered the ideal setting for the relaxation that we craved, with the total absence of the vulgar imperfections of the city that surrounded us hidden from our view by the artistry of nature. Even so, we were to be denied the luxury of complete freedom from fear. Since the introduction of the flying bomb, Greater London was under constant air raid alert, with only local sirens being sounded when one or more of the bombs was known to be headed in that direction. The wailing of a new alert had just been silenced when the peace and quiet of the park was again broken by the unique note of one of the bombs as it approached. Because we could see no shelter nearby, we stopped to watch its progress, and were relieved to see that the craft would pass about a mile to the east - provided it stayed on course. At first it was just a speck in the cloudless sky but, as it grew nearer, I could clearly distinguish its rugged shape - the pointed, cigar-shaped body; the stubby, square-cut wings; the squat engine unit mounted above the tailplane. This was a throw-away weapon, designed to make just one flight, and it embodied only that which was necessary to the execution of its basic function - its capacity to deliver death and destruction to the British people. It had none of the refinements one would expect to see on a service aircraft. Even the finish was utilitarian. A drab black matt colouring which served to emphasize the sinister intention for which the weapon had been created.

As I watched its progress, I began to appreciate something of the degree of demoralizing uncertainty that accompanied the sudden appearance and performance of such a devilish and diminutive craft. Rosanna had witnessed the arrival of quite a number of them since their introduction on the 13th June, and she was busily describing to me what I could expect to see happen as it neared the end of its journey. Its steadfast flight had by then taken it past us, and I calculated its altitude to be about two thousand feet. However, it was travelling much faster than any other aircraft I had seen previously - probably in excess of four hundred mph. Suddenly, and without any prior indication, the engine silenced itself, and the thing immediately nosed over and plunged into the city at a location which I reckoned would be somewhere south of the Thames. Although distant, the resulting explosion could be clearly heard, and the spot was marked by a cloud of smoke and dust that rose into view above the trees that surrounded us.

I was later to learn that the action taken by these bombs when the power was cut didn't always follow a distinct pattern. On occasions the craft would fly on for some distance in a shallow glide, or might even perform a series of erratic and unpredictable manoeuvres before finally coming down to earth. But generally, it plummeted down as soon as the engine cut, leaving those beneath it precious few seconds in which to take shelter.

During the course of my leave, I was to experience quite a few such unwelcome visitations, and I was particularly impressed by the traumatic effect that the sudden appearance of a "doodle-bug" could produce. As one of the things throbbed steadily in your general direction, you found yourself willing the engine to stop before it reached you. Then, as it neared your vicinity, you prayed that it wouldn't. Once it had passed overhead, you felt reasonably safe, unless - as previously stated - it turned around and headed back towards you. Irrespective of the ultimate action it took, the near presence of one instilled in me a state of near panic which was not to be expected of someone dressed in uniform. I was involved in the business of delivering bombs to the enemy, but I didn't very much relish the idea of being on the receiving end.

One afternoon while out walking, Rosanna and I were confronted by the fearsome spectacle of a flying bomb coming straight down the street towards us, with its engine still running. I at once bundled her into a nearby shop doorway, where we finished up in an ungainly heap, with me on top. The bomb went hurtling past and crashed into the roadway further down the street. Having escaped unhurt, we disentangled ourselves, only to be confronted by an equally frightened and understandably irate ARP Warden who wanted to know why the hell we weren't in one of the shelters provided for us.

Despite the disruptive efforts of the enemy, my period of leave proved to be the most restful and rewarding of the many I had enjoyed so far, and this was entirely due to the comforting presence of Rosanna. I remembered my earlier leaves spent in wandering the streets of London alone, wishing that I could get back to the entente cordiale of squadron life. Now that my priorities had been totally reversed by the effect that she was having on me. I was loath to return to the rigours of warfare, and desired nothing more than a life devoted to an existence with her. Her presence supplied for me a degree of friendship and intimacy that no fellowship could ever provide, and I found that all other aspects of living palled in significance to the desire I had that I might spend the rest of my life with her. During the leave, I again

COMMISSIONED RANK

made known the depth of my feelings, and once more broached the subject of our future together. But she remained firm in her insistence that we should not commit ourselves while I was still fighting a war. She again pointed out that, because we both enjoyed so much the love and companionship that the existing arrangement provided for us, we should leave things as they were. There was no doubt that we fulfilled a need in both of us, and she sincerely hoped that I would survive the conflict, after which time she would no doubt agree to the suggestion.

Wednesday, July 19th., 1944 brought the end of my leave. Back on the squadron, I learned that losses had been light during the previous two weeks, with only one aircraft, ND-966 (OL/C) failing to return from a raid on St Leu d'Esserent, one of four French targets that the squadron had attacked during that time. OL/C had been flown by Flying Officer Griffiths. There was just one other item of bad news for us: our own aircraft, ND-4654 (OL/S) had crashed and caught fire soon after takeoff on a daylight flight test on the 16th. There had been no survivors.

On the following afternoon, we got the news that Bill Siddle had been promoted to Flight Lieutenant, but the customary celebrations had to be postponed because we were on the battle order that night. Instead, we did a night flying test on ND-930 (OL/Q) prior to taking her to war. Q was to remain with the squadron until her failure to return from a raid a few weeks later. It was perhaps appropriate that my first attack after leave should be against a flying bomb launching site. The location was a place called Wizernes. The one-hundred-and fifty minute flight passed without incident, and all of the squadron's aircraft returned to base safely. In later years I was to have the satisfaction of learning that we had performed our task well on the night, when I was told by an ex-British soldier that, on recapturing the site, his platoon found a large hole in the ground where the launching ramp had once been.

Next day I was told that I was to be considered for promotion to commissioned rank, and was ordered to report to the C.O.'s office for an interview. The C.O. (Wing Commander Deane) had been in charge of the squadron since April. The RCAF had always insisted that each airman serving on an English squadron should, on reaching the rank of Warrant Officer, be monitored for possible promotion at regular intervals, and to this end had supplied a Form R.211 for the purpose. The Wing commander had called me in on two previous occasions in order to inform me of his assessments, and neither of these had been favourable. His comment on the latest of these had read 'This man shows lack of leadership and initiative. He has the ability of these assets, but he must prove this to me'. In conclusion he had appended, 'He is not yet recommended for promotion, but is to be considered in one month's time'. This time, the procedure differed from previous interviews I had attended in that I was to be assessed first by the Squadron C.O., followed by the Station Commander, and finally by the Base commander. I was under the impression that the game called for a favourable recommendation for all three, but that a score of two would suffice. So, clean shaven, and with uniform well brushed and pressed, I presented myself at the C.O.'s office.

The Wing Commander invited me to be seated and handed to me the latest Form R.211 for my perusal. The form consisted mainly of a questionnaire, and listed the various desirable qualities, against each of which was shown a selection of four possible assessments, ranging in degree from (a) 'excellent' to (d) 'poor'. On reading it, I was pleased to notice that, although I hadn't scored a lot of a's, there were no d's indicated, and only one c assessment. But, at the end of the two-page document, immediately above the C.O.'s signature, were the words, 'This man is not recommended for promotion'.

On reading the document, I placed it on the desk and remarked, "So I'm not being recommended for a commission, Sir".

"I'm afraid not".

"May I ask why?"

"You may. It's because I consider you too young to handle the responsibility that the rank would carry".

Being aware that there were a few junior officers of equally tender years on the squadron, I chose to disbelieve the C.O.'s excuse, suspecting instead that my recent tangle with his pet mongrel might have a bearing on the issue.

I could see no logic in subjecting myself to a character change in order that I might qualify for a rank that I didn't seriously aspire to, so decided against pressing my case any further with the man. Instead, I thought it wise that I should avoid being subjected to further criticism by withdrawing from the contest, so I rose from my seat, intending that I should bring the interview to a close.

At this, the Wing commander raised his hand in restraint. "I've arranged for you to be interviewed by the Station Commander in his office at fourteen-thirty hours today", he said, then added, "Good Luck, Moore". I thanked him, saluted, and left.

During lunch, I formulated a plan of campaign for the coming sessions with the Station and Base com-

COMMISSIONED RANK

manders, having decided that, although I held no hope of succeeding, there was much to be said for trying if only to prove to myself that I was officer material. Of the two officers yet to be dealt with, the Base commander (Air Commodore Sharp) was unknown to me, but the Station Commander was no less a person than Group Captain Evans-Evans, with whom I had flown on the trip to Alconbury a few days earlier. I had been impressed by his jovial and easy-going disposition, and I had formed the opinion that he was a man that I could talk to.

After lunch I made my way back to the Admin block and took a seat in the corridor to await my summons to the Group Captain's office. As I waited, a decidedly repulsive individual, attired in scruffy army greatcoat, and looking as if he hadn't been washed in weeks, entered and sat down in the chair next to mine. I was about to get up and move some distance down the corridor from him when a faint glimmer of recognition came over me. My second take of the unwashed face beneath the stubble satisfied me that the bedraggled uncouth character sitting uncomfortably close to me was none other than Sergeant Munro, with whom I had trained in Edmonton and McDonald back in 1942. He recognised me in the same instant, and the resulting exchange was showing promise of being a lengthy one when I was called to the Group Captain's office. During our brief exchange, I learned that he had "just walked back from bloody Germany" and, being a member of one of the squadrons attached to the Base, had been called so that he could be briefed on his experiences by the intelligence Officer. Unfortunately, my being summonsed for my interview prevented us from ever meeting again.

I had hopes that the interview with 'Evans-Squared' would prove a bit more congenial than the set-to I had had with the Wingco earlier in the day, so it was with some trepidation that I knocked on the door marked 'Station Commander'.

The Group Captain began by asking a number of technical question, most of which were concerned with the science of ballistics. At one point he wanted to know how I would deal with an attack taking place at forty-thousand feet. In reply I pointed out that, with respect, such an altitude was beyond the maximum ceiling of a Lancaster, to which he replied that the question was purely hypothetical, and insisted on an answer. Because I had never considered the possible effect that such a rarefied atmosphere might have on the trajectory of a .303 bullet (and because mathematical calculation was not a strong point of mine), I was unable to supply an accurate answer to the question. Instead, I admitted that I didn't know the exact deflection to allow, and specified that, in such an unlikely circumstance, I would make use of the 'hosepipe' technique, and this appeared to be to his satisfaction.

As the interview neared its end, the exchanges between us became more concordant, and I suspected that his action in drawing me into a seemingly off-hand discussion on bombing techniques was designed to reveal more of my character. The topic drifted to daylight bombing, and I at once expressed my dislike of the idea. The Group Captain refrained from making known any views of his own on the subject, but appeared to be interested in mine. At that point in time, neither one of us could foresee his death on one such raid a few months later.

In signalling the end of the interview, he said, "I'm recommending you for a commission, Moore. Now the procedure is this: You'll be given a seventy-two hours pass; a travel warrant; some clothing ration coupons, and an advance of pay so that you can go out and purchase your items of uniform. I suppose you'll be going to London for them?"

"Yes, Sir".

"Then I suggest you get measured by Burton's in The Strand. They always supply my uniforms, and I've yet to fault their service. It'll take them a few weeks to make your order up, so I'd advise you to hang on to your Warrant Officer's uniform. Get your batwoman to change the rank markings on it, then you can keep it as a beer suit.

"There's one other thing", he added "You'll probably find that you won't have enough clothing coupons. That's where the black market comes in handy". He then proceeded to supply me with the address of a black marketeer in Soho, and assured me that this man would supply my needs if I mentioned his name.

The interview having ended, I found myself wondering if the Group Captain was a bit premature in his assessment of my chances. After all, I had failed to meet the Wingco's standard, and there was still A/Cdr. Sharp to contend with.

In addition to my involvement in the promotion stakes, the crew itself was at this time undergoing some changes, the most notable of which had been the sudden departure of Paddy Blanche, who had opted for a transfer to 617 ('Dambusters') Squadron, after having completed only one trip with us - a raid on a French target at St Vitry le Francoise on June the 27th. Fortunately, the vacancy had been speedily filled by Pilot Officer Hine, a man of undoubted experience and ability. He began his term of service with the crew when he accompanied us on the

COMMISSIONED RANK

Wizernes trip, during which I had been impressed by his calm efficiency.

My tilt at being promoted was interrupted on the afternoon of July the 23rd., when a number of squadron aircraft (ourselves and our own OL/Q included) were ordered down to our old base at Wyton. It appeared that we and the others were being seconded to the hard pressed 8 Group in order to assist in marking a couple of targets that needed the technique in which we were experienced. That night we carried out an attack on the docks at Keil. All of the squadron's aircraft and crews returned safely from the trip, but we lost ND-922 (OL/J), piloted by Flight Lieutenant Banfield, an Australian. On the following night, when we took off from Wyton to attack Stuttgart. OL/J went down with eight crew members including a spare bomb aimer.

On the afternoon of the day following our return to Coningsby, Bill called an emergency crew conference, at which we were told that our newly-acquired mid upper gunner and Clem, the wireless operator, had both been posted away from the squadron. When pressed for a reason for this, Bill insisted that none had been given, but both of these men had already left the station, and could not be expected to return.

I had known this to happen to other crews, and had learned that the swift and unexplained disappearance of someone in this way meant that the person concerned had either committed a serious breach of conduct, or had been declared LMF (lacking in moral fibre). Usually looked upon as cowardice, the latter was a condition which affected not just those who were new to the rigours of serial warfare, but it could suddenly become manifest in the makeup of men with many trips to their credit. I had noticed that mostly, the men who cracked under the strain were men of intelligence, and I suspected that this was because they had succeeded in assessing the odds against them, as I had done, and had allowed the element of self-preservation to outweigh their fear of the shame and dishonour that opting out would bring. Having taken such action, they were instantly grounded, banished from the scene, and would be reduced through the ranks and allocated the most menial of tasks as a punishment.

In my estimation, the subjecting of oneself to such shame and degradation called for a far greater degree of personal courage than I possessed, and I found myself questioning the crude justice to be meted out in the circumstances. It wasn't as if these men had been new to the game. Clem, for one, had completed more than a first tour with the crew, under some of the fiercest opposition to be met. I knew little of P/O Hine's record, but there was no doubt in my mind as to his ability as a gunner, and I failed to see how anybody could consider either of these men to be a coward.

We had already been allocated a new wireless operator in the person of Flying Officer Alan MacDonald, but there was a shortage of mid upper gunners on the squadron at the time, so we would have to depend on there being a spare one around for our use in the immediate future.

Alan MacDonald was a fellow Canadian whose home town was far remote from mine, he being a native of a place called Marble Mountain, in the east coast province of Nova Scotia. Fair haired, handsome, and with an air of quiet efficiency, Alan was destined to become a valuable asset to the crew in the months ahead.

COMMISSIONED RANK

CHAPTER 22

BACK TO THE BIG TIME

Later that afternoon (Wednesday, July 26th., 1944) the squadron was again alerted for operations, and we found ourselves on the battle order for the third night out of four. We at once took PB-230 (OL/V) up for a night flying test. V had just seventeen more days of service left with the squadron, and would fail to return from a raid on Brunswick on the 12th August. We had Sergeant Gorham with us as mid upper gunner for this one, so we did a spot of fighter affiliation with a Hurricane while we were up, so that he and I could get used to working together.

This time, our target was Givors, a few miles south of Lyon, and not far from the Swiss border. We lifted off just after nine p.m. on what was to prove one of the most tiring and exacting eight-hour flights we had ever undertaken. The Met office had got it wrong this time, and we found ourselves flying in thick cloud for most of the outward flight. Then, just as we neared a point about half an hour from the target, we started to ice up badly, so Bill decided with reluctance that we should abort the mission and head back to base.

Despite the gloom and murk that was all around us. I continued to carry out a search for any fighter that might have managed to get off the ground in the prevailing conditions. I had my turret on the starboard beam when I saw what looked like the lighted windows of a farmhouse drifting past beneath us. I at once called Bill and asked:

"What's our height, Skipper?"

"Fifteen thousand. Why?"

I reported what I had seen, then added, "There goes another one, and it's above us this time"

Realising the full significance of the mysterious lights was immediate. Because we had turned around we were now flying directly into the path of the advancing bomber stream, and the 'lighted windows' I was seeing were the exhaust flames of other Lancasters as they roared pas us in the opposite direction, and it was with some alarm that I envisaged the fireworks display that would result from a head-on collision between two bomb-laden Lancasters.

"Hang on, everybody", Bill announced. "We're going down", and I at once felt my turret shoot skywards into the pitch darkness that surrounded us.

The manoeuvre served a dual purpose. Not only did it remove the danger of collision, but the lower altitude alleviated the icing problem. Furthermore, now that we were free agents, untroubled by a preconceived operational flight plan, we could plot our own course and altitude for the return flight. But the situation had some disadvantages. for one thing, we no longer had the collective security that the main bomber stream would provide. We were alone, and our trace would stick out like a sore thumb on the German radar screens. But there was plenty of cloud cover around, and this would make it difficult for an enemy fighter to locate us. There was one other problem: the fact that we carried a full bombload, so it was decided that we would jettison this at the earliest. So it was that an unfortunate German village was treated to a somewhat noisy awakening as we made our way back home.

My log book entry for the trip bears the suffix DNCO (duty not carried out), and is the only such entry to be found in it. The squadron operational record lists the loss of ND-856 (OL/E), Squadron Leader Eggins and crew, and gives the information that the aircraft had not been heard from after 02:30 hours - at about the time that we had given up and turned for home. Because our duties had not been carried out, I was led to understand that the flight could not be counted as an operational sortie, but I drew consolation from the fact that a number of other crews had also aborted.

Following on the Givors raid, there came a period of relative inactivity on the squadron, and this at last enabled us to hold a celebration in recognition of Siddle's promotion to Flight Lieutenant. For this, the crew assembled in a Coningsby ale house, with each member intent of getting as blotto as his personal finances would allow. The proceedings began with the customary round of drinks being supplied by the person promoted (Bill), after which a 'kitty' was set up in order to finance the festivities for the remainder of the evening. Bill began to pound the old piano, and we were soon joined by a number of other revellers in giving voice to the kind of lyricism for which airmen are noted. Although I was tempted to raise a glass or two in recognition of the one success I had so far scored in my own tilt at rank advancement, I decided that such an act might be tempting fate, so promised myself that I would hold a celebratory binge - or a drowning of my sorrow - once I knew the result of the pending interview with the Air Commodore.

My meeting with Air commodore Sharp was held on the morning of the following day. The session proved terse and businesslike, and was markedly devoid of

BACK TO THE BIG TIME

the free-and-easy aura which I had enjoyed during my visit to the Group Captain's office. I had again decided on projecting assertiveness and self-confidence in the face of whatever test was put to me.

Prior to entering the Base Commander's office, I recalled an incident which had taken place some weeks previously. I and some of the crew had visited the Admin block on some sort of business and, whilst waiting to be dealt with, I had playfully altered the painted sign on the Air Commodore's office. it read "AC Sharp, Base Commander". To the initials "AC" I had carefully appended the numeral 2, thereby reducing the great man to the lowest rank in the air force. Now, before knocking on the door, I noted that the numeral had been painstakingly and effectively obliterated.

The preliminaries over, A/Cdr Sharp got the interview under way.

"I understand that you have been unofficially appointed Deputy B Flight gunnery Officer", he remarked.

"Yes Sir"

"And I also understand that, in that capacity, you regularly carry out inspections of the guns and turrets of the B Flight aircraft".

"That is correct".

"And what are your findings in this respect?"

"In general, I find the standard of maintenance to be good", I replied.

"In general, but surely not in total", he asserted.

"There is the odd occasion when I find the cleanliness and synchronization of guns to be short of the criterion I set".

"And what action do you take?"

"I then approach the gunner concerned and order an improvement".

"But you don't report it to your superior?"

"No. Sir".

"Why not?"

"Because there usually follows an immediate improvement in the standard of servicing carried out by the man concerned".

"But why don't you refer the matter higher up at once?"

"Because I don't see the need to, not unless there isn't an improvement, in which case I would then submit a report to the Flight Gunnery Leader, a situation which has not yet presented itself".

I got the impression that the Air Commodore was not too happy with my response to his close and persistent questioning on the subject. However, I remained adamant in my choice of action when pressed even further, and the interview gradually developed into an exchange of conflicting ideals on the matter of command and leadership. Because I had in the past found my method of dealing with the occasional problem to be effective I could see no need to resort to the role of an informer. By acting as I had in the past, I held the respect of my fellow gunners, and I considered this to be of importance.

The quality of the interview continued to decline until, after having fired a few more questions at me, the Air commodore suddenly indicated that it was ended. No mention had been made as to whether or not I was considered a suitable candidate, so I took the pessimistic conclusion. As I left the office, I was filled with the belief that I had blown it, and that my dogged resolve to 'stick to my guns' had put paid to any hopes I had of being promoted, and that I would be obliged to remain a Warrant Officer for the remainder of my service career.

The remainder of July and all of August 1944 brought a period of enforced inactivity for the crew because of our shortage of members. We were still without a mid upper gunner, and gunners were in great demand due to the commencement of the daylight attacks, on which the front turret was usually manned. The daylight raids began on July 30th., and the squadron took part in seven of these between that date and August the 6th. These were followed by night raids on Secque Ville and Bordeaux. On the August 6th raid, ND-930 (OL/Q) - the aircraft we had flown from Wyton - was lost. On this occasion, Q had been manned by Flight Lieutenant Drinkall and crew. The target had been Boise de Casson and - because it was a daylight raid - the aircraft had carried an extra gunner. Because of my aircrew grade (and because I was still on the list of volunteer gunners), I was also in danger of being nobbled, but had somehow managed to miss out on the daylight flights, not that I was unduly perturbed about that. My name came to the top of the list on Friday, August 11th., when I was listed as replacement tail gunner with Flight Lieutenant Young's crew.

Young, a New Zealander, was an experienced pilot with an experienced crew, so I didn't mind having to dice with them. A night attack, the target called for my return to Givors, and I suspected that this was because of the undisputed failure of the Command's visit some two weeks previously.

The weather report was better this time, and I got the impression that the crews were keen to make up for the earlier disappointment. During the briefing, I had a word with the mid upper, Pilot Officer Craig, on the crew's evasion tactics, and was relieved to find that these were similar to our own. Prior to closing the briefing, the Wing commander (a recent replacement for Dixie Deane) rose to give the customary summing-up. This usually consisted of words intended to instill confidence, and invariably ended with the C.O. wishing the men a good trip and good luck. Not this time, however. He began his tirade by pointing out the failure of those involved in the previous attack on the target, and pressed home his insistence that a better show was to be expected this time. He then polished off the pep talk by saying, "This is war, and somebody's got to die!", then strode from the room, leaving behind a deathly silence.

We lifted off with PB-240 (OL/J) at nine-fifty p.m. and climbed into the darkening sky in the direction of the continent. As we crossed the English coast at our operational height. I listened to the business-like exchanges between the various members of the crew, and drew comfort from the impression of quiet efficiency and discipline that I got. I hadn't flown with the crew before, but I felt confident that it was every bit as good as our own, and this was evident from their previous trouble-free operational record.

The flight, although met with little enemy opposition, was a lengthy one lasting eight gruelling hours, and we were all feeling shattered when we finally touched down at Coningsby. After the de-briefing, we trooped into the mess for breakfast before. I retired to my room and locked the door before falling into bed. I couldn't recall ever having felt so totally exhausted, and I had a blinding headache again, so didn't want to be disturbed for some hours. Within a few minutes of hitting the pillow, I was out for the count.

I remained in a blissful state of unconsciousness until well after five p.m., at which time I got up and had a refreshing shower before going for a meal. Down in the mess room, I met Dick Lodge.

"Where the hell have you been?", he wanted to know. I answered the question, then asked him to explain his concern.

"You're on with Young's crew again tonight. They've been trying to raise you all afternoon, so you'd better get down to the flights right away".

Although feeling half starved, I immediately left the mess and hurried over to the gunnery office for instructions.

Over at the flight offices, I was told that the Gunnery Officer was already attending the briefing, and that this had begun ten minutes earlier. I was also told that, since I couldn't be found, Warrant Officer Beck had been detailed to fly in my place.

Since the last-minute swap was out of the question, I returned to the mess and collected a meal from the serving hatch. After eating, I went back to the flights, intent on finding Warrant Officer Beck. After a while the operational crews began to drift in, having had their pre-flight meal of two eggs, etcetera. On finding Beck amongst the throng, I proceeded to apologise to him.

"That's alright, mate" he assured me. "Anyway, I want to get some ops in". Beck was a quiet but jovial Londoner with good looks and an ever-ready smile. He had been with the squadron for some time, and I had heard that he was married, with children.

"I went to Givors with Young last night", I told him. "They're a damned good crew, so you should have a safe enough trip. What's the target?"

"Brunswick. Looks like a maximum effort. Take off is set for nine o'clock".

I wished him luck and set off over the field for the long walk to the caravan, where I joined the assembled 'press on gang' of well-wishers waiting to watch the aircraft taking off. J-Johnnie was in the leading lineup of Lancasters waiting near the caravan, and I got a wave from Flight Lieutenant Young before she began to roll. When the rear turret bounced past, I gave Beck the thumbs up and got a broad grin in reply. Once the remaining aircraft had taken off, I walked back to the mess for a few drinks and a singsong around the old piano before I retired to my room with a mug of coca and a plateful of Leicester cheese chunks and bread buns. Once settled in, I proceeded to write a few letters as I disposed of the snack.

I awoke the following morning feeling refreshed as a result of the lengthy rest I had enjoyed during the previous twenty-four hours. As I walked into the mess for breakfast, I was struck by the unusual silence of the assembled diners. Gone was the familiar babble of conversation and laughter, and the resulting sombre atmosphere caused me to suspect something was seriously wrong. I collected my breakfast from the serving hatch and joined Jock

BACK TO THE BIG TIME

Wilson at his table. He was staring disconsolately at his plate, and didn't see me as I sat down across from him.

"Good morning, Jock". he looked up to greet me, but with only the ghost of a smile.

"It's no' such a good yin", he answered. "Last night was the biggest chop night the squadron's had for months".

"How many?"

"Three"

"Good God!. Who?"

"Keeling, Erritt and Young".

"Young!", I echoed with disbelief. I didn't know Flight Lieutenant Keeling's crew very well because they were on A Flight, but Pilot Officer 'Tubby' Erritt had shared my room in the Sergeant's mess until a few weeks ago, when he had been granted his commission. It was the news about Young that really stunned me. I should have been with that crew. I had flown with them in J the night before last, and now they were gone, and Warrant Officer Beck had taken my place because I had failed to report in time for the flight. I tried to imagine what had gone wrong with such an efficient body of men. No doubt they had been feeling tired. Most crews on the squadron, with the exception of our own, had been pressed almost to the limit since the invasion started, and there was a point beyond which even young men could not progress before their vigilance and efficiency suffered.

The news brought home to me the realisation that I had once more managed to cheat death. Such were the stakes in the game of aerial warfare. Once the cards were dealt, you picked up your hand, and you played it out to the best of your ability. If luck was on your side, you might be able to cut your losses, or you might even win. It all depended on how many aces you held. Luck had been with me last night, but not with Beck, and I felt nothing but shame because his going had been because of me. Maybe, I thought, things would have been different had I been with them. Then again, maybe not. There were so many imponderables. You weaved to port instead of starboard, and this brought you within view of an enterprising Jerry fighter pilot, or it placed you at the exact spot at which the next flak shell was going to burst. Maybe some members of the crew had been feeling the strain of too many nights over Germany. Being tired played tricks with your ability to remain alert, and it affected your eyesight. Under this condition, your imagination began to dupe you into seeing things that didn't exist, and you sometimes failed to notice those that did.

Of the squadron's losses for the night, Flying Officer Keeling had been flying FB-230 (OL/V) - the aircraft we had taken on the abortive trip to Givors on July 26th - and Flight Lieutenant Young had taken with him PB-240 (OL/J).

The month of August proved disastrous for the squadron. Six more aircraft and crews were to be lost during the remaining seventeen days, bringing the total for the period to nine. ND-854 (OL/F), Flight Lieutenant McLean (an Australian) failed to return from Brest on the 14th. Then, PB-362 (OL/W), Flight Lieutenant Saunders i/c. was seen to go down during a daylight raid on L'isle D'Adam on the 18th. This aircraft had only completed a total of nine hours in the air since its manufacture. On the 25th., we lost two more on Darmstadt: PB-345 (OL/Q), with Squadron Leader Williams and crew, and ND-455 (OL/U), Flight Lieutenant Meggeson and crew. The next night, we lost PB-292 (OL/S) on a trip to Koningsberg. Three nights later, on a return to the same target, PB-249 (OL/C) - another new aircraft - was lost. It was piloted by Wing Commander Sparks, the A Flight Commander, who was heard to make a report on VHF radio at 01:37 hours.

Despite all this, plus our enforced state of inactivity, the month had its compensations for the crew and for myself. Bill Siddle was awarded the Distinguished Flying Cross, and some of the others received the Distinguished Flying Medal. The batch of awards included nothing for me however, so I had to be content to adorn myself with nothing more prestigious than the Canadian Operational Wings, which served to signify that I had completed a tour of thirty trips against the enemy.

Also during the month of August I had been summonsed to appear before a group of invigilators so that my ability to carry the King's Commission could be further assessed. The test was designed to determine the extent to which I could control a body of men on the parade square. On arrival I was presented with a collection of about thirty men which I formed into a squad. Having done this, I was instructed to size the squad, an order which filled me with dismay because of the problems I had encountered two years earlier at Edmonton, when I had been instructed to carry out the same drill at the passing-out parade. As I brought the men to attention and marched them out onto the cricket pitch, I racked my brain in an attempt to remember the required commands and their sequence, but to no avail. having made certain that I had moved the men beyond ear shot of the examining flat-hats, I halted them and turned them into line, then asked quietly,

"Do any of you know the commands for this bloody drill?"

I got an affirmative response from an LA/C in the front rank, so together we conspired to hornswoggle the hierarchy into thinking that I knew what I was doing. In return for my promise of a couple of pints of ale, the LAC proceed to whisper the commands to me, after which I bawled them out for the benefit of the examining officers.

The conspiracy achieved the desired result. The LA/C got blotto that night at my expense, and I got my commission the following day (Tuesday, August 15th, 1944). Once the promotion was granted, little time was wasted in getting me dressed for the part. Before night had fallen, I was installed in a private room in the Officer's Mess (but sharing a bathroom with the Wing Commander!); had my W/O's uniform converted to that of a P/O by my batwomen (a petite Scottish girl whose name I cannot recall), and had been supplied with all that I required for a seven day trip to London for my kitting-out. I had been granted a week because the crew would have been due to this in September but, because of crew shortage, and because Bill and some of the others had been invited to attend an investiture at Buckingham Palace, the leave had been brought forward.

Soon after my arrival in London, I caught a tube train across to the Strand with the intention of getting measured by Burton's as soon as possible in the hope that they might have my new uniform ready for collection before the leave period was up. I had with me a list of my requirements, to which I had added a few extras such as shirts, underclothing, socks and ties, etcetera. With the exception of the uniform, all of these were to be had off the shelf, so that I soon had all that I needed, with the exception of shoes. These I was unable to purchase because my supply of clothing coupons had run out.

I was unconcerned about the shortage of footwear because I had tucked away in my tunic the address of the black marketeer that the Group Captain had given me, and I planned on visiting Soho the following day.

I had no difficulty in locating the designated clothier's shop, which I found to be deserted except for the Proprietor, an elderly gentleman of obvious Jewish parentage. After we had exchanged the customary greetings and remarked on the weather (it was raining at the time), I announced my requirement.

"Certainly, Sir. You have the clothing coupons?", he asked.

his display of shock and indignation on being told that I didn't posses sufficient stamps to legalize the transaction, but was hoping to get shoes without them, bordered on the theatrical. However, my incantation of the magic words "Group Captain Evans-Evans" brought about an instant change in the man's demeanour, and I was soon on my way, complete with my new footwear, but minus a cash payment which was far in access of the retail mark-up price.

By the afternoon of my second day in London, I had collected all the required items, except for the tailor-made dress uniform. I was not to take delivery of this for some months because of the profusion of orders waiting to be filled.

I spent much of the afternoon at the club pressing and ironing my new clobber in readiness for a date with Rosanna later that evening. After dressing, I viewed the result in a full-length wardrobe mirror. The Warrant Officer's uniform, although of inferior quality to the one I had ordered from Burton's looked impressive despite this. The tunic bore the Canada shoulder flashes, and the left breast sported the Air Gunner's wing; a selection of campaign ribbons; the brass pathfinder's wing (the albatross), and the gold-plated Canadian Operational wing. On each cuff was the Pilot Officer's ring of rank, and the whole caboodle was topped off by a spanking new peaked officer's cap with the familiar crown, albatross and oak leaves insignia mounted above the peak.

Because of my preference for the casual and much more comfortable battledress tunic and trousers that we wore around the squadron (except in the Mess), I felt uncomfortable and over-dressed in the new get-up. Despite my sense of pride in the uniform I was wearing. I couldn't avoid thinking that I resembled a glorified tram conductor.

BACK TO THE BIG TIME

CHAPTER 23

END OF SECOND TOUR

The remainder of my leave period was spent in the company of Rosanna - all except for one unfortunate evening, that is. We had arranged to meet in Piccadilly Circus at seven p.m., after which we were to have dinner and spend the night together in a rented hotel room. On the morning preceding the event, I awoke to find that I was again suffering from one of the frequent severe headaches to which I had grown accustomed in previous months. It was accompanied by the feeling of nausea, and my field of vision was again limited so that I felt blinkered. I was indeed grateful that I wasn't flying on operations at the time, but, being intent on getting myself in shape for the coming event, I had a light breakfast and downed a handful of aspirin before returning to bed. I had been told that woman sometimes developed a headache under the circumstances, but I considered that it was not in the nature of a man to behave in such a way.

Some hours later I awoke from my drug-induced slumber to find that I was feeling fully refreshed and ready for anything, Thankfully, the headache had passed. So unfortunately had the appointed hour of seven p.m.!

Cursing my stupidity all the while, I hurriedly dressed and caught the tube to Piccadilly Circus, where I twice circled the sand-bagged and boarded-up statue of Eros, the god of love, in search of Rosanna. She wasn't there, but this didn't come as much of a surprise to me because I was by then more than ninety minutes late for the meeting. Because it seemed unlikely that there would be time in which to reorganize a rendezvous for that night, I cancelled the room I had booked at the Regent's Palace Hotel and returned to the club. After about an hour, I phoned her flat and apologised for my absence, and gave an account of the reason for my stupidity. With a graciousness that was typical of her loving personality, she laughingly issued her admonishment, then suggested that we try again on the following night, the last of my leave.

The next evening, we met in the lounge of the Regents Palace Hotel. This time there were no complications, and I felt so proud as Rosanna made her way over to our table. She looked like a princess in her elegant and carefully-chosen attire, and I sensed that all eyes were on us as I placed the chair for her and ordered our drinks. She projected an aura of beauty and refinement that demanded the admiration of all those present. After we had dined, we returned to the lounge for more drinks before retiring to our room for the night, where she was at once transformed from a princess into the most loving and sensuous girl I had ever known.

The month of September, 1944 was to be a busy one, both for the squadron and for our crew. Soon after our return from leave, we were allocated PB-368 as a replacement for our ill-fated ND-464 (OL/S) in which we had completed nine raids, including the opening of the invasion. Because we were by then one of the more senior crews operating with the squadron, we qualified for a Lancaster fresh from the manufacturers, and the new OL/S was a delight to fly. We soon had her trimmed to our liking, and we were delighted with her performance during a series of day and night training trips that we made with her during our first week back from leave.

The realization that we were a senior crew was brought home to me, not only by the new aircraft, but by a large wall chart in the Squadron Gunnery Office. This listed the gunners down the left-hand side, and running out to the right was a series of blacked-in squares, each one representing a raid which the particular gunner had completed. The blackened squares opposite my name now extended far across the chart, and numbered thirty-nine. Of all the others, only two came near to my score to date, with most having reached on average a total of just ten or twelve. In quite a few instances, a line had been drawn through the name, indicating the gunner concerned was no longer with us.

The chart was no doubt intended as a means of boosting the morale of the new crews by giving them a target to aim at, and by showing them that success could be achieved. In truth, it had the opposite effect on many. To those new to the squadron, the number of names that had been deleted indicated something of the odds facing them, and served as a pointer to those who (like myself) had put up a good score that the day of judgement must be near.

The thought of opting out of operational flying was one that had troubled me during my career. Within a matter of weeks after my first posting to a squadron, I had come to realize the unlikelihood of survival. The excitement and romance of flying had gone, and was replaced by the belief that I didn't stand a chance. This produced fear, and fear affected different people in different ways. There were those who recognised the danger, and those who did not. The latter was a man who would walk through a mine field, not knowing that it was there. He was a fool, not a hero. The other man, showing great courage, would try to find a safe way through. But what if he couldn't see an alternative route? What action would

END OF SECOND TOUR

he then take? This depended not only on the strength of his fear, but on his survival instinct. Plainly, he had but two options: he could trust to luck and continue (there were many who did, and I had witnessed the terrible price that they paid), or he could opt out, as two of my crew had already done.

Following on the leave period I had spent in London with Rosanna, my mind was again concentrated on the question of my involvement in further action against the enemy. There was no doubting my love for Rosanna now, and, in addition to the physical aspect of our relationship, I knew that we were ideally suited to each other. It remained for me to complete a further six trips in order to finish my second tour, and this I was keen to do. Once I had accomplished this, it was my intention that I should then withdraw from further operational flying.

Our first op in OL/S took place on sunday September 10th., when we attacked the German town of Munchen Gladbach. We were still without a permanent mid upper gunner, and it was only because flight Sergeant Gorham had volunteered as a spare that we were able to take part in the operation. Our new Lancaster performed perfectly, and the 3½ hour trip proved mostly uneventful.

On the following evening, we were again called upon to join the squadron in an attack, this time on Darmstadt, an industrial target about twelve miles south of Frankfurt. For this trip, the mid upper turret was occupied by Sergeant Froud. The first half of our flight presented no serious problems, although the increased activity and determination of the German defences in the area of the target was very much in evidence.

The drift to increased German defences was one that I had noticed ever since the opening of the second front. The Fatherland was no longer the aggressor, but we were being made to face up to the tenacity and fighting skills of a cornered animal. Nevertheless, it wasn't until we had carried out our attack that the real troubles began, although these were not entirely due to the action of the enemy.

Our homeward route took us out over the American sector of the advancing Allied armies, and we were well aware of the Yanks' habit of letting fly at anything larger that a barn owl that dared to venture within range of their anti-aircraft guns. These fired shells to which were fitted 'proximity' fuses which were capable of 'sensing' the nearby presence of a metal object, whereupon the shell would detonate. Unfortunately, the inventiveness of man had not progressed to the state of enabling the device to identify the country from which the metal object had originated. Because of this, and because of the apparent lack of liaison between the factions involved, we were again subjected to a few anxious moments, as had been our experience during our more recent crossings of the battle lines. Fortunately, our 'nose down and get to hell out of it' tactic again proved to be effective, and we managed to ward off the unwanted attention of both friend and foe!

The following evening (September 12th) found us on the battle order for the third consecutive night. This time, our objective was to be Stuttgart, a town deep inside Germany, and one which we had attacked on two previous occasions. For this trip, we again carried a stand-in gunner, Sergeant Seager. The briefing was unusually early, because a new tactic was to be tried. We were to take off at 5:40 p.m. and hedge-hop in daylight almost to the Allied lines before climbing to our operational height, by which time darkness would have fallen. The tactic was designed to avoid radar detection so that the deployment of the German fighter squadrons would be delayed through lack of any advance warning or our approach.

After takeoff, we at once set course for Beachy Head, following closely as possible the contours of the terrain, and keeping it just a few feet beneath our heavily laden bomb bays. As we flew down England, the big black Lancasters were all around us, bobbing and weaving like porpoises as they skimmed over and around each obstacle that they encountered. Old Bill was thoroughly enjoying the task, and I was glad that he had in the past indulged his fondness of low flying at each given opportunity. As a result, he was expert at handling a fully-laden Lancaster at 'zero' feet, and this caused me to regret having once accused him - in a light-hearted manner - of suffering from acrophobia.

The sun was just beginning to touch the horizon as we dropped still lower and roared out over the English Channel. A few minutes later, the final segment of the solar disc disappeared as we rose over the coastline and headed into France, still hugging the ground. Now the landscape that slid out from beneath my turret presented a marked contrast to the early autumn tints of the English countryside we had left. Not because this was a foreign country, but because it bore the scars that had been left by the fierce battle that had raged there in recent weeks. Apparently deserted and lifeless, the fast-receding panorama closely resembled my concept of a moonscape, with a profusion of ugly bomb and shell craters spoiling what must once have been a scene of rural tranquillity. Roofless and wrecked farm buildings dotted the landscape, and even the trees and hedgerows had suffered from the carnage as it passed. Tank tracks were everywhere, some leading

END OF SECOND TOUR

to an abandoned and burnt-out wreck. The only living creature that I saw was a solitary cow trotting aimlessly in panic as it tried to escape the roar of our engines. Siddle reported that a Lanc had crashed into a tree ahead and to starboard. I rotated my turret to watch the burning hulk come into view, but couldn't read the squadron letters. What appeared to be the lifeless body of a crew member lay a few yards away from the wreckage, with flames enveloping his flying suit. I could see nothing of the other six, and thought it unlikely that there could possibly be any survivors.

Soon the daylight began to fade, and we and the others started the long climb to operational height. During the hedge-hopping part of the flight, I had been keeping a close watch on the sky above us, trying to visualise the abuse to which a gaggle of diving enemy fighters could put us, since we were without a fighter escort. Fortunately, we were spared such maltreatment, and were soon soaring into the friendly darkness of our otherwise hostile environment.

The remainder of the trip was fairly straightforward, with no hazards to be met other than those we were used to. Because of the new tactic, we arrived back at base just after midnight, and were de-briefed, fed and bedded down soon afterwards. There were no squadron losses.

Next afternoon, I was to meet our new mid upper gunner. Bill Trotter by name, he was a Warrant Officer with a string of previous trips to his credit, and I liked his carefree personality and his sense of humour. He told me that he was from a place called West Hartlepool, somewhere up in the north of England. Because he was our fifth 'permanent' mid upper to date, I had hopes that he might remain with us. We at once did a fighter affiliation flip, during which I introduced him to our version of the fighter evasion tactic, which he soon mastered, doubtless to the annoyance of an unfortunate Hurricane pilot who quite probably returned to base with a magazine full of blanks.

Trotter was the fourteenth man to have served with the crew. Of the original seven, only the pilot (Bill Siddle), the Navigator (Dick Lodge) and I remained. In the space of just fourteen months, we had suffered one killed, two grounded through injuries, two declared LMF, and two transferred to other squadrons or commands.

The squadron carried out an attack on Bremerhaven, again without loss, on the night of September 18th/19th. However, because we had been called upon to operate three consecutive nights earlier in the week, our crew got a well-earned night off. On this occasion, somebody else took OL/S out for an airing, while the seven of us staged a drinks session down in the village. Although it wasn't necessary to have a reason to get tanked up, we had one this time: Siddle had been awarded a bar to his DFC that afternoon. The party was soon under way. Bill was appointed piano pounder, and we had been joined by Wing Commander Gibson, V.C. of Dambusters fame. Guy was prone to making an appearance at such celebrations, and thoroughly enjoyed mixing it with the other ranks. Back at the station, he was a frequent participant in similar rituals, even those held in the Sergeants' Mess, at which he would appear dressed in the uniform of a non-commissioned officer, one which he had acquired for the purpose of dodging the forces protocol which he so openly disliked.

As the evening wore on, and minds grew lucid from the effect of liquid refreshment, the conversation became profuse on subjects ranging throughout service life and beyond. Glancing at the tunics worn by those around our table, I noticed that Mike and I were at that stage the only members of the crew still devoid of either a DFM or a DFC, and the reason for our celebration prompted me to ponder the chances of me ever getting such an award. There were two distinct grades of DFC - immediate and non-immediate. Whilst the immediate award was given in recognition of a single act of bravery, the other was in recognition of the recipient's qualities of efficiency and devotion to duty. In all modesty, I considered my success in having completed more than forty operations without the need to fire a single shot in defence of my aircraft and crew to be ample qualification, yet I had not been so honoured despite having been recommended for the award by Siddle. Toward the end of the evening, after a reasonably sober Guy Gibson had left the party, I questioned Bill on the matter, and he assured me that his application had been lodged, and that I should be receiving my 'gong' any day. It was well known in Air Force circles that gunners, being the poor relations of a crew, tended to be overlooked in this respect, unless they had succeeded in downing a couple of Jerry fighters. It followed that non-immediate awards of the DFM and DFC were scarce. Perhaps, I thought, my propensity for living in Rome and fighting with the Pope had a bearing on my failure.

Just before lunch the following day (Tuesday September 19th, 1944), a list of crews was issued for ops that night. We were included on the list, but only as the reserve crew. This meant that we must attend the briefing and hold ourselves in readiness to take the place of any designated crew that failed to take part for whatever reason. Such a contingency seldom arose, and it was generally accepted that the standby crew was guaranteed a night off, the one

END OF SECOND TOUR

drawback being that the members of that crew would be confined to the station for the night because of their knowledge of the target. The Mosquito squadron that shared the aerodrome with 83 and 97 Squadrons was to accompany the main force, and Wing Commander Gibson was to act as Master bomber. Dick Lodge had been provisionally selected to fly as navigator to Wing Commander Gibson on the trip, and he was delighted at the prospect of doing an op in a Mosquito with a holder of the Victoria Cross. Indeed, we ourselves derived pride and pleasure from the fact that he had been chosen.

Unfortunately, Dick's euphoria was to be short-lived. Just prior to the scheduled time for briefing, we were informed that the pilot of one of the crews had reported in sick, thus making it necessary for us to take their place, and that another navigator would be taking over the navigator's table in the Wing Commander's Mosquito.

We were told at the briefing that the target was to be Munchen Gladbach/Rheydt, two adjacent industrial towns with which we had become familiar in recent times. Takeoff was scheduled for ten minutes past seven p.m., and the trip was to take a little less than four hours. By a remarkable coincidence, the defaulting crew had been down to fly our own aircraft - OL/S. The attack proved to be one of the most concerted and successful we had shared in. The marking was excellent, and Wing commander Gibson was heard to congratulate us all on 'a good show' as we turned for home. Throughout the outward flight, Dick had been bemoaning his luck at having been tricked out of a flip with the V.C. but only until the skipper told him to 'shut up and get on with the job'.

On our return to Coningsby, we were shocked on hearing that Gibson's aircraft was overdue and presumed to be missing. The sad loss of 'Gibby', as he was known to those of us who had shared his friendship, was to stay with the squadrons based at Coningsby for as long as those who had known him remained. His boyish, quiet and cheerful disposition, together with his undoubted courage and flying ability had been an inspiration to us all, and I - together with many others - considered myself greatly honoured to have known him, and to have raised a glass with him on a number of memorable occasions. Those who knew him could not avoid being inspired by his courage and integrity.

The realization that an Officer so distinguished and experienced could be taken from us served to indicate once more the grimness of the lottery in which we were involved. The demon Valkyries responsible for the administration of 'The Chop' held no regard for the efficiency and reputation of those chosen. There was no doubting the competence of my crew, despite the desecration it had suffered since its formation more than a year earlier. But so too had many of the others I had known and respected. Crews which included high-ranking and experienced men, the kind who would never make mistakes. yet they had gone, and their passing could only be attributed to misfortune. Once again, my thoughts on the matter renewed the despondency in me, and caused me to wonder how long our luck could last out.

Our next venture into Germany was on September the 23rd., when the town of Munster became our reluctant host. As usual, we found the hospitality non-existent, and were subjected to a display of discourtesy which, although imposing, was of sufficient magnitude to scare the living daylights out of all seven of us. There was no doubt that the Germans were learning the art of defence, and the proof or their success was evinced by the number of aircraft seen being blown out of the sky as Siddle pressed home the attack, holding our aircraft straight and level through the fire and the noise of the flak that was bursting all around us.

On the return flight, I again found myself suffering from a sight problem, and this was as usual accompanied by the then familiar head pains and nausea. Although the condition had been evident for some months, it was the first time that I had experienced it during an operational sortie, so that I had come to believe that the use of oxygen over a period of hours might explain why I had been spared the condition until then. Now I was forced to accept that such a belief was unsound, and that I could no longer be depended upon to provide the degree of protection that my aircraft and crew required of me. The one thing that a night bomber crew could well do without was a gunner with a sight defect. I needed just one more sortie in my log book in order to complete my second tour, and I was keen to chance it, after which I would carefully reconsider my future with the crew.

Again, the squadron came through the raid unscathed. In truth, September had so far provided a marked contrast to the disastrous month of August. With the exception of the Stuttgart raid mentioned earlier, all of the September trips in which the squadron took part (eight in all) were undertaken in darkness, and without any loss.

Ops were again called for the night of 26th., when the target was Karlsruhe, but the crew was not listed amongst those crews selected to take part. There were no squadron losses.

END OF SECOND TOUR

The next night (Wednesday, September 27th., 1944) we made it on the list. This time, we were part of a force detailed to attack Kaiserslaughtern, a town about 25 miles west of Mannheim. I had hoped to land an easy target with which to finish off my second tour, but this one didn't look too promising in that respect. Although I had no previous knowledge of the place, the briefing served to show that Kaiserslaughtern was an industrial target, and that we could expect to find it well defended. This we did, and we had a few anxious minutes over the town before we managed to discharge our load.

The weather had presented problems during the outward flight, with violent electrical storms in abundance for much of the trip. As we turned for home, the darkness was frequently broken by brilliant flashes of lightening beneath us, and these served to illuminate other aircraft in our vicinity. Turbulence was a problem, and Bill had his work cut out just keeping on course. We were still over Germany when he announced the presence of a large cumulonumbus up ahead, and said that he was going to skirt around it rather than try to climb above it. As the stormcloud came into my view on the starboard beam. I could see that its interior was glowing continuously from the effect of the electrical charges within it, and I could clearly see other Lancasters silhouetted against its steep sides as it towered several thousand feet above us.

As we drew level with the cloud, I noticed that my guns were crawling with glowing electrical charges, and that the perspex cupola of my turret was similarly decorated with shifting rivulets of fire which closely resembled miniature streaks of lightning. Glancing to either beam, I could see that the trailing edges of the big elevators and rudders were also outlined in dancing white light. The phenomenon, known as St Elmo's Fire, was not new to me, but I had never before seen it so densely displayed. As I concentrated on searching the dark port side for a possible enemy fighter, my attention was drawn to a long streak of brilliant white light which extended from beneath my turret to a point some thirty yards behind the aircraft. In the same instant, I became aware of an ever-increasing buildup of static interference on the aircraft intercom system. I at once recognised the nature of the problem: Alan Macdonald, being cloistered in his radio compartment out of contact with the rest of the crew (and therefor unaware of the outside conditions), had reeled out his trailing aerial in order to improve his radio reception.

Although I knew little of the laws of physics, I had a suspicion of what was happening to us: Through the generation of static electricity, our Lancaster was fast becoming a small but volatile thunder cloud, and the process was being greatly accelerated by the presence of the trailing aerial.

I was uncertain as to whether or not the trailing aerial was adding to our problem, but decided that, since I was probably the only member of the crew (apart from Alan) who was aware of the aerial being deployed. I should warn the others. I switched my mike on and called the skipper, but was unable to make myself heard above the roar of static, so decided to leave my position and go forward to tell someone about it.

I was in the process of preparing to leave the turret when i witnessed a blinding flash, accompanied by the most ear-splitting CRACK! I had ever heard, at once followed by total darkness and a deathly silence. In almost the same instant, I became aware of a tumbling sensation, as if my turret was falling. My analysis of the situation was that we had suffered a lightning strike. Although I was uncertain as to what effect this could have on a Lancaster, I had heard of aircraft breaking up during such an occurrence. The Lancaster fuselage had a tendency to fracture at a point just behind the mid upper turret when subjected to violence (as happened with our crash landing). Furthermore, it was not unknown for the tail turret to part company with the rest of the aircraft. I reasoned that this accounted for my being unable to hear the engines, and it also explained the sensation of falling. Being seized by a state of panic, and feeling certain that I had arrived at the correct appraisal of the situation, I decided it was time to get out.

Cursing my luck at having been downed over enemy territory by the forces of nature on this, the last trip of my second tour, I hastily set in motion the drill I had practised so many times in the past: turret facing the port beam; seat belt unfastened; sliding doors fully open; flying helmet off; tuck the knees up and roll out backwards. As I proceeded with the drill, I was unable to see anything in the turret. Only my familiarity with my surroundings enabled me to function.

I was about to remove the flying helmet and bale out when I discerned a faint yet familiar voice in my earphones.

"Is everybody alright?", it asked.

It was the voice of Bill Siddle requesting a report from each crew position in turn. The static was gone from my earphones now, and I could at last see and recognise my immediate surroundings. What was more, the sensation of falling out of control had left me.

END OF SECOND TOUR

It wasn't until after I had reported my state of wellbeing that I came to realise just how close I had been to spending the rest of the duration in a prisoner of war camp. Had Bill's call come just a split second later than it had, my helmet would have been removed, and I would have been descending into Germany.

During the return flight, the reality of what had happened gradually came through to me. We had been struck by lightning, and the resulting flash had served to bring temporary blindness to all of those with visual access to the sky around us. In addition, the thunderclap had rendered us deaf for a short period. Because he could no longer see and read his instrument panel, Bill had lost control of the aircraft, and it was probable that we had been performing all manner of aerobatics, including inverted flight, during the time that his eyesight was affected.

A cursory examination of the aircraft on our return to base showed that OL/S had not one aerial left intact. All had been reduced to droplets of molten metal, and these were no doubt now deposited in some far-distant German corn field.

Ours was the only aircraft to have returned in a damaged condition, and the squadron had again suffered no losses on the raid.

CHAPTER 24

FRENCH LEAVE

Now that I had completed a second tour, I applied for and was granted a bar to my Canadian operational wings. In the meantime, a crew conference had been held, at which the opinion seemed uppermost that we should continue together until the war ended. There was little doubt that the Allies were winning the fight, and most believed that victory was little more than a few weeks away. In the circumstances I agreed - with reluctance - to comply with the decision.

The month of October began with the crew getting involved in a lot of flying training, from which it became obvious that the squadron was again to take part in the recently inaugurated daylight bombing technique. On the morning of Thursday, October 5th., 1944, we took off in OL/S for what was to be a large formation exercise on London. The weather was mainly fine, with only a few scattered, fleecy clouds around, and most of these had disappeared by the time we reached the London area en masse just before noon. From my lofty vantage point, I could clearly see the landmarks with which I had become familiar during the many enjoyable leave periods I had spent in the metropolis.

As we traversed the vast expanse of the greater London area, familiar landmarks began to present themselves. The first that I recognised was Buckingham Palace, followed by Piccadilly Circus over on the starboard side, with the hotel where Rosanna and I had stayed wedged between Shaftsbury Avenue and Coventry Street. Then came Hyde Park Corner and the park itself with Marble Arch standing at the north-east corner. As each of these slid from beneath my turret I was reminded of the happy times we had spent there together. Carefree times, so far removed from the deadly conflict in which I and my crew were involved. A conflict to which in my mind there could only be one conclusion.

Next in view came Paddington station, near to which Rosanna lived. Although I was unable to locate her exact address amid the conglomerate of streets, avenues and terraces that made up the area, I knew that she was down there somewhere, and I wanted more than anything to be with her. I had no doubt concerning the future that awaited Rosanna and me once the war was at an end. A life filled with love, happiness, contentment, freedom and security, and with a natural span that would stretch into the far-distant future. As we left the great city of London behind us and headed north towards Lincolnshire, I realised that I had reached the stage in my career at which I should give more consideration to our destiny and less to that of the war and the fighting unit of which I was a part.

Much of the return flight was spent in conducting an appraisal of my past accomplishments. In the space of just fourteen months, I had served on two squadrons, both of which had been in the thick of the action. I had made many friends during the period, but most of those had either been killed or posted missing. Of those with whom I had shared my training in Canada, many were known to have met a similar fate. Only Eric Plunkett had enjoyed my good fortune, and he, together with his pilot, Squadron Leader Mitchell, (having completed their second tour a week ago) had left the squadron. In all, I had witnessed the loss of more than fifty aircraft and crews during my service with the two squadrons, and this number represented more than the total strength of the two units concerned. In terms of personnel, this meant the almost certain death of close on four hundred men, the majority of which had been highly skilled in their profession. What was more, almost all of the aircraft I had flown in at one time or another had come to grief at the hands of our enemy, or had crashed during training with equally disastrous results. There was no doubting the proficiency of my crew, but that quality alone was not enough. Luck had played a significant part in our survival, and I considered it unlikely that such good fortune could be expected to remain with us for many more trips, especially if we were expected to get involved in the daylight bombing campaign.

There was one other point for reflection, and this I considered to be of far greater importance than all the rest because it concerned the safety and welfare of the crew. During the year that had elapsed since the crash, I had suffered frequently from the after-effects of the injuries I had sustained at the time. Whilst I could endure the pain and nausea that accompanied the condition, it was the brief deterioration of my eyesight during the symptom that troubled me. As a gunner, my prime duty was the protection of the aircraft and crew against the onslaught of an enemy night fighter. In order that I might perform this function with any degree of proficiency, I must first be able to detect the presence of the enemy, and this could not be expected if my vision was impaired. Foolishly perhaps, I had decided against mentioning the ailment to anyone, largely because I had not experienced the difficulty during operational flying - at least, not until the Munster raid. One other matter for concern was my behaviour during the recent Kaiserslaughtern flight. Although My physical reaction to the lighting strike could be understood, I had been so overcome by panic that I became incapable

FRENCH LEAVE

of assessing the situation with any degree of logic. I had come to believe that the tailplane had broken away, in which case I would have been unable to operate the turret by any means other than manual, because the hydraulic power necessary for control was supplied by a pump which was fitted to one of the port engines, but I had not realised it.

My thoughts strayed to my native Canada, with its vast prairies; its majestic mountain ranges; its countless lakes; the friendliness of my fellow Canadians, and the lifestyle that differed so greatly from that of the English people that I had come to know and admire. They had been affected by the disruption, the distress, and the shortages that the horrors of war could inflict on them, yet they had met those hardships with an unyielding sense of determination and courage that defied comprehension.

Rosanna, under the influence of my many descriptions of Canada and its people, had expressed a desire to visit my homeland on some future occasion, and there was no doubt in my mind that she could soon adapt to the vastly different lifestyle that she would find there. I wanted to marry her. She already knew this, but had insisted that a proposal could not be considered until such time as my involvement in combat flying was at an end. I had completed two tours, and this was in excess of the achievement of most members of aircrew. in truth, I was to learn later that a mere two percent could be expected to complete as many trips and survive. My crew had elected to continue, yet it was an accepted RCAF ruling that a man who had reached that score was entitled to a period of rest.

By the time we touched down at Coningsby, I had decided to withdrew from further combat flying.

On the morning of Thursday, October 6th., 1944, I made my way over to the Office block after breakfast, intent on arranging an audience with the Wing commander, and was surprised to find the bomb aimer seated in the corridor.

"Morning Mike", I said. "What're you here for?"

"I'm waitin' to see the C.O.", he replied, then added "I'm packin' it in, Clayton".

"Me too", I told him. "What's your reason?"

"Well, I think we're pushin' our luck too far, and I don't like the idea of these bloody daylight raids they're plannin' for us".

"Nor do I", I affirmed. "Anyway, I think we've done our bit, don't you?". He nodded, and we launched into a discussion on what our respective futures might hold. Like me, he had hopes of getting in a spell on Training Command, by which time the war would probably be over. He had completed a total of forty-eight trips-three more than I. Our conversation was cut short when he was summonsed to the Wing Commander's office. It was to be the last time that we would meet until many years after the war. After he had left, I visited the Adjutant's office and arranged an appointment with the C.O. for later that afternoon.

As I expected, my meeting with the Wing commander, although brief, was far from congenial. From the moment that I announced my wish to take a rest from operations, I got the impression that he despised me for it, and that he considered me a quitter. In the circumstances, I drew comfort from the private knowledge that, although I wanted to terminate my commitment to operational flying, it was not entirely because of the fear that was ever present in the minds of those involved in the fight. If the Wingco wanted to think otherwise, that was his prerogative.

When the interview ended, I was instructed to return to the mess and await further orders. On the way up to my room, I collected a letter from my pigeon hole. It was from Edith, and it contained news that she had recently given birth to Dick Jones' child in St Mary's Hospital, Newcastle on Tyne. The letter went on to say that both she and the baby (a girl) were well, then remarked on the lack of information about the crew and me.

I resolved to write a letter of congratulations to her that evening, in which I would tell her about my withdrawal from combat, and arrange to visit her at a future date, but my good intentions were thwarted by a call over the Tannoy requesting me to report to the Adjutant's office at once.

On entering the Adjutant's office, I was at once impressed by the friendly reception I got from the man behind the desk - a contrast in demeanour so different to that which the Wing Commander had adopted. I was invited to be seated, and was at once afforded some quite unexpected praise for my flying record, followed by a mild comment on my list of earlier misdemeanours - two charges and a reprimand, the latter for persistently failing to turn up for morning parades. After a few more cordial exchanges, he informed me that I was to be posted away from the squadron immediately, and that I was to catch a train that evening for an RCAF unit at a place called Houghton Green, near Warrington in Lancashire. In answer to my question on what my future prospect might be, he was unable to comment, saying that this would now be up to the Canadian unit to which I was being posted. At this point, the interview came to an end, so we shook hands, I saluted and left.

That evening, after I had hastily satisfied the requirements of the unescapable clearance chit, I visited both messes in the hope of finding some of the crew. But the weather had clamped down on all flying, so I guessed that they must be down in the village enjoying a tipple or two. Back in the Officer's Mess, I was just downing a last pint prior to catching my train when the Adjutant came in and joined me at the bar.

The Adjutant ordered a drink then, after taking a sip said, "Before you go, Moore, a batch of DFC's arrived in my office last thing today. I haven't had time to go through them yet, but I think there's one there for you. If there is, I'll send it on to you, of course".

I thanked him, drained my pint, then asked, "Sir, have I been declared LMF?"

"Not to my knowledge, you haven't. And why should you? You've done more than your share. The C.O.'s orders were that I arrange with the RCAF for your immediate posting, and that's all I know about it".

I thanked him again, shook his hand for the last time, and stepped out into the pouring rain to catch my transport down to the station. There wasn't time to call at the pub, so I boarded the train for Lincoln without having the chance to say goodbye to my old crew. as my train pulled away from the platform. I wondered how they would take the news that I had left them so abruptly. Would they think that I had 'chickened out', just as I had thought when Clem and Hine had vanished from our midst in circumstances which were probably identical to my own? Perhaps I and the crew had been wrong in reaching such a conclusion, but any information which might have indicated the truth had been withheld from us.

Because my ultimate destination was located on the opposite side of the British Isles to Coningsby. I again found myself faced with the same series of interruptions and delays that I had met with on my earlier trip - the one in which I had been misdirected to Warrington in Lancashire instead of Waddington in Lincolnshire. The only difference this time was that everything was in reverse order. As a result, the town or Warrington was just beginning to show signs of life when the last of the many connections I had caught during the long and sleepless night finally steamed into the station. Air Force transportation being conspicuous by its absence. I loaded my kitbags and other bits of luggage into a taxi and set out for the short journey to Houghton Green on the northern outskirts of the town. During the train journey, I had been wracking my brain to recall to memory the presence of a Canadian squadron near the west coast of England, but without success.

I was met at the gatehouse by a friendly Sergeant wearing Canada flashes on his shoulders and a broad grin on his face. In answer to my question, "What the hell is this camp, anyway, Sergeant?, he replied, "It's the Royal Canadian Air Force Repatriation Centre, Sir. Aren't you glad?" The statement rocked me back on my heels. So that was it. I was being sent back to Canada!

"I'm not sure that I am, Sergeant", I replied.

A few minutes later I was loaded into a Morris van for the short trip to my quarters, where I had a shave and got cleaned up before having breakfast.

The mess hall was occupied by a mixture of Canadian aircrew, some non-commissioned, but most of Officer rank, and I was at once impressed by the lack of class distinction to which I had grown so accustomed during my service with the English squadrons. Those present were all experienced and time-expired men, and their impatience to get home was made obvious by the exchanges that were taking place at my table. I learned from my fellow diners that the average wait for a ship was about a week, possibly two, depending on what turned up at the ports. Of the troopships plying the Atlantic route, there was much talk about the need to avoid boarding one called The Andies, a vessel of uncertain origin and construction which had earned itself a reputation for being almost totally devoid of comfort and safety.

Although I was equally keen to get back to Canada, I still had some unfinished business to attend to: now that my combat flying was finished, I could at last propose marriage to Rosanna, and I was confident of her acceptance. It followed that I must procure a special licence but, I was due to end of tour leave, so decided to pay a call on the Adjutant after breakfast. I was due to the customary fourteen days, but considered that seven would suffice.

I expected the Adjutant to project the same air of friendliness that I had received from the others on the camp, but my expectations in this regard were to be thwarted from the outset. On entering the office, I found seated behind the desk a Flight Lieutenant in his late forties. His tunic was without any ornamentation other than his rank, the Canada flashes, and a solitary 1939 Star ribbon. When he finally looked up begrudgingly to acknowledge my presence, I saw before me the face of a man who hated all aircrew, regardless of their rank or operational achievement, and I could foresee some difficulty in getting my argument across.

FRENCH LEAVE

I was right. His reaction to my request for leave, and my stated reason for requesting it, made it plain that I had no hope of succeeding.

"You've been posted back to Canada, and you'll be on the next ship out".

I tried to reason with him, but he stubbornly refused to listen, and ordered me to leave his office, which I did. Having learned that the best way of getting something done in the Air Force was to go straight to the top, I walked along the corridor and knocked on the door marked 'Commanding Officer', only to be told by a man polishing the corridor lino that the Group Captain was on seven days' leave.

By the time I reached the billet I had decided on a plan of action: the next ship leaving for Canada would be sailing with an empty bunk because I wouldn't be on it, and damn the consequences! My future with Rosanna was at stake, and it was obvious that I was not going to get any help from my superiors in dealing with the problem. I was being forced to take drastic action if I was ever to see her again. In doing what I intended, I would thus qualify for yet another charge, but I considered her to be well worth it.

I at once packed a suitcase and set out for the main gate, where I was confronted by a fellow Canadian wearing the rank of a Corporal. His friendly and well-intentioned greeting was met with an outburst of indignation, during which I demanded to know why he had failed to salute me, and why his cap was not set at the prescribed angle. The ploy produced an effect for which I was somewhat unprepared, not having used my rank for such a purpose previously. The corporal quickly adjusted his cap before peeling off a smart salute, and returned to the guardroom in a state of confusion without having asked to inspect my non-existent leave pass.

I strolled out of the camp in the direction of the nearest bus stop. The first hurdle had been successfully dealt with, but I feared that there might be others ahead.

It turned out that my fears of being caught in the act were unfounded, and my train, hauled by the majestic Flying Scotsman, steamed into Euston station in the late afternoon. I at once booked a room in the Regent's Palace Hotel, thinking it wise to avoid the service clubs in case they were to be checked on. Once established in my room, I wasted no time in getting cleaned up to catch a tube train over to Rosanna's place.

She was delighted to see me, but expressed surprise at my reappearance so soon after my previous leave period. Because I wished to postpone the announcement of my purpose until conditions were exactly right, I side-stepped the issue and invited her to have dinner with me at the hotel, where I had booked a table for two for that evening.

The dinner was a success, with a setting that served to create the kind of atmosphere usually to be found only in a scene from some romantic movie. Our conversation was free-flowing, with no mention being made of the war. Once we had finished dining, I took her into the lounge, where I found a small table in a quiet corner and ordered drinks. Rosanna had never looked more beautiful, and I couldn't help but notice the attraction she held for all those present, so magnetic was the charm of her poise and her personality.

As the evening wore on, and the feeling of mutual togetherness between us increased. I sensed that the time was right for me to steer our conversation towards the topic uppermost in my mind. I began by breaking the news that I had been withdrawn from further operational flying, and that I was to be sent back to Canada at once. I also told her that I had applied for leave in order that I could come to London and see her before sailing, but that this had been refused, so I had gone absent without leave in order that I could deal with matters concerning our future.

"I love you. Rosanna, and I'm asking you to marry me now so that I can make plans for you to follow me out as soon as the necessary arrangements can be made.

She didn't reply at once, but gazed into my eyes as if trying to read my innermost thoughts. Gradually, the familiar smile that I had grown to love was replaced by a look of solemn consideration and tenderness. This I understood. Although my intentions had been made clear in the past, she was now faced with an immediate decision. The risks must have seemed considerable to a girl in her situation. Not only was I asking her to marry me, but her acceptance would make it necessary for her to leave all her friends and the familiar surroundings of her homeland to live in a strange and distant country of which she had little knowledge.

She continued to study me in silence for some time, and I detected a look of concern and sadness in her adorable eyes that was so unworthy of the happy, carefree girl I had come to know. Then, she reached across the table and placed a hand on mine, and, with the tears beginning to well up, she said:

"Clayton, I'm sorry, but I can't marry you".

"Rosanna", I said, "I know it's a big decision for you to make, but I can promise that you'll never be sorry if you marry me. I can understand it if you don't want to go to Canada. That's alright with me. I'd be only to willing to share my life with you here in England. That's how dearly I love you. Now, will you reconsider?"

Her tears were flowing freely as I pressed her extended hand in both of mine and waited for her response.

"Clayton, I can never become your wife because I am already married. My husband is a serving officer with the British Army in Italy. Before that, he was in the North African campaign, so I haven't seen him for more than three years. And I have another shock for you: we have a daughter, and she was evacuated to Wales just a week before Rose and I met you and Eric in the West End".

Needless to say, I was devastated by her reply. From early in our year-long relationship, I had made my intentions towards her clear, and I had believed that she would accept my proposal when it came, because I knew that we were both in love. I had bowed to her refusal to discuss possible marriage while I was still involved in operational flying. That made sense. But I couldn't understand her reason for deliberately deceiving me, so asked for an explanation.

"As I'm sure you can imagine, I was feeling desperately unhappy at having to send our baby daughter away. I was alone and miserable. Rose suggested that we should have a night out in the West End. I didn't want to go, but she insisted that I was in need of being cheered up, so I agreed. That night, we met you and Eric, and you know the rest".

"But why didn't you tell me that you were married?"

"I fully intended to, believe me. But somehow, I just kept putting it off".

"Why?".

"For a number of reasons. First of all, I knew that it was unlikely that you would survive the war. I admired you, and I felt a genuine sorrow for you, and I was feeling sorry for myself, too. Then, you visited me again on your next leave, and I began to realise that we enjoyed each other's company so much. I wanted to tell you then, but it was already obvious that you were in love with me. I knew that the news would only hurt you, and I didn't want that to happen. Then I began to see that we fulfilled a need in each other, and, selfish though I was to do so, I decided against the early ending of a beautiful relationship that I feared would end in tragedy anyway. For just a little while, we were both happy, and I could see no harm in that".

Although the rejection had made me feel almost sick with disappointment, her reason for allowing the continuation of a relationship that she knew couldn't last indicated something of the emotional torment she was prepared to accept on my behalf, and I could understand that. We were just two of the many who had been thrown together by the prevailing circumstances. Our affair (for that's what it was), although unrewarding in the long term, had, if only for a few short months, provided us both with a modicum of sanity in a world that had gone mad. My biggest regret was in the knowledge that our relationship could never be allowed to run its natural course.

"So this is Goodbye, Rosanna", I remarked. In reality, I knew it to be a statement of fact. By definition, it was plain that the relationship must end at once.

"Clayton, I'm both sorry and pleased that it is. I'm sorry that we have to part at all, particularly in this way, and I want you to know that I'm going to miss you terribly because you've been such a comfort to me. But I'm so happy to know that you've survived, and that I was able to provide for you something of the companionship and normality that you needed. You're a young man with most of your adult life still in front of you. In time, you'll meet someone else, and you'll forget all about me. I want you to, Clayton, and you must".

Despite the distress that it caused me, I could see the validity of her reasoning. In similar circumstances, some might have considered her action in not telling me that she was married to be selfish. To some extent it was. But she had been alone and in need of the love and the friendship that I had so willingly provided. Similarly, there was no question of the benefit I had derived from having known her and enjoyed the care and generosity of her personality. From its beginning, the relationship had been based on a lie, but she had withheld the truth from me in the knowledge that it would only cause me hurt and disappointment.

The parting was not immediate. We spend several days just being together and reliving all the many pleasures we had enjoyed in the past. We dined. We strolled arm-in-arm through the parks that we knew so intimately. We saw an Ivor Novello show, and we again visited the near-by Mitre - the public house where we had first met.

FRENCH LEAVE

On our final evening together, we booked a hotel room for the night. Early the following morning, we went down for breakfast, and I booked a taxi for ten a.m. before we returned to the room. We had agreed that we should say our last goodbyes there in private, and that she would then leave, after which I would go down and pay the bill before catching my taxi.

Although we tried so earnestly to part as we had planned, we found that we just couldn't bring ourselves to do it. Finally, Rosanna accompanied me to Euston in the taxi. As the train began to move slowly out of the station, I released her hand for the last time and heard her tearfully speak the words that were to remain with me for all time:

"Have a nice life, Clayton", she called after me.

I leaned out of the carriage window and waved to her until her petite form had faded into the distance.

CHAPTER 25

HOMEWARD BOUND

As was to be expected, my eventual return to the RCAF Repatriation Centre at Warrington was not without incident. I was quite prepared to face up to the indignity of being locked up in the guard house on arrival, but was surprised to find that I was allowed to re-enter the camp without being challenged, so made my way to the dormitory, where I found my bed space and locker as I had left them. For a time I considered the possibility of rejoining the system without detection, but soon realised the folly of such an idea, it being unlikely that my absence at the roll call for eight consecutive days would have passed without notice. On learning from those present in the dormitory that three ships had sailed for Canada in the past week, it became obvious to me that I would not be able to evade the consequences of my action. I therefore concluded that I would simply have to face the music, and that the first overture would have to take the form of a courtesy call on the decidedly unfriendly Adjutant. In this respect, I considered that whatever evil my adversary might choose to inflict on me would pall in significance to the despondency I had experienced since I had learned the truth about Rosanna. To me, nothing else mattered.

The Adjutant wasted no time in subjecting me to a string of verbal abuse. At first, this concerned the nature of the offence I had committed so I made no attempt to intervene on my behalf, knowing that my guilt was without question. It wasn't until he started to attack my character that I began to speak out with equal ferocity, pointing out his downright refusal to recognise the urgency of my situation, thus making necessary the action I had taken. The exchange then deteriorated into a slanging-match which ended with the expected charge being made, after which I was ordered out of his office and told that I would be confined to my quarters. I at once left his office and walked down the corridor to a door marked 'Commanding Officer' and knocked.

A voice from within bade me enter, so I opened the door to find myself confronted by a Group Captain seated behind the desk. As I saluted, I noticed that his tunic bore Canada flashes, pilot's wings, and two rows of campaign medals and other decorations. I was later to learn that his hame was Massey, and that he was a brother to Sir Vincent Massey, a name which was vaguely familiar to me as some high-up Canadian personage. I thanked him for seeing me, and apologised for having sought an interview without prior arrangement. This he accepted, then invited me to be seated while I gave an account of my reason for such unorthodox behaviour.

Group Captain Massey listened as I gave a detailed and honest account of the problem. When I had finished, he asked:

"How many sorties have you done?"

"Forty-Five, Sir".

"With what squadron?"

"I completed sixteen with number nine Squadron, Bomber command, and the rest on eighty-three Squadron, Pathfinders, Sir".

There followed a lengthy pause while he appeared to consider the validity of myself and the information I had given, before he at last announced his decision.

"You were wrong to go absent as you did, of course, but I think you got a raw deal in the circumstances. I'm impressed by your operational record, and it is this that goes in your favour. You've done your bit, and I'm ordering you to get back home. Then, perhaps, you'll be able to forget the whole unfortunate episode".

"Thank you, Sir. And what about the charge?", I asked.

"You can forget about that, too", he assured me.

At the conclusion of the interview, I left the C.O.'s office and returned to the dorm, feeling elated at having overcome the inflexible attitude that some people held regarding the rules of the game. The Group Captain had shown that he was not afraid to bend the rules when he thought it necessary, and it was to be regretted that his Adjutant had been lacking in such initiative.

I considered that my brawl with the Adjutant was ended, but was forced to accept the folly of this when the man stormed into the dormitory half an hour later and confronted me once more.

"I bet you think you're really somethin!", he bellowed from the entrance so that all those present could hear. In the circumstances I considered it best that I should not allow myself to be drawn into any further conflict, but that I should let him give full vent to his anger.

This he did, and it became evident from his unbridled fury that he had just taken delivery of a high

HOMEWARD BOUND

powered rocket from the Group Captain. At last, having seemingly exhausted his extensive vocabulary of abuse, he fired a question at me:

"I understand you've got a DFC coming to you. Am I right?".

Recalling that Bill Siddle had put me forward for one, and remembering what the 83 Squadron Adjutant had told me on the night I left Coningsby, I considered his belief to be correct. In any case, it was probable that he was already in possession of my documents. For what other reason would he be asking the question?

"Yes", I replied, "I understand that I have". I deliberately neglected to append the word 'Sir'.

"Then you'll never see it!", he scowled, as he turned and left the room.

I was aware that, had I been given such a decoration, it would have been a 'non-immediate' award, and as such, could be withdrawn if I was convicted of misconduct. But no disciplinary action had been taken against me in this instance, and I considered the Adjutant's threat to be nothing more sinister than a desire on his part to wreak vengeance on me for having jumped the chain of command. Furthermore, I thought it unlikely that he would succeed in his purpose, so I decided against a further visit to the Group Captain's office.

Three days later, on Tuesday, December the 19th., 1944, I boarded the Dutch cruise liner "Nieu Amsterdam" at Greenock, bound for Halifax, Nova Scotia. The crossing took considerably longer than it would have taken on one of "The Queens", but the food and the accommodation was excellent, so there was a total absence of complaint from the many time-expired fellow Canadians on board. For us, the war was ended - at least, we were given to believe that it was. But, on Christmas Day, we got an unpleasant reminder that we were still within a war zone. We were nearing the port of Halifax, and I had just entered one of the dining halls, intent on enjoying my third Christmas Dinner away from home, when an announcement came over the ship's Tannoy, ordering all passengers below decks. No reason was given, but the urgent tone of the message and the sound of bells ringing all over the ship made it plain that we must be under attack. The order was followed by numerous others, but these, being directed at the crew, were in Dutch, a language foreign to most, if not all of us.

During the voyage, I had become friendly with a fellow RCAF officer, and he, being with me when the balloon went up, suggested that we should make our way up top to see what was going on. This we did, and were thus afforded an unrestricted view of the action from our carefully selected vantage point behind one of the lifeboats.

Our ship was engaged in some quite violent evasive action, and we could see a Sunderland flying boat approaching from a westerly direction. As we watched, we saw a salvo of depth charges leaving the Sunderland, and these splashed into the water about half a mile off our starboard beam, but we were unable to observe anything other than the waterspouts that they produced. The Sunderland, apparently having exhausted its supply of depth charges, then turned and left the action, but was soon replaced by a Catalina. This dropped two more 'ash cans' in the same area, after which it began to circle where they had fallen. At last my companion and I were able to see something of what had caused all the confusion, as a German U-boat rose slowly to the surface. As we watched, a number of dark figures were seen to leave the conning tower and move out onto the narrow deck. One was waving something white at the 'Cat', which then turned in a westerly direction and disappeared over a gathering grey fog bank. The Nieu Amsterdam ceased its weaving and sailed steadily past the unfortunate German submariners and their stricken craft, not daring to stop for survivors because of the danger of coming under attack from another member of the pack.

The action was over, so my friend and I returned below and joined the lineup for our Christmas fare.

Later that evening (Christmas Day, 1944) our troopship docked at Halifax to find the city blanketed in thick fog, and with the temperature well below freezing. As we lined up on the dockside in the bitter cold to be processed, I found myself wondering how the German U-boat crew had fared out there in the icy waters of the Atlantic. Had they been picked up, or had they just been left there to die? During the past two years I had watched many of my friends and colleagues perish at the hands of the same enemy, such were the horrors of war. But I couldn't help hoping that the U-boat crew had been picked up and taken prisoner.

Next day we boarded a train for an RCAF collecting depot at Lachine, Quebec. There we were held for a further three days before being checked out and granted thirty days of disembarkation leave, plus whatever time it took us to travel to our respective home towns. In my case, it took me three days to make the journey, with the result that it was late on New Year's Eve that I got down from my train at Saskatoon, two years (almost to the hour) from the time I had left to go overseas. There was a party on when I got to the house in Avenue C south, just as there had been on the night that I left two years before - just as if it had been going non-stop all that time, just as if nothing had changed.

But there had been changes nevertheless. Our country band had broken up because of the depletion of its members through enlistment, and because of the death of one of them. An uncle had passed away, and most of the many friends I had known were serving in the Canadian armed forces. Margaret had married, and had moved with her husband to the Peace River district of western Canada. In general, living conditions were about the same, although I heard much complaining about shortages. At first I felt shame for my fellow countrymen because of this, then I came to realise that they couldn't begin to appreciate the hardships being borne by the courageous people of war-ravaged Britain unless they had witnessed them personally, as I had done.

After a short stay in Saskatoon, I caught a ride on 'The Skunk' up to Prince Albert. As I stepped down from the train I got a handshake from a uniformed member of the Canadian Legion. It appeared that his duty was that of greeting each returning veteran and presenting him or her with a couple of packs of Players cigarettes, while a small band played a tuneful ditty to welcome us back. Father was also at the station with the horse-drawn sleigh which was to be our only means of making the seven-mile journey through the snow-laden Nesbit pine forest to Whitfield and home. He was unable to conceal his pride in me and the uniform I was wearing, but I was wishing that I had something more substantial to wear during the cold journey that lay ahead.

Because it was mid winter, the roads beyond the town were mere tracks through the deep layer of crisp snow that was everywhere, and I found the Christmas card landscape with its snow covered pine trees a sharp contrast to the environment I had become accustomed to during the previous two years. The scene was one of unbridled natural beauty, with only the deep sleigh tracks to betray the vulgar presence of man. The pine-scented air was crisp and clean, and the afternoon sunshine made it look as if the snow-laden branches of the tall pine trees were bejewelled with diamonds and sapphires.

Mother had prepared a special spread for the occasion, complete with a late farmhouse lunch that included all my favourite dishes, followed by a generous helping of her home-made wines. After we had dined, some of the neighbours called in, and - as a result of the subsequent drift of conversation, I found myself being pressed for details of my exploits and experiences. Whilst I could appreciate their interest in such matters, I realised that I was being looked upon as something of a hero, an accolade of which I considered myself undeserving in view of more recent events, and I was possessed of a desire to forget all about the war, particularly the part I had played in it.

After our visitors had left, Dad asked me about my plans for the future, and I had to admit that I had not yet decided on what to do. During my voyage on the Nieu Amsterdam, I had been called to an on-board office, where a Squadron Leader remarked favourably on my war record and suggested that I should consider an extension to my period of service. He pointed out that officers of my experience were needed in an instructional capacity, and he assured me that I would be granted an immediate bump-up in rank if I agreed to the offer. I was at first tempted to accept, but thought it wise to explore the pro's and con's first. On the credit side, there was the immediate promotion, plus the possibility of going even higher. I felt confident that I could handle the job of instructing new aircrew, and this would involve flying, which was a job that I liked. Job security was the one thing that troubled me. There was little doubt that the war would soon be over, and a marked reduction in the Canadian armed forces could be expected once it was. I had been accepted into the RCAF 'For a period of National emergency', and it was unlikely that I would be granted a permanent commission in peacetime. Then there was the matter of the administrative inflexibility I had met with during my service career. The imposition of petty discipline. The charges which had been levelled against me. The restrictions. The lack of personal freedom. Then I had remembered the attitude of the Canadian Adjutant at Warrington, and this had induced me to decline the offer.

Because my five brothers had all been married, and each had taken up employment elsewhere, Dad wanted me to assist in the running of the farm. I told him that I had already opted to leave the Air Force, but was still undecided on what my future might be, and that I wanted some time in which to make up my mind. Having decided to give up flying, I had tried to map out a plan, but found that the state of restlessness I was then experiencing as a result of recent events was hampering any hope of practicality. At the back of my mind was the knowledge that the Canadian Department of Veteran's Affairs was active in offering assistance in the rehabilitation of ex-service men and women, and that the scheme included a selection of courses designed to prepare one for civilian employment. Things mechanical had always held a fascination for me, and I wanted to find out what was on offer in this field before reaching a final decision. Besides, I wasn't keen on farming.

HOMEWARD BOUND

I was under orders to report to No 2 Aircrew Release Centre in Winnipeg on the twenty-sixth of February, 1945. On presenting myself, I was surprised to learn that no one there had any knowledge of me. After much searching of files, and the making of a number of long-distance telephone calls, it was established that my records had been mislaid, after which I was granted indefinite leave, and given orders to return home to await further instructions by post.

Prior to leaving Winnipeg, I had enquired about the courses on offer, and was told that one covering Diesel engineering was available at the Vancouver technical college. I at once made application for it, and arranged for my release to take place in Vancouver instead of Winnipeg.

Back home, I found that my further instructions were a long time in coming. Because my documents were missing, I was not drawing any pay, and personal finances were becoming something of a problem. At the end of six weeks of unrelenting boredom and deprivation, my impatience got the better of me, so I again boarded a train bound for Winnipeg, where I was at once arrested. In reply to my angry reaction to this, I was told that I was a deserter, and that I must therefore be court martialled. Sensing that someone somewhere had dropped a colossal clanger, I demanded a full rundown on my alleged transgression, and was told that, once my documents had been recovered, I had at once been transferred to No 8 Aircrew Release Centre in Vancouver, but that repeated letters to that effect had been totally ignored by me. When I insisted that I had not received any such letters, the address to which the orders had been sent was produced, thus enabling me to point out with aclacrity that they had been sending the letters to the wrong address. In fact, it was one that I had never heard of.

Once my freedom from guilt had been established, little time was wasted in projecting me through the system. So it was that, on Tuesday the twentieth of March, I took up my final posting with the RCAF - this time in Vancouver.

My arrival at the Aircrew Release Centre signalled the beginning of my last skirmish with 'The Powers that Be'. Because I was still suffering from the after effects of the crash, I was intent on getting to the roots of the problem, and had resolved to insist on a thorough medical examination prior to my release.

The examination was part of the standard release procedure, which in total was intended to ascertain whether or not the person being released was reasonably fit; had surrendered all items of issue, and had paid any outstanding mess fees or other dues. On having satisfied these requirements, the officer was then asked to sign his release. After the tests, I was told that my medical category had remained unchanged throughout my period of service. Knowing this to be untrue, I refused to sign until a more detailed appraisal of my condition had been made. During the next three days I was subjected to numerous tests, at the conclusion of which it was ruled that I was suffering from a severe migraine condition which could not in any way be attributed to the injuries I had sustained in the flying accident.

Finally, on Tuesday, April the 17th., 1945, with a feeling of frustration and disgust, I was at last forced to accept the quite unsatisfactory judgment of a superior power, so presented myself within a tiny office for the final act in my conversion to civilian status. As I entered the room I saw seated behind the desk a friendly and much-decorated Squadron Leader who smiled, shook my hand, and asked me to be seated. In the course of the ensuing conversation I was congratulated on my past record of service, and my plans for the future were discussed with genuine interest. I was told that a sum of money in the form of war gratuity was due to me, and that this I would be receiving soon. I was also informed that I had been promoted to the rank of Flying Officer with effect from the 25th of February, and that back pay for this would also be forthcoming. I then enquired as to whether or not I had been awarded a DFC, and the Squadron Leader expressed surprise, in view of my operational record, that there was no mention of such an award in my documents. It then crossed my mind that the Adjutant back in Britain had done a good job of making sure that his threat to me had been carried out, which might explain the reason for my records having gone missing for a time. Finally, I was asked to sign my release paper, and was then supplied with an address in North Vancouver where temporary accommodation could be had. As I turned to leave, I noticed a sign above the door which read "CIVVY STREET". I turned the knob and stepped outside.

The city of Vancouver was bathed in brilliant spring sunshine as, one hour later, I boarded a trolley bus for the ride to my digs. As the bus silently made its way along the tree-lined avenues, I reflected on the brief but action-packed period from which I had just emerged. In the time span of just two years and nine months, I had learned many things that I wouldn't have learnt had I chosen not to enlist, and I was aware of the debt I owed to my past experiences, and to the Royal Canadian Air Force for having provided me with the opportunity to take an active part. I had witnessed at first hand the horror and brutality of war. I had made many friends, and I had watched many of them die. Of my own crew, only two of the original seven were still involved in the struggle - the pilot and the navigator. One had been killed, two had been so badly injured that they could no longer fly, one had mysteriously disappeared from the crew, and I had returned home to Canada. Then there were the many replacements - seven in all. Of these, two had transferred to other squadrons, yet another had disappeared mysteriously from the crew, one had left at the same time that I left, and three were still flying with Bill Siddle and Dick Lodge. I had taken part in forty-five raids on some of the most heavily defended targets in Western Europe. We had been holed by flak, chased by fighters, and coned by searchlights on numerous occasions. Our Lancaster had been struck by lightening, and we had suffered a crash.

I had progressed through the ranks to Flying Officer, and had been offered further promotion. I had completed two tours without having fired a single shot in anger, and this accomplishment alone indicated something of the luck we had enjoyed as a small fighting unit. But there was no doubting the fact that our overall efficiency had figured largely in our ability to avoid trouble. All things considered, I had been fortunate - indeed honoured - to have served with Flight Lieutenant Siddle and the others.

As I left the bus and walked up the pathway to my digs at 214 West 14th Street, North Vancouver (the home of the Kosgroves), I reflected on how the events of the past thirty-three months had transformed me from a naive, adventure-seeking and rebellious youth into a young man with an awareness of duty and responsibility that belied my age.

My search for adventure had been met, and I had survived despite all the odds. It was a pity that I couldn't go out and celebrate in the way to which I had become accustomed. My twenty-first birthday - the date from which I could legally partake of intoxicants - was still eighteen days hence.

HOMEWARD BOUND

CHAPTER 26

WHERE ARE THEY NOW

PILOT

F/Lt William E (Bill) Siddle, DFC & Bar

Place and date of birth unknown. Formed the crew on June 23rd, 1943 at Upper Heyford. Remained on active service until the cessation of hostilities, having completed more than sixty operational sorties. On discharge from the RAF, he concentrated on running the family business (the Crown Hotel in Penrith, Cumberland). Last visited in the summer of 1955. On the failure of the business, it is understood that he was divorced, after which he took up residence in Grimsby, working as a chef for a steamship company there. He re-married, but no details are available on any descendants. He died in 1970.

NAVIGATOR

Warrant Officer Richard (Dick) Lodge, DFM
A Volunteer Reserve entrant, served throughout the war, completing more than sixty trips with Siddle, ending with the repatriation of Allied prisoners of war from Germany, Married to Gwendoline. Two children (Stephen and Barbara). Director of company involved in the manufacture of neon signs, including those installed at the BEA and BOAC terminals at Heathrow airport. Died 23rd of November, 1977, Gwendoline died on the 3rd September, 1990.

1st BOMB AIMER

F/O K T (Ken) Hill, DFM

A Londoner, he Joined the crew at its formation. He was involved in the crash on September 7th., 1943, and was excused further flying duties as a result of injuries sustained, having completed only eight trips with us. Little is known of his further RAF activities, or his date of discharge. The author visited him and his wife and family in mid-1957, at which time he was living at Cheshunt, East London, and was believed to be involved in a large market gardening business. No further information is available.

2nd BOMB AIMER

Warrant Officer Norman (Mike) Machin, DFC
Joined the crew at Bardney in late 1943, and completed a total of forty-eight sorties, most of these with Siddle. Left the crew with the author, but remained in the RAF until 1949. Married to Dorothy, a WAAF Wireless and Teleprinter Operator. Two children and one grandchild. On discharge, took up employment as an engineering buyer for M.I.P.S. of Coventry. Now retired and residing at Ferryhill, County Durham.

WIRELESS OPERATOR

Sgt Clem Culley

Believed to be from Loughborough in Leicestershire, he joined the original crew at Operational Training Unit in early 1943. Remained with us until September, 1944, during which time he completed some thirty-five sorties with us. The author has had no further contact with him since the date of his departure.

WHERE ARE THEY NOW

2nd WIRELESS OPERATOR

F/O Alan MacDonald, DFC.

A member of the Royal Canadian Air Force, he joined the crew in early September, 1944, and remained with it until the cessation of hostilities. On discharge, he took up residence in Britain, working for Imperial Chemical Industries Billingham, during which time he resided in West Hartlepool with the author before his marriage to Bunty (the sister of F/Lt Siddle) in the summer of 1947. He and Bunty emigrated to Canada some time later, and are now retired and residing at Marble Mountain, Nova Scotia, where he set up a radio repair business. They have raised six children.

FLIGHT ENGINEER

Sgt R W (Reg) Moseley

Born in Bristol. Joined the crew at Winthorpe in June, 1943. Married to Edna on August 16th of that year. Completed eight trips with the crew, ending in the crash. After this he undertook a number of ground crew postings as an engine fitter to various places, including Burma, where he was serving at the conclusion of the war with Japan. Was discharged from the RAF in December, 1946. Was employed as a fitter for British Overseas Airways Corporation at the Brabazon hangar, Filton, Bristol, and for Bristol Aero Engines. Was involved in the development of the Britannia, and did some work on the lubricating system of the ill-fated Brabazon. Edna died in 1980, aged 58, and Reg re-married in 1983, after which he and his new wife, Bridget, took over the tenancy of a public house in Devon for a period of three years. His only daughter, Carol, died suddenly in May, 1991, aged 44. Reg and Bridget now reside in Bulkington, Coventry.

2nd FLIGHT ENGINEER

Warrant Officer Alan (Jock) Wilson, DFM.

Born in Glasgow, Scotland in 1920. Joined the crew in early October, 1943 after having lost his own crew, with which he had taken part in seven raids. Completed an additional thirty-seven sorties with F/Lt Siddle's crew which he left in January of 1945. On discharge from the RAF he took up employment as shop manager (later chief buyer) at British Celanese of Ilkeston. In 1964 he established his own business (A R Wilson (Packaging Limited) in Nottingham. Married to Mary, who had been serving with the NAAFI at Bardney, in October, 1944. Four sons and two daughters from the marriage. Died in Nottingham on the 13th of December, 1981, aged 61 years. Mary died on the 7th January 1993.

MID UPPER GUNNER

Sgt R E (Dick) Jones

Born in Wales, 1921. Joined the crew at Winthorpe on June 23rd, 1943. completed eight raids with the crew, plus an unknown number of others with other crews. Was involved in the crash in September, 1943, and was married to Edith Malcolm of Easington Colliery, County Durham on November 13th., 1943. On return to the squadron, he flew with another crew on December 3rd., 1943, but the aircraft was shot down near the base by an intruder aircraft on return from Berlin, and he was one of those killed. One daughter Gloria Gwynneth, now married and living in Cleveland.

WHERE ARE THEY NOW

2nd MID UPPER GUNNER

Warrant Officer G (Gerry) Parker, DFC

Citizen of the United States. Was attending an English university when war was declared, and enlisted in the RAF. Joined the crew in October, 1943 as temporary replacement for Sgt Jones. Completed twenty-three operational flights with the crew prior to his transfer to the US 8th Army Air corps in late June, 1944. No further contact.

3rd MID UPPER GUNNER

Warrant Officer J J (Paddy) Blanche

A native of Northern Ireland, had completed a tour in North Africa prior to being accepted by our crew in late June, 1944. After taking part in just one raid with us, he transferred to 617 (Dambuster) Squadron, with which he completed a further five trips. Moved to 227 Squadron, but was subjected to court martial proceedings (nature of offence not known) and was reduced through the ranks to AC2 on the 19th of February, 1945. Was discharged on the 12th of December that year. Worked as a ganger for Wimpy Construction Co. Found dead in a London street some time during the seventies. married. Two sons. Age not known.

4TH MID UPPER GUNNER

Pilot Officer E D Hine

Believed to be a Londoner, joined the crew in July, 1944. Previous operational record unknown, but completed three sorties with the crew before being posted to '54 Base' in August 1944. No further contact.

5TH MID UPPER GUNNER

Warrant Officer W G (Bill) Trotter, DFM

Believed to be a native of West Hartlepool, County Durham. Joined the crew in September, 1944. Had completed three raids with the crew when the author left, but is believed to have remained with it for the remainder of the war. No further contact.

TAIL GUNNER

Flying Officer Clayton C Moore (the Author)

Discharged from the RCAF in April, 1945. Returned to England. Employed as engine fitter at Wimpey's repair depot, Southall for one year. Moved to West Hartlepool, County Durham. Motor mechanic for one year, then seven years as bus driver (United Automobile Services, West Hartlepool). After this, served with the local Fire Brigade for twenty-four years, then set up in business making pedal steel guitars. Retired in 1983. Now residing at Billingham, Cleveland, with Edith, the widow of Dick Jones (the 1st Mid Upper Gunner), who he married on the 30th November, 1946. One step daughter (Gloria Gwynneth) and one son (Clifford Nelson), both married with families, and living in the Cleveland area.

THE END

WHERE ARE THEY NOW

Left
Fig 17. The author 1945

Fig 18.
Below.
Flying Officer Andrew Mynarski, V.C.
by artist Chris Sheehan.

WHERE ARE THEY NOW

Fig 19. Above.
Edith in front of the Oak Tree, once favourite haunt of the members of 419 ("moose") squadron. R.C.A.F. which was then stationed at nearby Middleton-St-George, North Yorkshire.

Fig 20. Left

Edith at home, 1952

WHERE ARE THEY NOW

Fig 21. Left

The author in his role of rythm guitarist in a small Hawaiian band, Hartlepool, Cleveland, 1963

Fig 22. Below.

The author during a visit to his brother Charlie's farm at Debolt, Alberta, Canada, 1978. The wagon is the same one used at the smallholding in whitfield, as mentioned in Chapter one.

WHERE ARE THEY NOW

Fig 23,24 above

The author's small workshop, Middlesborough, 1980 making Mustang pedal steel guitars.

Fig 25. Left.

Edith at home, 1992

WHERE ARE THEY NOW

Fig 26. Right

The Battle of Britain Memorial Flight Lancaster in IX Squadron Markings.

Fig 27. Below

A gathering of ex air-gunners at a recent get together.

Standing L to R: George Hunter, 114 Sqd-1 tour, The author 9&83 Sqd's-2 tours, Alf Heathcote 218 Sqd-1 tour Sonny Green 50 Sqd-1tour, 1 enemy a/c shot down, 1 probable. George Moon 115,515,192 Sqd-3 tours.
Seating L to R Tom Mclean 102,617 Sqdns,7 enemy a/c shot down, 2 probables. Harry Mallaby 22,39,47,217 Sqdns. Albert Leonard 230 (flying boat) Sqdn-half tour. Frank Sumpter 50 Sqdn. Harry Blagg.

WHERE ARE THEY NOW

Fig 28. 83 Squadron Standard on display in Lincoln Cathedral where it was laid up when the Squadron was disbanded.

Fig 29 top right. Grave of Dick Jones in the Rake Lane cemetary, Wallasey, Cheshire.

Fig 30 right. Don Hibbert pictured beside a memorial which he presented to the Yorkshire Air Museum at Elvington. Don completed more than 60 raids as an air gunner, and was awarded the DFM (immediate) and the DFC. He completed his first tour with 10 Squadron, his second with 158 Squadron, where he held the post of gunnery leader. He then joined Transport Command, in which he continued to serve until well after the cessation of hostilities. Having started at the bottom of the ladder, he gained promotion to the rank of Wing Commander, and has the distiction of being one of the few air gunners to take command of a unit or squadron. He was credited with shooting down one enemy aircarft.

WHERE ARE THEY NOW

Other Reading

Of other photographs which relate strongly to the text, but which are subject to copyright restrictions are: Page 73 "Guns in the Sky" by Chas Bowyer, published by Dent. This shows the late Dick Jones with a number of gunners under instruction. On page 83 is a photo of Andrew Mynarski, V.C. who trained with me.

On page 36 of "Lancaster at War", part 4 (Ian Allan) is a picture of Wing Commander Guy Gibson, V.C., with whom I was well acquainted, as I was with Air Commodore John Searby on page 99. On page 117 is a picture of a 9 Squadron aircraft mentioned in the text (WS/J 'Johnnie Walker'-the insignia now carried by the battle of Britain Memorial Flight Lancaster)

EPILOGUE

ON REFLECTION

A half century has passed since the events about which I have written took place. In the interim I have devoted some time to a critical examination of the effect that the experience has had on the lives of both myself and those who shared it, and on the reason why we chose to become involved in the conflict.

In age, the vast majority of we who volunteered for aircrew duties were in our late teens or early twenties. Although patriotism and the defence of freedom played a part in influencing our decision, by far the greater attraction was the element of adventure and glamour which attended a career in flying. We knew something of the dangers with which we would be faced, although the media tended to exaggerate our successes and overlook our failures in the interests of maintaining national morale. Not until we had begun our flying training were we able to recognise something of the dangers associated with our chosen profession.

As was to be expected, training brought with it flying accidents, and these resulted in the death and injury of young men who we had known mostly for only a short time. Once we had been posted to an operational squadron, the true extent of the danger to which we would be subjected became calculable, and the result bred a feeling of cynicism and despair. The absence of familiar faces at the bar - all of these enabled us to calculate our chances of surviving even one tour of operations, and the result was frightening to men of such tender years.

However, only a few found it impossible to withstand the fear and the pressure. In the main, we tended to outwardly ignore our fears. Such misgivings were never aired, although they were ever present in our private thoughts Instead, we consoled ourselves with the belief that it could never happen to us - that divinity and luck would protect us. That a well trained and efficient crew would somehow survive.

Then, as the number of targets listed in our log books reached double figures and the percentage of losses grew steadily, we were compelled to accept that such factors as courage and crew efficiency gave no guarantee of survival. It was true that inexperienced crews were in danger of becoming a statistic, but so too were those made up of high-ranking officers and section leaders, and this brought home to us the realisation that luck played an important part in the outcome.

To dwell on such uncertainties was to create a lowering of morale. However, the majority, knowing the effect that this could have on our ability to function as a fighting unit, did all that we could to dispel such despondency. Of those who failed, a few withdrew from the conflict, while many became resigned to the probability of early extinction.

To declare oneself LMF (lacking in moral fibre) was in itself courageous when one considered the degradation such action brought. One was immediately reduced from aircrew status to the lowest rank, was usually banished from the squadron, and was assigned to the most arduous of tasks. As a consequence, most continued to take part, in the forlorn hope that their luck would prevail.

In the case of our pilot, our navigator, and myself (the only members of the original crew to remain together throughout two tours of operations), it can be said that luck remained with us. Whilst it is true that in the main, we took part in attacks on the most heavily defended targets of the German homeland, suffered a crash, sustained flak damage, were coned by searchlights, pursued by fighters, and were struck by lightning, we enjoyed a good measure of luck. During our term of service with the two squadrons, the equivalent strength of both units (in terms of crews and aircraft) was lost and replaced.

Post war statistics show that a total of fifty-five thousand allied airmen were killed during the conflict, of which ten thousand were fellow Canadians. Also indicated is that, of all the heavy bomber crews, only two percent went on to survive the completion of two tours against fortress Europe. To those who remain lies the obligation to ensure that future generations are made aware of the costly contribution made by those who gave all in the furtherance of peace and normality.

There can be little doubt that the experience had an indeterminate effect on the personality of all those who survived. We had witnessed the horrors of war at first hand. We had seen the death of so many of our friends - and our enemies, and the memory of this was to stay with us throughout the remainder of our lives.

In recent times, the media has questioned the morality of our actions in the bombing of civilian populations. But it had to be done. In those times, the bulk of armament production was located within the major cities of Germany. These had to be destroyed if we were to win the war. It was the German High Command which failed to introduce a policy of mass evacuation of non-essential persons from these target areas. As a consequence, we and Sir

ON REFLECTION

Arthur Harris in particular - have been targeted as the instruments and perpetrators of indiscriminate bombing. Yet, no other weapons could have been more indiscriminate than the V-1 and the V-2.

The author invites any correspondence to be sent to :

**Clayton Moore
4 Edgehill Way
Billingham
Cleveland
TS23 3LE
England**